GREAT PERFORMANCES

SYMPHONY LEAGUE OF TUPELO, MISSISSIPPI

Since 1972 the Symphony League of Tupelo has been committed to the financial support of the Tupelo Symphony Orchestra. Proceeds from the sale of *Great Performances* will help insure that the orchestra can continue to perform the highest quality concerts for Northeast Mississippians and special concerts for elementary school children for years to come. The Symphony League of Tupelo dedicates this cookbook to our community and to the many friends and volunteers whose generous help have made it possible.

Additional copies of *Great Performances* may be obtained by writing:

Great Performances
The Symphony League of Tupelo
P. O. Box 474
Tupelo, MS 38802-0474
(601)842-8433

First Edition   November 1990   10,000 copies
Copyright © 1990
by
The Symphony League of Tupelo
Tupelo, Mississippi
All rights reserved

ISBN: 0-9627598-0-5
Library of Congress Catalog Card Number 90-71199

CHAIRMEN AND EDITORS
Nancy Bostic Diffee and Mabel McClanahan Murphree

STEERING AND POLICY COMMITTEE

Julia Dodge Blakey	Joyce Causey Johnston
Patty Wood Block	Carol Spight Leake
Tommie Wright Bourland	Jane Spight Riley
Beth Boozer Brevard	Ann Shannon Springfield
Cindy Jones Brooks	Judy Bornscheuer Thomas
Grace Strickland Clark	Charlotte Tannehill Westbrook
Judy Joyner Hodges	

GRAPHIC DESIGN	FOREWORD	PHOTOGRAPHY
Sandy Heard Ford	Peggy Webb, Novelist	Scott Ramsey

COMMITTEE CHAIRMEN

Testing ....Camae Purvis Tharp
Editing and Proofing .... Emily Sims Westbrook
Indexing .... Audrey Jerue Schreiner
Publicity .... Karen Kahler Holliday
Photography Arrangements............................Charlotte Tannehill Westbrook
Jane Spight Riley

RECIPE SELECTION COMMITTEES

Appetizers
Patty Wood Block
Hilda Stewart Boyd
Donna Neaves Hambrick
Ann Shannon Springfield

Beverages
Sue Oldham Imbler
Diane Evans Tannehill

Soups
Adrian Leist Caldwell
Frances Workman Foy
Mabel McClanahan Murphree

Salads
Mary Ann Lee Caldwell
Martha Tate Stokely Dodge
Jane Spight Riley

Vegetables
Joyce Causey Johnston
Virginia Timbes Mathews
Betty Fields Reed

Meat and Game
Cindy Jones Brooks
Frances Purvis Reed
Charlotte Tannehill Westbrook

Poultry
Lisa White Reed
Willa Searcy Smith
Mary Elizabeth Phillips Williams

Fish and Seafood
Julia Dodge Blakey
Sandy Heard Ford
Gretchen Long Ramsey

Eggs, Cheese and Pasta
Camille Reed Clayton
Michelle Barnhill Hutto

Bread
Tommie Wright Bourland
Carol Spight Leake

Accompaniments
Louise Rodgers Bland
Nancy Bostic Diffee

Desserts
Judy Joyner Hodges
Lee Purnell Walsh

Cakes
Grace Strickland Clark
Margaret Stevenson Ray
Carolyn Loper Sharp

Pies
Rosemary Rich Bryan
Cindy Little Mathis

Cookies and Candy
Sonja Anne Jenkins
Catherine Reed Mize
Cathy Timbes Sparks

Casseroles
Beth Boozer Brevard
Barbara Christensen Zander

TABLE OF CONTENTS

FOREWORD

From the concert hall to the kitchen, from the ballet to the board room, from the art gallery to the factory, from the theatre stage to the cotton fields, from the arts festivals and schools and libraries to the small cottage lit by the glow of television — Tupelo resounds with the sounds of a great performance, a magnificent symphony whose varied melodies blend together in perfect harmony.

This cookbook is a part of that symphony, a coming together of Tupelo's many different performers to bring you the best in Southern cooking. Each page sings its own song; each section dances to its own rhythm.

Catch the beat; join the song and, above all, please your audience with a symphony of good cooking. The Tupelo Symphony League wishes you a great performance in your kitchen and many encores.

Peggy Well

"Come the Spring with all its splendor…" Henry Wadsworth Longfellow

Warm weather, spring rains, Tupelo gum trees…Painters, sculptors, runners…Parties for artists and out-of-town guests…

GUM TREE BRUNCH

THE ABLE NAVEL

GUM TREE BRUNCH CASSEROLE

AMBRE FRUIT

GRAHAM WHEAT ROLLS

APRICOT REFRIGERATOR CAKE

"Thank God for tea!…I am glad I was not born before tea." Samuel Taylor Coleridge
Linen napkins, lace-edged…translucent china cups…bridal teas, membership teas…a friend's visit.

AFTERNOON TEA

PINEAPPLE MERINGUE TORTE

PUMPKIN TARTS

TEACAKES   PECAN CRISPS

FANTASTIC COOKIES

PEPPERMINT PARTY MERINGUES

FRESH FRUIT

FAVORITE GREEN DIP FILLED CHERRY TOMATOES

PARTY SHRIMP SANDWICHES

TEA AND COFFEE

"It's clever, but is it art?" Rudyard Kipling
Ceilings tall, marble hall, landmark…pictures in an exhibition…toast the artist…new friends, old friends, sparkling wine, mellow cheese…

COCKTAILS AT THE GALLERY

PICKLED SHRIMP

CHICKEN SALAD SUPERB IN MINIATURE PUFF PASTRY

CAVIAR DELICIOUS   HOMEMADE RONDELÉ

ASPARAGUS CANAPÉS   DILLED CARROTS

FRESH FRUIT WITH COCONUT RUM FRUIT DIP

SUNSHINE PUNCH

CHAMPAGNE

"The play's the thing!" William Shakespeare
At TCT on Broadway…Showboat, Camelot, make-believe, what's the plot…pre-theatre dinner… bravo! Take a bow!

DINNER BEFORE THE THEATER

SALMON PÂTÉ

SPICY SPINACH SALAD

INDIVIDUAL TOMATO PIES

NO KNEAD ROLLS

CHOCOLATE POTS de CREMÉ

"Sizzling summer sun slips silently toward stardust." Anonymous
Long summer evenings…friends' laughter, reminiscing…gas grills, patio furniture, citronella candles…

DINNER ON THE GROUNDS

MARINATED EYE OF ROUND

SUMMER SURPRISE SALAD

RANCH POTATOES

LIMA BEAN CASSEROLE   GARDEN STUFFED YELLOW SQUASH

VEGETABLE MEDLEY SALAD

REFRIGERATOR ROLLS

BLACK RUSSIAN CAKE

LEMON CHESS PIE

STRAWBERRY TEA

"Twas the night before Christmas...." Clement C. Moore

Green trees, red balls, silver tinsel...church bells caroling, presents...snow—we hope!...Santa Claus, oh, please!...family, close friends, fireside. Peace on earth!

CHRISTMAS EVE SUPPER

EASY FAMILY EGGNOG

OYSTER STEW

SLICED COUNTRY HAM IN CORN LIGHTBREAD
WITH MUSTARD SAUCE

CRANBERRY SOUFFLÉ

SOUTHERN GINGERBREAD
WITH OLD FASHIONED ORANGE SAUCE

"The daintiest last, to make the end most sweet." William Shakespeare

Beethoven and Sondheim...violins and applause...sweet ending to a great performance...Play, Maestro, play!

DESSERT AFTER THE SYMPHONY

FRUITED CHEESE BALL WITH CRACKERS

DEVILISH-CHOCOLATE CAKE
WITH ANGEL FROSTING

RASPBERRY FLUFF

FRESH FRUIT AND CHEESE

WINE

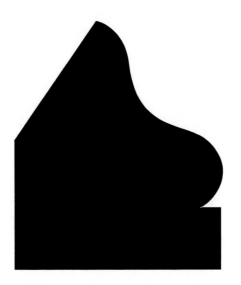

APPETIZERS

CAVIAR DELICIOUS

2 Tablespoons unflavored gelatin
¼ cup cold water

4 Tablespoons fresh lemon juice

Egg Layer:
4 hard boiled eggs, chopped
½ cup mayonnaise
¼ cup minced fresh parsley
1 green onion, minced

¾ teaspoon salt
Dash of Tabasco
Dash of white pepper

Avocado Layer:
2 medium avocados
1 green onion, minced
2 Tablespoons fresh lemon juice
2 Tablespoons mayonnaise

½ teaspoon salt
Dash of Tabasco sauce
Dash of black pepper

Sour Cream Layer:
1 cup sour cream
¼ cup minced onion

2 ounce jar black caviar
Lemon juice

Soften gelatin in lemon juice and water. Melt over hot water. Set aside. Prepare a 7-inch springform pan by spraying with no-stick cooking spray. Egg layer: Combine ingredients with 2 Tablespoons dissolved gelatin mixture. Neatly spread egg mixture into prepared pan and smooth top. Avocado layer: Purée one avocado in processor or blender. Dice remaining avocado. Place avocados in medium bowl and add remaining ingredients. To avocado mixture add 2 Tablespoons gelatin mixture. Blend and place over egg layer in pan. Smooth top. Sour cream layer: Mix sour cream, onions, and 4 Tablespoons gelatin mixture. Blend well and place on top of avocado layer. Smooth top. Cover pan tightly with plastic wrap and refrigerate overnight. Just before serving rinse caviar in strainer under running cold water. Sprinkle with lemon juice and drain well (this will keep sour cream layer from turning gray). Remove sides from pan. Transfer mold to serving dish. Spread caviar over top. Serve with Melba rounds.
Serves: 12 to 14

At Christmas use red caviar to make a very festive appetizer.

CAVIAR-CHEESE RING

2 pound round Brie Cheese
2 (3½ ounce) jars red lumpfish caviar
½ cup whipping cream

8 ounces cream cheese, softened
Salt to taste
Freshly ground pepper to taste
½ cup walnut halves

Using a 2-inch biscuit cutter, cut center from Brie. Set center aside for another use. Cut ring in half horizontally, making 2 rings. Reserve 2 Tablespoons caviar for garnish, spread remaining caviar over bottom ring. Beat cream until stiff peaks form, set aside. Beat cream cheese until fluffy. Fold whipped cream into cream cheese. Season cream cheese mixture with salt and pepper. Spoon one half of the cream cheese mixture over the caviar filling. Place other half of Brie ring on top. Press walnut halves into side of ring. Spoon remaining cream cheese mixture into pastry bag fitted with a medium open-star tip. Pipe cream cheese mixture decoratively on top of ring. Garnish with reserved caviar. Serve with assorted crackers.
Serves: 10 to 12

EGGPLANT CAVIAR

½ cup olive oil
6 cups peeled and diced eggplant
1 large onion, chopped
¾ cup diced green bell pepper
2 (4 ounce) cans chopped mushrooms, drained
5 cloves garlic, crushed
12 ounce can tomato paste
4 Tablespoons red wine vinegar
2 cups chopped green olives

2 Tablespoons sugar
2 teaspoons oregano
2 teaspoons salt
2 teaspoons black pepper
¼ cup Worcestershire sauce
2 bay leaves
½ cup mild picante sauce
10 ounce can Rotel tomatoes
1 teaspoon basil

Heat oil in large skillet. Sauté eggplant, onions, pepper, mushrooms and garlic. Cover and cook 30 minutes over medium heat. Add remaining ingredients and cook slowly for 2 hours. Remove bay leaves. Cool. Pour into blender and blend until smooth. Reheat and serve hot with corn chips or crackers. Best made a day ahead to allow flavors to blend.
Yield: 4 to 5 cups

HAM BALLS

1½ pounds ground pork sausage
1 pound ground ham
2 cups saltine cracker crumbs

2 eggs
1 cup milk
Pinch of Accent

Sauce:
1 cup packed dark brown sugar
1 teaspoon dry mustard
½ cup vinegar

½ cup hot water
½ cup seedless raisins

Mix ham ball ingredients and shape into balls about the size of walnuts. Bake at 350 degrees for 10 minutes. Mix sauce ingredients. Pour sauce over meatballs and bake 40 minutes. Stir once or twice while baking. Serve hot.
Yield: 80 ham balls

SAUSAGE CANTONESE

8 ounce can whole water
   chestnuts, quartered

1 pound pork sausage
½ cup hot spicy mustard

Cover each water chestnut with sausage. Shape into a ball. Place balls in a shallow pan and bake at 350 degrees for 15 minutes or until browned. Serve on wooden picks, dipping into mustard.
Yield: 45 balls

PEPPERCORN LIVER PÂTÉ

1 cup unsalted butter, divided
1 pound chicken livers
½ clove garlic, minced
2 green onions, chopped
¼ teaspoon basil

2 Tablespoons cognac
2 Tablespoons peppercorns
1 large hard boiled egg, chopped
Coarse ground pepper for garnish

In a large skillet melt ½ cup butter and sauté livers for 5 minutes. Remove livers and cool. Place livers in a blender. Add remaining butter, garlic, green onions, basil, cognac, peppercorns and egg. Blend until smooth. Pack into a buttered 2-cup mold and refrigerate overnight. Unmold. Sprinkle with coarse ground pepper. Serve with whole wheat or rye crackers.
Yield: 2 cups

CATFISH MOLD

1 pound catfish fillets
8 ounces cream cheese, softened
¼ cup mayonnaise
1 teaspoon Worcestershire sauce
1 Tablespoon fresh lemon juice

½ teaspoon onion juice
1 teaspoon garlic powder
1 teaspoon paprika
Salt to taste
Pepper to taste

In a large skillet place fillets and add water to cover. Poach fillets for 10 minutes. Drain and cool. Flake fish into tiny pieces. In a mixing bowl combine cream cheese and mayonnaise with an electric mixer. Add catfish and mix well. Add remaining ingredients and mix on low speed until well blended. Pour mixture into an oiled 3-cup mold. Refrigerate until set. Unmold and serve with crackers.
Yield: 3 cups

SALMON PÂTÉ

8 ounces cream cheese, softened
2 Tablespoons chili sauce
2 Tablespoons chopped fresh
  parsley

2 Tablespoons chopped onion
½ teaspoon hot sauce
16 ounce can red salmon, drained
  and boned

Place all ingredients in food processor or blender; process until smooth. Pour into an oiled 2-cup mold. Cover and refrigerate overnight. Unmold on serving dish and serve with crackers.
Yield: 2 cups

HOT CRAB DIP SUPREME

16 ounces cream cheese
½ cup mayonnaise
2 teaspoons prepared mustard
1 clove garlic, minced

2 Tablespoons minced onion
¼ cup sherry or brandy
½ pound crabmeat

Melt cream cheese in top of double boiler. Add mayonnaise, mustard, garlic, onion and sherry. Mix well. Drain and flake crabmeat. Add crabmeat to melted cream cheese. Heat, but do not boil. Serve hot in chafing dish or hollowed out round loaf of bread. Serve with crackers or toasted bread.
Yield: 2½ cups

CRABMEAT IN PHYLLO CUPS

16 ounce package phyllo pastry
  sheets
½ cup butter, melted and cooled
6½ ounce can crabmeat, drained
  and flaked
6 ounces Cheddar cheese, grated

¾ cup mayonnaise
¼ cup grated Parmesan cheese
Salt and pepper to taste
Dash of Tabasco sauce, optional
2 teaspoons fresh lemon juice,
  optional

To assemble phyllo for cups place 1 sheet of pastry on a flat surface and brush lightly with butter. Top this with another sheet and brush with butter. Continue this process until 7 phyllo sheets are buttered and stacked. Using kitchen shears, cut dough into 2-inch squares. Gently place in miniature muffin tins sprayed with no-stick cooking spray. Bake at 350 degrees for 15 minutes. Repeat process until all dough is used. Store cups in airtight container. In a large bowl mix crabmeat, cheeses, mayonnaise, salt, pepper, Tabasco and lemon juice. Mix well. Fill phyllo cups with crab mixture and place on baking sheet. Place under broiler and broil until mixture bubbles.
Yield: 72 pieces

SEVICHE

1 pound bass or orange roughy
  fillets, diced
2 bay leaves
1 cup fresh lemon juice
½ teaspoon oregano
⅔ teaspoon garlic salt
Salt and pepper to taste

1 medium onion, chopped
1 green bell pepper, chopped
2 ribs celery, chopped
1 tomato, chopped
2 cups mild white vinegar
⅔ cup water

Layer fish, bay leaves, lemon juice, oregano, salt and pepper in a plastic bowl. Refrigerate overnight. In another container, mix onion, bell pepper, celery, tomato, vinegar and water. Marinate for 2-3 hours. Drain fish and vegetables. Gently combine fish and vegetable mixtures. Place in serving bowl and serve with round butter crackers.
Serves: 8 to 10

Try apple rounds instead of bread for serving pâté.

SENSATIONAL SEAFOOD APPETIZER

16 ounces cream cheese, softened
10 ounce bottle cocktail sauce
2 pounds cooked shrimp, chopped
1 pint cherry tomatoes, halved
   and seeded
4 green onions, chopped

4 ounce can pitted black olives,
   drained and chopped
12 ounces mozzarella cheese,
   shredded
Grated Parmesan cheese

In a glass pie plate, or a dish of a similar size, spread cream cheese in bottom. Layer remaining ingredients in order listed. Sprinkle Parmesan cheese on top. Wrap with plastic wrap and chill until ready to serve. Serve with crackers or corn chips.
Serves: 18 to 20

PICKLED SHRIMP

2½ pounds shrimp, cooked and
   peeled
2 large onions, sliced into rings
1½ cups vegetable oil
½ cup cider vinegar
½ cup fresh lemon juice

2½ teaspoons celery seed
⅓ cup sugar
½ teaspoon salt
1½ Tablespoons capers and juice
½ teaspoon Tabasco
4 bay leaves

Layer shrimp and onions in a bowl. Combine remaining ingredients and pour over shrimp and onions. Refrigerate at least 24 hours. Drain and serve.
Serves: 6

SEAFOOD DIP

8 ounces cream cheese
2 cups cottage cheese
2 cups mayonnaise
2 teaspoons Worcestershire sauce
Salt and pepper to taste
½ cup finely chopped celery

⅓ cup finely chopped onion
1 Tablespoon fresh lemon juice
6½ ounce can crabmeat, drained
4½ ounce can shrimp, drained
6½ ounce can minced clams,
   drained

Blend all ingredients together. Chill. Serve with chips or crackers.
Serves: 30 to 40

CHILI DIP

8 ounces cream cheese
16 ounce can chili, with or
  without beans

¼ cup chopped green onions
¼ cup chopped black olives

In a saucepan melt cream cheese over low heat. Add chili and heat until well blended. Pour into serving dish. Top with green onions and olives. Serve hot with corn chips.
Yield: 2 cups

COOL JALAPEÑO SPREAD

1 pound Velveeta cheese,
  grated
1 small onion, finely chopped

2 hot pickled jalapeño peppers,
  chopped
¾ cup mayonnaise

In a large bowl combine cheese, onion, jalapeño peppers and mayonnaise. Mix thoroughly. Cover and refrigerate. Serve at room temperature with crispy tortilla chips. Best made 24 hours before serving.
Yield: 2 cups

This is very good spread on French or Italian bread and toasted.

HOT SALSA

6 large ripe tomatoes, finely
  chopped
1 clove garlic, crushed
1 small white onion, quartered
1 bunch green onions, chopped
½ bunch fresh parsley, chopped
½ bunch fresh coriander or
  cilantro, chopped

1 teaspoon seasoned salt
½ teaspoon sugar
½ teaspoon white pepper
1 Tablespoon safflower oil
1-2 fresh jalapeño peppers,
  seeded

Combine all ingredients, except peppers, and place in food processor. Process until coarsely chopped. Add jalapeño peppers a little at a time. Continue processing for a few seconds. For chunkier texture, save ½ cup tomatoes and add after processing. Add more salt to taste before serving if preferred. Serve with tortilla chips.
Yield: 1½ quarts

CHILI AND TAMALE DIP

2 pounds Velveeta cheese, cubed   **15 ounce can tamales**
15 ounce can chili, without beans   **⅔ cup mild picante sauce**

Place cheese in microwave proof bowl. Add chili and tamales. Heat on medium high until cheese is partially melted and the tamales have softened. Add picante sauce. Mix together and heat thoroughly. Serve hot with tortilla chips. For spicier dip, use medium picante sauce or a dash of cayenne pepper.
Yield: 8 cups

A good and easy favorite Mexican dip.

TORTILLA ROLL-UPS

12 (14-inch) flour tortillas   **12 ounces sharp Cheddar cheese,**
8 ounces cream cheese, softened   **grated**
1 cup sour cream   **3 Tablespoons sugar**
4 ounce can chilies, chopped   **1 cup picante sauce**
3 Tablespoons minced onion

In a medium bowl combine cream cheese, sour cream, chilies, onion, Cheddar cheese and sugar. Mix thoroughly. Spread onto tortillas and roll up. Cover and chill for 2 hours or overnight, keeping tightly covered while refrigerated. When ready to serve, slice each roll into ½-inch pieces. Serve in basket or on tray with picante sauce.
Yield: 100 pieces

CHILIES AND CHEESE SQUARES

8 eggs   **12 ounces small curd cottage**
½ cup all-purpose flour   **cheese**
1 teaspoon baking powder   **2 (4 ounce) cans California chilies,**
½ teaspoon seasoning salt   **chopped and drained**
4 cups shredded Monterey Jack
cheese

Beat eggs until frothy. Add flour, baking powder and salt. Blend well. Fold in remaining ingredients. Pour into greased and floured 9X13-inch baking pan. Bake at 350 degrees for 30 minutes or until golden brown on top and center is firm. Cool for 10 minutes. Cut into 1-inch squares and serve. May be frozen. Thaw and reheat at 325 degrees for 5-10 minutes or microwave 2-3 minutes.
Yield: 120 pieces

CHUTNEY CHEESE SPREAD

8 ounces cream cheese, softened
4 ounces Cheddar cheese, grated
¼ teaspoon salt
½ teaspoon curry powder

4 Tablespoons dry sherry
¾ cup chutney
3 green onions, chopped
3 strips bacon, fried and crumbled

Mix cream cheese, Cheddar cheese, salt, curry powder and sherry. Form into a flat circle on a serving dish. Chill. Before serving, spread chutney, green onions and bacon on top. Serve with bacon flavored crackers.
Yield: 2 cups

FRESH BASIL CHEESE SPREAD

3 cloves garlic
5-6 fresh basil leaves or 2-3
   teaspoons dried basil leaves
16 ounces cream cheese, softened

½ cup olive oil
1 cup grated Parmesan cheese
1 cup walnuts
Fresh basil for garnish

In a food processor process garlic and basil until finely chopped. Add cream cheese, olive oil, Parmesan cheese and walnuts. Blend well until walnuts are pulverized. Place in a bowl for serving. Garnish with fresh basil leaves. Serve with wheat crackers or toasted French bread rounds.
Yield: 3 cups

BEER CHEESE

8 ounces sharp Cheddar cheese,
   cubed
¾ cup beer, divided
8 ounces cream cheese, softened

1 clove garlic, minced
Dash of red pepper
Dash of salt
Paprika for garnish

In blender or food processor cream Cheddar cheese and ½ cup beer. Add cream cheese, garlic, ¼ cup beer, salt and pepper. Blend well. Place cheese in bowl and refrigerate. Garnish with paprika. Serve with large pretzels.
Yield: 2 cups

HOMEMADE RONDELÉ

1 cup butter, softened	**¼ teaspoon salt**
16 ounces cream cheese, softened	**¼ teaspoon basil**
¼ teaspoon oregano	**¼ teaspoon garlic powder**
¼ teaspoon thyme	**¼ teaspoon coarsely ground**
¼ teaspoon dill	**black pepper**
¼ teaspoon marjoram	

Cream butter and cheese together until light and fluffy. Add spices and mix well. Form into a ball or place in a serving dish. Cover and chill. Serve at room temperature with crackers or dark bread. For a pretty party appetizer, add an extra 8 ounces cream cheese and ¼ cup butter when mixing rondele. Reserve 1¼ cups rondele for decorating. Line a 3-cup mold or a bowl with plastic wrap. Pack cheese into mold. Cover and chill thoroughly. Unmold on green leaf lettuce. Smooth top and sides of cheese mold with a knife. Place reserved rondele in pastry bag fitted with a medium open-star tip and decorate base and top of mold. Be creative! Will keep for several weeks refrigerated.
Yield: 3 cups

Wonderful for unexpected company.

BUTTERED PIMIENTO SPREAD

½ cup butter, softened	**⅛ teaspoon freshly ground black**
4 ounces cream cheese	**pepper**
2 ounce jar diced pimientos, drained	**1 Tablespoon minced green bell pepper**
1 Tablespoon grated onion	**1 teaspoon caraway seed**
½ teaspoon Worcestershire sauce	**2 ounce can anchovies, drained**
1 teaspoon lemon juice	

In a large bowl cream butter, cheese and pimiento. Add remaining ingredients and blend well. Chill. Serve with Melba rounds.
Serves: 6 to 8

When serving sliced apples and pears as an accompaniment for Brie, Camembert or Cheddar cheese, the fruit may be kept fresh and will not turn brown if marinaded in canned pineapple juice. The juice also enhances the flavor of the fruit.

CHEESE APPLES

Apples, sweet Delicious (as many as needed)

Italian dressing
Grated Parmesan cheese

Wash and dry apples. Slice each apple into 12 slices. Place in a plastic bag. Pour only enough dressing into bag to moisten apples. Marinate at least 4 hours or overnight in refrigerator. Sprinkle cheese into paper bag and drop apple slices in bag and shake to coat. Arrange attractively on serving dish. The number of apples used will be determined by the number you wish to serve.
Yield: 12 slices per apple

BLEU CHEESE BALL

8 ounces cream cheese, softened
4 ounces Bleu cheese
4 ounce can pitted black olives, chopped
¼ cup butter

Dash of Worcestershire sauce
1 Tablespoon horseradish
½ cup chopped pecans
⅛ cup chopped chives

Blend all ingredients except pecans and chives. Chill. Form into a ball. Roll in pecans and sprinkle with chives. Serve with wheat thins.

FRUITED CHEESE BALL

6 ounces dried apricots
16 ounces cream cheese, softened
1½ cups grated Monterey Jack cheese

½ cup golden seedless raisins
8 ounces chopped dates
Cream cheese for garnish

Soak apricots 5 minutes in warm water to cover. Drain and dice apricots. Cream cheeses together. Add apricots, raisins and dates. Shape into a ball or mound. Cover and refrigerate overnight. Frost with softened cream cheese and serve at room temperature with saltines or gingersnaps.
Yield: 4 cups

ASPARAGUS CANAPES

20 fresh asparagus spears, uncut
3 ounces Bleu cheese
8 ounces cream cheese

1 egg, beaten
1 loaf very thin sliced bread
½-1 cup butter, melted

Drop asparagus into boiling water for 2 minutes. Rinse with cold water, drain and pat dry. Beat together Bleu cheese, cream cheese and egg. Trim crust off bread. Roll bread slices flat with rolling pin. Spread cheese mixture on bread. Place one asparagus spear on each slice of bread and roll up tightly. Dip each roll into butter and refrigerate. Spray baking sheet with no-stick cooking spray. Bake at 400 degrees for 10-15 minutes. Serve immediately.
Yield: 120 pieces

BLEU CHEESE MUSHROOMS

12-14 extra large fresh
  mushrooms
¼ cup chopped green onions
¼ cup butter

¼ cup Bleu cheese, crumbled
⅓ cup fine, dry bread crumbs,
  divided
Salt and pepper to taste

Remove stems from mushrooms. Chop stems. Cook stems and onions in butter until tender, but not browned. Add Bleu cheese, 2 Tablespoons bread crumbs and salt and pepper. Fill mushroom crowns with mixture. Sprinkle with remaining bread crumbs. Place on cookie sheet. Bake at 350 degrees for 12 minutes.
Yield: 6 servings

Everyone will love these.

DILLED CARROTS

1 pound carrots
Juice from 16 ounce jar dill pickles

Dill weed

Pare, wash and cut carrots into sticks. Simmer in saucepan with pickle juice until tender-crisp. Chill carrots in juice. Drain and sprinkle with dill weed.
Serves: 8 to 10

BACON OLIVE DIP

5 slices bacon, cooked crisp and
  crumbled
8 ounces cream cheese, softened
¼ cup skim milk
1 cup chopped ripe olives

2 Tablespoons grated onion
1 teaspoon salt
1 teaspoon Worcestershire sauce
5 drops Tabasco sauce

Mix all ingredients together. Serve with fresh vegetables.
Yield: 1½ cups

BLACK-EYED PEA DIP

3 (15 ounce) cans black-eyed peas,
  drained
1 teaspoon bacon drippings
2 (10 ounce) cans Rotel tomatoes,
  drain and reserve juice

2 teaspoons lemon pepper
1 Tablespoon grated onion
Dash of garlic powder

Heat peas in saucepan with bacon drippings. Chop tomatoes in blender. Mix all
ingredients in blender, adding tomato juice as needed for right consistency. Serve as
a dip with miniature hushpuppies.
Yield: 15 servings

A Southern delight.

FAVORITE GREEN DIP

20 ounces frozen chopped
  spinach
16 ounces nonfat plain yogurt
1 cup mayonnaise
2 teaspoons dried onion
1 Tablespoon dried dill weed

1 teaspoon dried salad herbs
1 package dry ranch dressing mix
½ teaspoon seasoned salt
2 Tablespoons fresh lemon or lime
  juice

Steam spinach in strainer over boiling water for 10 minutes. Strain and squeeze most
of moisture out. Cool to room temperature. Place all ingredients in processor and
process until fluffy and well mixed. Mixture will be thick and bright green. Chill. Serve
with fresh vegetables. Best made several hours or overnight before serving.
Yield: 4 cups

Great for St. Patrick's Day celebration.

MARINATED MUSHROOMS

1 pound fresh mushrooms
⅛ teaspoon thyme leaves,
  crumbled
3 whole black peppercorns,
  crushed
⅛ teaspoon fennel seeds,
  crushed
1 bay leaf

½ teaspoon garlic powder
1 teaspoon onion powder
1 teaspoon chopped parsley
3 Tablespoons red wine vinegar
2 Tablespoons olive oil
¼ teaspoon lemon peel
2 teaspoons seasoning salt

Clean mushrooms and trim stems off. Mix remaining ingredients in large skillet. Place mushrooms, cap side down, in skillet. Cook over low heat, turning frequently until tender. Place in bowl, cover and refrigerate overnight.
Serves: 6

DIP FOR RAW VEGETABLES

8 ounces cream cheese
1 cup sour cream
2 packages dry green onion dip
Dash Worcestershire sauce

½ teaspoon dry mustard
1 Tablespoon ketchup
½ teaspoon garlic salt
1 teaspoon prepared horseradish

Combine all ingredients in small bowl and mix until smooth. Refrigerate until ready to serve. Serve with fresh vegetables.
Yield: 2 cups

COCONUT RUM FRUIT DIP

8 ounces cream cheese
1 cup sour cream
¼ cup powdered sugar
¼ cup white rum

¼ teaspoon nutmeg
½ cup flaked coconut
½ cup flaked coconut, toasted

Mix all ingredients, except toasted coconut, in blender. Blend until smooth. Chill. Top with toasted coconut. Serve with fresh fruit. To toast coconut place on a shallow pan. Bake at 350 degrees for 7 minutes, stirring occasionally.
Yield: 2 cups

Pretty served in a coconut shell for a patio party.

BRIE IN CROCK

16 ounces Brie cheese, cubed and
   at room temperature
8 ounces cream cheese, softened
3 Tablespoons butter, softened

1 cup chopped pecans, toasted
2 Tablespoons fresh lemon juice
2 Tablespoons chives

In processor mix Brie and cream cheese. Stir remaining ingredients into Brie mixture. Pack in crock. Cover with plastic wrap and refrigerate. Serve with assorted crackers.
Yield: 3 to 4 cups

MARY VICKERS

1 loaf thin sliced white bread
½ pound Cheddar cheese,
   shredded
6 slices bacon, fried crisp and
   crumbled

⅔ cup slivered almonds
1 onion, finely chopped
1 cup mayonnaise
Salt and pepper to taste

Preheat oven to 400 degrees. Remove crusts from bread. Mix remaining ingredients together. Spread each slice of bread with cheese mixture. Cut into strips, triangles, or any desired shape. Bake 10 minutes or until browned. May be frozen before baking. Freeze on cookie sheets and store in plastic bags in freezer.
Yield: 36 pieces

GOLDEN CHEESIES

2½ cups all-purpose flour
1 cup butter, softened
1 cup sour cream
Seasoned salt to taste

Pepper to taste
3 cups shredded Cheddar cheese
Paprika

Combine first 3 ingredients. Mix well. Divide into 4 portions. Wrap and chill until firm. Roll out dough one portion at a time on floured surface to 12X6-inch rectangle. Sprinkle each rectangle lightly with salt, pepper and ¾ cup cheese. Starting at the 12-inch side, roll up. Seal edges. Place seam side down on cookie sheet. Using a sharp knife, cut rolls half-way through at I-inch intervals. Sprinkle with paprika. Bake at 350 degrees for 30-35 minutes.
Yield: 48 pieces

These are wonderful served hot or cold.

CRISP PARMESAN STICKS

1 loaf very thin sliced bread
1⅛ cups butter, softened
2 teaspoons Dijon mustard

¾ cup grated Parmesan cheese
¾ cup corn flakes, crushed

Freeze bread. Trim crusts. Return bread to freezer. Combine butter and mustard. Spread this mixture evenly on bread slices. Mix cheese with corn flakes and sprinkle over bread slices. Cut each into 5 strips using shears or sharp knife. Bake at 350 degrees for 7-8 minutes. Can be returned to oven later if not crisp enough or turn oven off and let remain in oven a few minutes. Freezes well.
Yield: 120 pieces

CHEESE TEMPTERS

1 cup butter or margarine,
  softened
1 cup grated sharp Cheddar
  cheese

2¼ cups all-purpose flour
½ teaspoon salt
2 cups finely chopped pecans
Grated Parmesan cheese

Combine butter with grated cheese. Add flour and salt. Mix well. Blend in pecans. Shape into 1-inch balls. Bake on ungreased cookie sheet at 350 degrees for 15 minutes or until very lightly browned. Gently roll in Parmesan cheese while still warm. Cool completely on wire rack. Store in airtight container. May freeze if not to be used for long period of time.
Yield: 100 pieces

LAKE FOREST HERB TOAST

1 loaf thinly sliced white bread
½ cup butter, softened
1 Tablespoon minced parsley
1 clove garlic, mashed
¼ teaspoon basil

¼ teaspoon oregano
Freshly ground black pepper to
  taste
1 teaspoon sesame seeds

Trim crust from bread. Mix butter with remaining ingredients. Spread generously over bread. Cut each slice into 3 or 4 strips. Bake at 350 degrees for 15 minutes or until browned and crisp. Store in an airtight container.

Nice for the cocktail hour.

ESTERETTES

8 ounces sharp Cheddar cheese,
  shredded
½ cup butter
1½ cups all-purpose flour

¼ teaspoon red pepper
8 ounces whole dates, pitted
60 pecan halves

In a mixing bowl cream cheese and butter. Add flour and pepper mixing until dough consistency. Stuff each date with a pecan half. Pinch off enough dough to form a marble size ball. Flatten the dough ball with palm of hand. Wrap dough around each date, keeping dough as thin as possible. Bake at 375 degrees for 15-20 minutes or until lightly browned.
Yield: 60 pieces

MUSHROOM AND CHEESE SNACKS

3 ounces cream cheese, softened
4 ounce can mushroom stems and
  pieces, drained and minced
2 Tablespoons chopped pimiento
1 Tablespoon Dijon mustard

8 ounce can refrigerated crescent
  dinner rolls
Poppy, caraway or sesame seeds
1 egg, beaten

In a small mixing bowl combine cream cheese, mushrooms, pimiento and mustard. Blend well. Separate crescent dough into four rectangles. Firmly press perforations to seal dough together. Spread each rectangle with ¼ of the mushroom mixture. Starting with long side, roll up, jelly roll style. Cut each roll into 6 pieces. Place seam side down on greased cookie sheet. Brush with beaten egg and sprinkle with seeds. Bake at 375 degrees for 12-15 minutes or until golden brown.
Yield: 24 pieces

Cheese "families" have similar flavor and texture, and often a new cheese can be substituted for a familiar one to liven a recipe. Substitute colby, Edam or Gouda for Cheddar. Substitute Asiago, Fontina or Romano for Parmesan. Substitute Neufchatel for cream cheese. Substitute Brie for Camembert.

BEVERAGES

BEVERAGES

MINT COOLER

8 cups boiling water
7 small mint tea bags
1 small plain tea bag
2 tubs sugarfree Crystal Light
   lemonade mix

8 cups cold water
8 to 10 individual packets sugar
   substitute

Add tea bags to boiling water and steep for 10 minutes. Add lemonade mix to 8 cups cold water. Remove tea bags from tea mixture and squeeze. Add lemonade mixture and sugar substitute to taste. Tea will keep for several weeks refrigerated.
Yield: 1 gallon

Refreshing and low calorie.

STRAWBERRY TEA

6 ounces frozen lemonade,
   thawed
10 ounces frozen strawberries
½ cup sugar

⅓ cup plain instant tea
5 cups water
Mint for garnish

Place all ingredients in blender. Mix until smooth and of pouring consistency. Pour into ice-filled glasses. Garnish with a sprig of mint.
Serves: 8

Easy and pretty.

TOMATO MIST

46 ounces tomato juice
¼ cup fresh lemon juice
1 teaspoon sugar

½ teaspoon onion salt
2 teaspoons Worcestershire sauce
2 teaspoons prepared horseradish

Combine all ingredients. Mix well and chill.
Serves: 6

Ideal for a ladies luncheon.

Add a pinch of cinnamon to coffee grounds before perking or dripping a pot of coffee for an exotic "coffee house" taste.

COFFEE PUNCH

For 1 quart:
1 cup strong hot coffee
¼ cup sugar
Pinch of salt
½ teaspoon nutmeg

1 teaspoon vanilla extract
3 cups milk
1 pint vanilla ice cream

For 1 gallon:
4 cups strong hot coffee
1 cup sugar
¼ teaspoon salt
2 teaspoons nutmeg

4 teaspoons vanilla extract
12 cups milk
1 quart vanilla ice cream

Dissolve sugar in hot coffee. Add salt, nutmeg, vanilla and milk. Mix well. Refrigerate. When ready to serve, unmold frozen coffee ice ring in serving bowl. Pour milk mixture over ring, and place scoops of ice cream on top.

Coffee Ice Ring
1 Tablespoon instant coffee   **l cup water**

Mix instant coffee and water at above ratio to fill mold of desired size or ice trays. Freeze.
Yield: Quart serves 6 to 8, gallon serves 25 to 30

For a brunch add bourbon for a delicious milk punch.

CAFÉ FINALE

1½ ounces Kahlua liqueur
1 ounce brandy
½-¾ cup hot coffee

Whipped cream
8-10 drops Galliano liqueur
Maraschino cherry for garnish

Into a coffee mug pour Kahlua and brandy. Fill with coffee. Spoon on whipped cream. Slowly drop Galliano on top of whipped cream. Do not stir. Garnish with cherry. Sip through a small straw.
Serves: 1

Cold water is recommended for coffee because hot tap water extracts too many of the impurities embedded in the water pipes.

FROZEN CRANBERRY PUNCH

4 cups orange juice
1 cup fresh lemon juice
¾ cup fresh lime juice
3 (46 ounce) cans unsweetened
  pineapple juice

4 cups sugar
48 ounces cranberry juice
Ginger ale, chilled

Combine orange juice, lemon and lime juice. Add pineapple juice, sugar and cranberry juice. Mix well. Pour into 7-8 quart containers. Freeze. When ready to serve, thaw desired amount until "mushy". Mix 1 quart punch concentrate with 2¾ cups ginger ale.
Yield: 2½ gallons

A year round pleaser.

GOLDEN ANNIVERSARY PUNCH

5 cups water
2 cups sugar
3 ounces lemon gelatin
4 cups pineapple juice

1 cup fresh lemon juice
1 Tablespoon almond extract
1 quart ginger ale, chilled

In a saucepan bring water to a boil. Add sugar and cook until sugar is dissolved. Remove from heat and stir in gelatin until dissolved. Add pineapple juice, lemon juice and almond extract. Chill or freeze. When ready to serve, thaw punch if frozen, and add ginger ale.
Serves: 20 to 25

A good punch for a 50th wedding anniversary. "Golden" in color.

EASY FAMILY EGGNOG

2 (32 ounce) cans eggnog, chilled
½ gallon premium quality vanilla
  ice cream

Nutmeg

Pour eggnog into punch bowl. Spoon ice cream into bowl and break up with a punch ladle. Sprinkle generously with nutmeg.
Serves: 18 to 20

SUNSHINE PUNCH

12 ounces frozen orange juice, thawed
12 ounces frozen lemonade, thawed

46 ounces pineapple juice, chilled
2 quarts ginger ale, chilled
Mint leaves for garnish
Orange slices for garnish

Combine orange juice, lemonade and pineapple juice. Mix well. When ready to serve, pour mixture into a punch bowl. Add ginger ale and ice ring. Garnish with mint leaves and orange slices.

Ice Ring
12 ounces frozen orange juice, thawed
12 ounces frozen lemonade, thawed

6 cups water

Combine orange juice, lemonade and water. Pour into fluted tube pan. Freeze. Remove the ring from freezer about 15 minutes before serving. Unmold and place in punch bowl.
Serves: 40

This recipe can be halved. This is a lovely punch for a ladies' luncheon or a graduation party.

THE BEACHED NAVEL

¾ ounce vodka
¾ ounce peach schnapps
¾ ounce Grand Marnier or triple sec
1 ounce pineapple juice

3 ounces orange juice
½ ounce grenadine syrup
1 cup crushed ice
Lemon twists for garnish

Blend together and serve in wine glass with 2 twists of lemon.
Serves: 1 to 2

The ingredients speak for themselves.

CHAMPAGNE PUNCH

3 fifths dry white wine, chilled
2 (46 ounce) cans pineapple-
grapefruit juice, chilled

12 ounces frozen lemonade,
thawed
2 fifths champagne, chilled

Combine wine, pineapple-grapefruit juice and lemonade. Mix well. When ready to serve, pour juice mixture into a large punch bowl. Pour in champagne and add strawberry ring.

Strawberry Ring
1 cup strawberries, halved
½ cup fresh lemon juice

Water

Place strawberries in a fluted tube pan. Pour water into pan to cover fruit. Freeze. When frozen, add lemon juice and water to fill pan to within ½ inch of top. Freeze. Serves: 50

Can be halved easily.

HEARTY BLOODY MARY

46 ounces tomato juice
10½ ounce can beef bouillon
2 Tablespoons Worcestershire
sauce
8-10 drops Tabasco sauce
1 teaspoon celery salt

1 Tablespoon sugar
1 teaspoon Krazy salt
¼ cup fresh lemon juice
¼ teaspoon pepper
2¼ cups vodka
Fresh asparagus for garnish

Mix together all ingredients except vodka. Refrigerate. When ready to serve, add vodka. Stir well. Serve over ice in tall glasses. Garnish with asparagus spears. (The vodka can be added on a per-drink basis instead of all at once. The mix is delicious without vodka).
Serves: 12

One of the best.

FIFTH AVENUE FREEZE

2 ounces Praline liqueur   **4 scoops vanilla ice cream**
2 ounces dark Crème de Cacao   **Nutmeg for garnish**

Place all ingredients in a blender, except nutmeg. Blend until smooth. Serve in stemmed glasses. Sprinkle with nutmeg.
Serves: 4

For a different taste substitute Amaretto and Kahlua.

IILINI POLAR BEAR

2 ounces Kahlua liqueur   **¾ quart vanilla ice cream**
3 ounces vodka

Place Kahlua, vodka and half of the ice cream in blender. Blend for a few seconds. Add remaining ice cream and blend until smooth. Serve in stemmed glasses.
Serves: 4

A delicious after-dinner drink.

THE ABLE NAVEL

¾ cup peach schnapps   **½ cup water**
¾ cup vodka   **12-24 ice cubes**
6 ounces frozen orange   **Mint for garnish**
** juice,thawed**   **Peach slices for garnish**

Mix peach schnapps and vodka with half of orange juice and water in blender. Blend at low speed. Turn to high speed and mix thoroughly. Add a few ice cubes and continue blending at high speed. Keep adding portions of orange juice and ice cubes until slushy consistency is reached. All ingredients should have been used at this point. Serve in a wine glass and garnish with mint leaves or a peach slice. May be made ahead and placed in freezer until 15 minutes before serving.
Serves: 6

A perfect morning cocktail for a brunch.

HOT MULLED WINE

½ gallon Burgundy wine
64 ounces apple juice
3 cinnamon sticks

1½ teaspoons whole cloves
1 teaspoon whole allspice
Cinnamon sticks for garnish

Combine wine and apple juice. Tie spices together in cloth bag, or put in a tea caddy. Add to wine and apple juice mixture. Chill over night. Bring to a boil and simmer 5 minutes. Remove spice bag. Serve in mugs with cinnamon sticks.
Serves: 16

A great warm-up drink.

SAN SIMEON II SANGRIA

½ gallon orange juice
3½ cups pineapple juice
½ cup fresh lemon juice
½ cup cream of coconut
½ cup orgeat syrup

1 cup grenadine syrup
1 gallon red wine (does not have
  to be a fine vintage)
Orange slices for garnish
Cherries for garnish

In a jug or container which can be shaken, mix orange juice, pineapple juice, lemon juice, cream of coconut, orgeat syrup and grenadine syrup. Add wine and shake. Serve over crushed ice in large wine glasses. Garnish with orange slices and cherries. May be prepared 12 hours or more prior to serving, but do not add wine until serving time.

Substitute for orgeat syrup:
¼ cup simple syrup
1 Tablespoon almond extract

3-4 drops bitters
3 Tablespoons water

Mix together and stir briskly.
Yield: 2 gallons

Simple syrup, sugar syrup or bar syrup is simply sugar dissolved in water. To make it, measure one part water to two parts sugar. Mix and boil for 5 minutes. Cool, bottle and refrigerate. Use for mixing cocktails.

SOUPS
AND
SANDWICHES

CREAM OF ALMOND SOUP

3 cups chicken broth
3 Tablespoons chopped onion
2 cups finely chopped celery
2 cups milk
1 cup half-and-half cream
3 Tablespoons butter

3 Tablespoons all-purpose flour
1 teaspoon salt
⅛ teaspoon pepper
Dash of Tabasco sauce
¾ teaspoon almond extract
⅓ cup chopped toasted almonds

Combine broth, onion and celery in medium sauce pan. Bring to a boil. Cover and simmer 20 minutes. Blend in blender until smooth. Stir in milk and cream. Melt butter in medium sauce pan; stir in flour, salt and pepper. Gradually stir in broth mixture. Cook over medium heat until thickened and smooth. Remove from heat. Stir in Tabasco and almond extract. Sprinkle with toasted almonds when ready to serve.
Serves: 8

Everyone loves this!

BROCCOLI SOUP

2 cups water
4 teaspoons chicken bouillon
  granules
2 cups cubed potatoes
2 cups chopped celery

2 cups chopped broccoli
2 (10¾ ounce) cans cream of
  chicken soup
1 pound Velveeta cheese, cubed

Bring water to boil and dissolve bouillon. Add potatoes and celery. Cook 15 minutes. Add broccoli and cook 10 minutes. Stir in soup and cheese. Heat until cheese melts. Serve piping hot!
Serves: 6 to 8

CREAM OF CORN SOUP

1 Tablespoon butter
1 small onion, chopped
½ cup chopped celery

17 ounce can cream-style corn
2 cups milk

Mix all ingredients together and simmer for 30-40 minutes. Stir occasionally to prevent soup from sticking to bottom of pan.
Serves: 4

Easy and delicious!

PIMIENTO SOUP

2 Tablespoons margarine
½ cup chopped onion
2 Tablespoons all-purpose flour
3 cups chicken broth
½ cup chopped pimientos,
   drained

½ cup whipping cream
½ cup milk
2 Tablespoons vermouth
¼ teaspoon white pepper

In a 2-quart saucepan melt margarine over medium heat. Add onion and sauté until soft. Stir in flour; reduce heat to low and cook 2 minutes, being very careful not to brown. Add broth and pimientos. Cook and stir until thickened. Cool to warm. Transfer to blender and blend until smooth. Return to saucepan. Stir in cream, milk, vermouth and pepper. Heat, but do not boil.
Serves: 4

Fantastic! You have to try it to believe it! Different as a first course. Serve with a sandwich and salad for a great lunch.

CREAM OF MUSHROOM SOUP WITH SHERRY

4 Tablespoons butter, divided
⅓ cup finely diced onion
½ pound fresh mushrooms,
   finely chopped
4 cups chicken stock

2 Tablespoons all-purpose flour
1 teaspoon salt
1 cup half-and-half cream
2 Tablespoons dry sherry
Whipped cream for garnish

Melt 2 Tablespoons butter in skillet. Add onion and sauté until soft. Add mushrooms and sauté for 2 minutes. Add chicken stock, cover and simmer for 15 minutes. Melt remaining 2 Tablespoons butter in large saucepan; add flour and salt and cook for 3-5 minutes, stirring constantly. Add mushroom mixture and cream, stirring until smooth. Add sherry and mix well. Strain soup and reheat. Serve with a dollop of unsweetened whipped cream on top.
Serves: 4

This is heavenly!

One 6 ounce can mushrooms, drained, may be substituted in a recipe calling for ½ pound fresh mushrooms.

ONION SOUP BEAUJOLAIS

2½ pounds onions, thinly sliced
1 cup butter
½ teaspoon thyme
1¼ Tablespoons all-purpose flour
3 (10½ ounce) cans beef broth
2 cups water
3 bouillon cubes
⅓ cup beaujolais or other dry
  red wine

Salt and pepper to taste
6 slices French bread, toasted and
  buttered on one side
1¼ cups shredded Muenster
  cheese
1¼ cup shredded Swiss cheese
½ cup grated Parmesan cheese

Sauté onions in butter for 35 minutes; do not brown. Add thyme and flour, stirring for 2 minutes. Add broth, water, bouillon cubes, wine, salt and pepper. Simmer 35 minutes. Pour into 6 (10 ounce) ovenproof bowls, leaving 1½ inches at top. Place bread in bowls and top with Muenster and Swiss cheeses. Sprinkle with Parmesan cheese. Bake at 400 degrees until lightly browned.
Serves: 6

One of the best!

SHRIMP CHOWDER

1 pound shrimp
6 green onions, sliced, including
  tops
2 Tablespoons butter
2 (10¾ ounce) cans cream of
  potato soup
2 cups milk

½ cup shredded mild Cheddar
  cheese
2 Tablespoons dry sherry or
  vermouth
Dash white pepper
Snipped parsley for garnish

Cook shrimp in boiling salt water until pink, about 5 minutes. Cool shrimp and peel. In a 2-quart saucepan, melt butter and sauté green onions. Stir in soup and milk. Heat to boiling over medium heat, stirring occasionally. Add cheese, sherry, pepper and shrimp. Cook for 5 minutes, stirring occasionally, but do not boil. Better made a day ahead. Garnish with parsley when ready to serve.
Yield: 6 cups

Great reheated the next day!

"SOUTHERN" NEW ENGLAND CLAM CHOWDER

4 slices bacon
1 large potato, cubed
1 rib celery, chopped
1 small onion, chopped
¾ teaspoon salt
⅛ teaspoon pepper

⅛ teaspoon thyme
2 (6½ ounce) cans clams, drain and reserve juice
¼ cup all-purpose flour
3 cups milk
⅓ cup grated Parmesan cheese

Fry bacon until crisp. Drain on paper towel. Crumble bacon and set aside. To bacon drippings add potato, celery, onion, salt, pepper, thyme and clam juice. Heat to boiling and simmer covered about 10 minutes or until vegetables are tender. Combine flour and milk, a little at a time to prevent lumping. Slowly stir into vegetable mixture. Cook over medium heat until mixture thickens, stirring occasionally. Stir in clams, bacon and cheese. Heat thoroughly, but do not boil.
Serves: 4

SEAFOOD GUMBO

3 Tablespoons oil
2½ cups sliced okra
1 large onion, chopped
2 cloves garlic, crushed
1 green bell pepper, chopped
1 rib celery, chopped
6 Tablespoons all-purpose flour
4 chicken bouillon cubes
8 ounce can tomato paste
8 cups water
2 bay leaves
1 teaspoon salt

1 teaspoon pepper
1 teaspoon thyme
½ teaspoon marjoram
½ teaspoon oregano
½ teaspoon basil
2 sprigs fresh parsley, or 1 teaspoon flakes
14 ounce can tomatoes
Tabasco sauce to taste
1 ham slice, chopped
1-2 pounds raw shrimp, peeled
1 pound crabmeat

In a large soup pot sauté okra, onion, garlic, bell pepper and celery in oil. While vegetables are sautéing, brown flour in a dry iron skillet on low to medium heat, stirring constantly until golden brown. When vegetables are tender, stir in browned flour. Add water and all remaining ingredients, except shrimp and crabmeat. Simmer 45 minutes. Add seafood and cook another 15 minutes. Serve over rice.
Serves: 8 to 10

An old Southern favorite.

CHICKEN-CORN CHOWDER

2 cups chopped cooked chicken
5 slices bacon
4 ounce can sliced mushrooms
½ cup chopped onions
10¾ ounce can cream of celery
  soup

½ cup chopped tomatoes
10¾ ounce can chicken vegetable
  soup
1¼ cups water
8 ounce can whole kernel corn,
  undrained

Cook bacon and drain, reserving 2 Tablespoons of bacon drippings. Crumble bacon and set aside. Sauté mushrooms and onions in reserved drippings. Add bacon and remaining ingredients. Heat thoroughly, stirring occasionally. Freezes well.
Serves: 6 to 8

Serve with a grilled cheese sandwich on whole wheat bread for a satisfying supper.

OYSTER STEW

4 Tablespoons butter
3 or 4 Tablespoons minced green
  onions or onion juice
1 pint oysters, drain and reserve
  juice
Oyster liquid and enough milk to
  make 3 cups

Herbs: garlic powder, oregano,
  marjoram, basil, thyme, parsley
  flakes (or chopped fresh), celery
  salt, rosemary, paprika, salt and
  pepper.

In a skillet melt butter and sauté onions until tender. Add oysters and cook until edges curl, being careful not to over cook. Remove from heat and set aside. In top of large double boiler, heat the milk and oyster liquid with a dash of each of the seasonings. Add oysters and sautéed onions; heat thoroughly, but do not boil. When using onion juice, add it when adding oysters to milk.
Serves: 4

A good Christmas Eve supper with a green salad and French bread.

VEGETABLE OVEN STEW

2 pounds stew meat, cubed
16 ounce can English peas
1 cup sliced carrots
1½ cups chopped onions
1 large potato, cubed

1 teaspoon salt
½ teaspoon black pepper
1 bay leaf
10½ ounce can tomato soup

In a Dutch oven layer ingredients in order given. Pour soup over top. Cover and bake at 275 degrees for 5 hours, or use a crock pot.
Serves: 4 to 6

CRAB ASPARAGUS SOUP

½ pound crabmeat
¼ cup chopped green onions
½ teaspoon curry
1 Tablespoon butter

2 (10¾ ounce) cans cream of
   asparagus soup
2 cups half-and-half cream
¼ cup sherry

Drain crabmeat if necessary. Remove any remaining shell. Sauté green onions and curry in butter. Stir in soup, cream and crab. Stir gently so that crab does not become stringy. Heat, stirring occasionally. Blend in sherry. Serve in mugs or bowls.
Serves: 6

Great for a new bride who wants to impress her in-laws!

TACO SOUP

1½ pounds ground chuck
1 onion, chopped
28 ounce can tomatoes
15 ounce can tomato sauce
2 (10¾ ounce) cans cream of
   potato soup

10½ ounce can beef broth
2 (16 ounce) cans kidney beans
1 (1.25 ounce) package taco
   seasoning mix
Corn chips
Shredded Cheddar cheese

In a Dutch oven brown meat and onions. Add remaining ingredients and simmer 20-30 minutes. Serve over crushed corn chips. Top with cheese.
Serves: 10 to 12

A great dish for children's or teenagers' party.

CHILI SOUP

2 pounds ground chuck
2 (14 ounce) cans stewed
  tomatoes
3 cups water
15 ounce can pork and beans
16 ounce can kidney beans
10¼ ounce can mixed vegetables

1 (1.25 ounce) package hot chili
  mix
1 teaspoon chili powder
½ teaspoon cumin
½ teaspoon salt
1 cup diced baked ham

Brown ground chuck; drain well. Add remaining ingredients except ham. Cover and simmer for 45 minutes-1 hour. Add ham and cook until hot.
Serves: 8 to 10

Super easy and good. Great performance just to open all these cans!

MEXICAN SOUP

½ pound pork sausage
1 medium onion, chopped
1 clove garlic, minced
2 (15 ounce) cans black-eyed peas
2 (14 ounce) cans stewed
  tomatoes

½ cup water
2 teaspoons chili powder
¼ teaspoon black pepper

In skillet cook sausage until done. Drain and crumble. Leave just enough drippings in skillet to sauté onions. Combine all ingredients in large pot and simmer over low heat for 20 minutes. Stir occasionally.
Serves: 6

Great recipe for using black-eyed peas.

Bottled minced garlic is convenient but less available than dry forms of garlic. Substitute ½ teaspoon for 1 clove fresh garlic. Refrigerate after opening.

SAUSAGE AND BEAN SOUP

1 pound pork sausage
2 (16 ounce) cans kidney beans, drained
28 ounce can tomatoes, chopped
4 cups water
1 large onion, chopped

1 bay leaf
½ teaspoon salt
½ teaspoon garlic salt
½ teaspoon thyme
⅛ teaspoon pepper
½ cup chopped green bell pepper

Cook sausage until browned. Drain and crumble. In large pot combine beans, tomatoes, water, onion, bay leaf and seasonings. Add sausage, cover and simmer for 1 hour. Add bell pepper and cook for 15-20 minutes or until bell pepper is tender. Serves: 6

Serve with corn bread for a complete meal.

COLD TOMATO SOUP

46 ounces tomato juice
2 Tablespoons sugar
1½ teaspoons salt
1 clove garlic, pressed
1 teaspoon Worchestershire sauce
2 Tablespoons lemon juice
1 cucumber, peeled and chopped

1 green bell pepper, chopped
3 tomatoes, chopped
14 ounce can artichoke hearts, chopped
1 cup chopped celery
¼ cup chopped green onions
1 cup shredded carrots

Mix together tomato juice, sugar, salt, garlic, Worchestershire sauce and lemon juice. Refrigerate overnight. Two hours before serving, add chopped vegetables. Mix well. Serves: 6 to 8

Better than gazpacho because it does not have oil!

Garlic salt is mostly salt. Begin by adding ⅛ to ¼ teaspoon, tasting for both garlic and salt.

COLD SPINACH SOUP

10¾ ounce can cream of potato
  soup
2½ cups milk
5 ounces frozen chopped spinach,
  thawed and drained

2 chicken bouillon cubes
1 teaspoon chopped chives
1 teaspoon chopped parsley
⅛ teaspoon Accent
Salt and pepper to taste

Place all ingredients in blender, reserving 1¼ cups of milk. Blend until smooth. Add reserved milk. Serve cold or hot. Variation: Add a few fresh oysters when serving soup hot.
Serves: 4 to 6

YELLOW SQUASH SOUP

2 medium onions, sliced
3 Tablespoons butter
12 medium yellow squash,
  sliced
1 cup chicken broth

Salt and freshly ground pepper
  to taste
2 cups half-and-half cream
Chopped fresh chives
Paprika

Sauté onions in butter until limp, but not browned. Add squash and chicken broth. Cover and cook briskly until squash is very tender, about 15 minutes. Cool. Purée in blender or food processor. Season with salt and pepper. Chill in refrigerator. Stir in cream when cold. Serve in chilled cups. Sprinkle with chives and paprika.
Serves: 6 to 8 large cups
14 to 16 demitasse cups

A very appealing soup course for a spring or summer luncheon!

Half-and-half contains a minimum of 10.5% milkfat to a maximum of 18%. Light cream contains no less than 15% milkfat, no more than 30%. Whipping cream begins at 30% up to a maximum of 36% milkfat.

CHICKEN AND RICE SOUP

4-6 chicken breasts
1 teaspoon celery salt
1 teaspoon onion salt
1 teaspoon garlic salt
Water, enough to cover chicken

4-5 ribs celery, chopped
1 large onion, chopped
1 cup raw rice
2 (10¾ ounce) cans cream of
chicken soup

In large Dutch oven cook chicken breasts in water seasoned with celery salt, onion salt and garlic salt, until tender. Cool chicken in broth. Reserve broth. Remove chicken from bone and cut into bite size pieces. Add celery, onion and rice to broth and cook for 15 minutes. Add chicken and soup. Simmer 1-2 hours. Add more water during cooking time, if necessary.
Serves: 12

Great to take to "sick" friend who needs a hot nourishing meal. Children and men love this!

FRENCH COUNTRY SOUP

2 pound chuck roast, cubed
8 cups water
2 (8 ounce) cans tomato sauce
with onions
2 beef bouillon cubes
1 Tablespoon sugar

¼ teaspoon black pepper
3 whole cloves
2 large turnips, pared and diced
¾ cup small elbow macaroni
16 ounce can cut green beans,
drained

In Dutch oven or kettle combine beef, water, tomato sauce, bouillon cubes, sugar, pepper and cloves. Bring to a boil. Simmer covered for 2 hours. Add remaining ingredients and simmer for 20 minutes uncovered or until macaroni is tender. Serve with cornbread or garlic bread.
Serves: 6 to 8

Hearty meal for cold winter night.

Substitute ⅛ teaspoon dried minced garlic for 1 clove fresh garlic.

BAKED HAM AND ASPARAGUS SANDWICH

12 slices bread, crusts trimmed
Butter
Mayonnaise
Mustard
6 slices baked ham
6 slices Swiss or American cheese

6 eggs
¾ cup milk
15 ounce can asparagus, heated
  and drained
Paprika

Spread each slice of bread with butter. Spread reverse side of 6 slices with mayonnaise. Place buttered side down on 9X13-inch greased baking dish. Top each slice with a slice of ham and cheese. Spread mustard on reverse side of remaining 6 slices and place on sandwich with buttered side up. Beat eggs and milk together and pour over sandwiches. Cover and refrigerate overnight. Before serving, bake at 350 degrees for 30 minutes. When ready to serve, cut into individual sandwiches and place on plate. Top with asparagus spear and ladle with sauce. Sprinkle with paprika.

Sauce
2 (10¾ ounce) cans cream of
  mushroom soup
4 ounce can mushrooms, drained
Dash of Tabasco

1-2 Tablespoons Worcestershire
  sauce
1 Tablespoon onion juice

In saucepan combine all ingredients. Cook over low heat until hot.
Serves: 6

A nice luncheon sandwich.

PARTY SHRIMP SANDWICHES

4½ ounce can shrimp, drained
  and mashed
2 Tablespoons grated onion
Lemon juice to taste

4-6 drops Tabasco sauce
3 ounces cream cheese, softened
Mayonnaise
Thin sliced bread

In a bowl combine shrimp, onion, lemon juice, Tabasco, cheese and just enough mayonnaise to make a spreadable consistency. Trim crust from bread. Spread filling on bread and assemble sandwiches. Cut into triangles or finger sandwiches.
Yields: About 16 sandwiches

Shrimp mixture can be stuffed into cocktail tomatoes for an appetizer.

PIMIENTO CHEESE

⅓ cup milk
1 pound Velveeta cheese
1 Tablespoon sugar
1 egg

1 Tablespoon vinegar
7 ounce jar pimientos, chopped
1 cup mayonnaise

Melt cheese with milk in top of double boiler or microwave. Add sugar, egg, vinegar, pimiento and cook 5-10 minutes over medium heat, stirring constantly. For microwave, cook 3-4 minutes, stirring at short intervals. Remove from heat and add mayonnaise, mixing well. Add additional mayonnaise if desired. Will keep in refrigerator for at least 2 weeks.
Yields: 4 cups

DEVILED CHEESE AND BACON SANDWICH

8 ounces Cheddar cheese,
  shredded
2 Tablespoons ketchup
1 Tablespoon minced onion
1 Tablespoon minced celery

1 Tablespoon butter, melted
1 teaspoon prepared mustard
½ cup fried and crumbled bacon
Mayonnaise to taste

Combine all ingredients. Spread on bread and toast. Even good cold. Wonderful on homemade bread.
Yields: 6 to 8 sandwiches

A delicious cheese sandwich. A nice change from pimiento cheese.

SUMMER EGG SALAD SANDWICH

3 ounces cream cheese, softened
¼ cup mayonnaise
½ teaspoon salt
¾ teaspoon dill weed
½ teaspoon dry mustard
6 hard-boiled eggs, chopped

1 cup sliced ripe olives
½ cup chopped celery
2 Tablespoons minced onion
1 Tablespoon chopped pimiento
3 pita breads, halved

Blend cream cheese, mayonnaise and seasonings thoroughly. Stir in remaining ingredients. Spread ½ cup mixture into each pocket bread half.
Yields: 6 sandwiches

A summertime favorite.

CHICKEN FILLED POCKET SANDWICHES

1 cup plain yogurt
1 package dry ranch dressing mix
2 Tablespoons mayonnaise
1 cup chopped cooked chicken
½ cup shredded lettuce
½ cup chopped black olives

6 ounce jar marinated artichoke
  hearts
4 green onions, chopped
1 medium tomato, chopped
1 small cucumber, chopped
4 whole pita breads

Mix yogurt, dressing mix and mayonnaise. Combine remaining ingredients, except pita bread, and toss with dressing mixture. Wrap pita bread in foil and heat at 300 degrees for 10 minutes. Cut bread in halves to form pockets. Fill with stuffing. Serve immediately.
Yields: 8 halves

CHICAGO CHICKEN CLUB SANDWICH

Roquefort cheese, crumbled
Mayonnaise
2 slices white or wheat bread,
  lightly toasted
Sliced chicken or sliced smoked
  turkey

2 slices bacon, fried crisp
Fresh ripe pear, peeled and sliced
Bibb lettuce

Mix desired amount of Roquefort cheese with mayonnaise. Spread on bread. Assemble sandwich adding remaining ingredients.
Yield: 1 sandwich

Surprisingly good and different!

CURRY-RIPE OLIVE SANDWICH

14 ounce can pitted ripe olives
1 cup finely chopped green
  onions and tops
3 cups shredded Cheddar cheese

1 cup mayonnaise
¾ teaspoon curry
½ teaspoon salt
6 English muffins, split

Chop olives. Add remaining ingredients, except muffins. Mix together and pile mixture high on each muffin. Place under broiler until puffy and lightly browned.
Serves: 6

Great with spinach salad!

MUFFALETTA WITH OLIVE SALAD

1 muffaletta loaf, hoagie bun or small loaf of French bread
Olive oil
4-5 slices provolone cheese

4-5 slices Genoa salami
4-5 slices ham
4-5 slices Swiss cheese

To assemble sandwich, slice bread in half horizontally. Drizzle each half with olive oil. Spread one side with generous amount of olive salad. Top with meats and cheeses. Cover with top of loaf. Serve at room temperature.

Olive Salad
⅔ cup chopped green olives
⅔ cup chopped black olives
¼ cup chopped pimiento
3 cloves garlic, minced
1 anchovy fillet, minced
1 Tablespoon capers

⅓ cup finely chopped fresh parsley
1 teaspoon oregano
¼ teaspoon pepper
½ cup olive oil

Mix all ingredients together. May be processed in food processor for short time to blend but not purée. Cover and marinate unrefrigerated at least 12 hours.
Serves: 4

HAM AND TURKEY POOR BOY

1 cup margarine, softened
2 Tablespoons prepared mustard
1 teaspoon poppy seeds
2 teaspoons grated onion
12 mini French rolls

12 slices cooked ham
12 slices salami
12 slices mozzarella or Swiss cheese
24 slices smoked turkey

Mix margarine, mustard, poppy seeds and grated onion, and spread on mini French rolls. Place 1 slice of ham, salami, cheese and 2 slices of turkey on each roll. Wrap in foil and bake in oven at 325 degrees for 20 minutes.
Yields: 12 sandwiches

Hearty enough to please a man, and just right for a ladies' luncheon.

HOT CRABMEAT SANDWICH

8 ounces cream cheese, softened
½ pound crabmeat
1¼ teaspoons grated onion
2 Tablespoons lemon juice
1 teaspoon Worcestershire sauce
¼ teaspoon Tabasco sauce

Salt and pepper to taste
4 English muffins, split
2 large ripe tomatoes, sliced
8 slices Cheddar cheese
8 slices bacon, cooked and halved

In a bowl combine the first 6 ingredients. Season with salt and pepper. Spread a generous portion of crab mixture on each English muffin. Top with a tomato slice, cheese slice and 2 halves of bacon slices. Bake at 325 degrees for 15-20 minutes or until hot and cheese has melted. The crabmeat mixture can be prepared ahead. Yields: 8

Delicious served with marinated vegetables for a luncheon.

BEEF DIP SANDWICHES

4 pound beef roast
Garlic salt
Pepper
2 Tablespoons oil
6-8 cups water
2 packages dry onion soup mix
2 Tablespoons Worcestershire
  sauce

Small or mini French bread loaves,
  one per person
1 onion, sliced and sautéed,
  optional
Monterey Jack cheese, sliced,
  optional

Salt and pepper roast. In a Dutch oven brown meat quickly on all sides in oil. Add water, soup mix and Worcestershire sauce. Cover and simmer over low heat until tender, approximately 2 hours. Slice French bread in half. Wrap in aluminum foil and heat in oven until hot. Slice roast thinly and place on bottom half of bread. Top with onions and cheese, if desired, and broil until cheese melts. Cover with tops. Serve broth from cooked meat in individual bowls for dipping sandwiches. Serves: 8

Serve with a green salad for a complete meal.

SALADS
AND
DRESSINGS

BEST CHICKEN SALAD IN THE WORLD

½ cup mayonnaise
¼ cup sour cream
1 Tablespoon sugar
1 teaspoon lemon rind
1 Tablespoon fresh lemon juice
½ teaspoon ginger
¼ teaspoon salt

2 cups cooked, chopped chicken
1 cup seedless green grapes
1 cup chopped celery
¼-½ cup sliced or slivered
  almonds, toasted
1 cantaloupe, peeled and sliced
  into rings

In a small bowl stir together mayonnaise, sour cream, sugar, lemon rind, lemon juice, ginger and salt. In mixing bowl combine chicken, grapes, celery and almonds. Add mayonnaise mixture and blend thoroughly. Cover; chill at least 2 hours before serving. Serve salad in melon rings.
Serves: 6 to 8

CHICKEN LUNCHEON SALAD

3 ounces cream cheese, softened
1 cup sour cream
Dash of salt
¾ cup chopped celery
½ cup chopped walnuts
2 cups cooked, diced chicken
  breasts

2 Tablespoons chopped green bell
  pepper
13½ ounce can pineapple tidbits,
  well drained
½ cup mayonnaise
1-2 Tablespoons fresh lemon juice

In a mixing bowl combine cream cheese, sour cream and salt. Add celery, walnuts and bell pepper. Mix well. Fold in diced chicken and pineapple tidbits. Chill. Before serving, mix mayonnaise and lemon juice. Place a dollop on each serving.
Serves: 5 to 6

Try chopped pecans in chicken, tuna or egg salads.

CHICKEN SALAD SUPERB

2 chicken breasts
½ cup chopped green onions
½-¾ cup sliced black olives
½ cup chopped water chestnuts

2 Tablespoons fresh chopped
 parsley
1¼ cups mayonnaise
Salt and pepper to taste

Boil chicken breasts. Allow chicken to cool in broth before removing. Shred chicken into small pieces. Add the remaining ingredients. Mix well and pour into a greased 4-cup mold. Chill. More mayonnaise may be added if mixture seems dry. This may be served as a main dish for a luncheon, or as a filling for miniature puff pastries. For a luncheon, place chicken salad in ½ cantaloupe or ¼ pineapple boat. The most important thing to remember about this recipe is to let chicken cool completely in the broth in which it was cooked.

Serves: 8

GUACAMOLE CHICKEN SALAD

Head of iceburg lettuce
2 medium tomatoes, chopped
¼ cup chopped green onions
1 cup broken taco flavored tortilla
 chips

3 cups cooked, chopped chicken
 breast
½ cup sliced black olives
½ cup grated Cheddar cheese

Break bite-sized pieces of lettuce into bowl. Add tomatoes, onions, chips, chicken and olives, reserving a few olives for garnish. Toss lightly with all of the avocado dressing just before serving. Top with cheese and reserved olives.

Avocado Dressing
½ cup mashed ripe avocado
1 Tablespoon fresh lemon juice
½ cup vegetable oil
1 teaspoon garlic salt

½ teaspoon sugar
½ teaspoon chili powder
¼ teaspoon Tabasco sauce

Combine mashed avocado and lemon juice. Add the remaining ingredients. Mix well and chill. May be made in blender.

Serves: 8

Good luncheon main dish.

CHICKEN BOUQUET

1 cup Italian dressing
¼ cup dry white wine
2 cups fresh broccoli flowerets
3 cups cooked, chopped chicken
2 cups cooked elbow macaroni
2 cups fresh mushrooms, sliced

¾ cup red bell pepper, cut into
  julienne strips
½ red onion, sliced and
  separated into rings
Salt and pepper to taste
¼ cup grated Parmesan cheese

Combine dressing and wine. Blend well. In large bowl combine broccoli, chicken, macaroni, mushrooms, red pepper and onions. Toss with dressing. Season to taste. Cover and refrigerate, stirring occasionally. Sprinkle with cheese before serving,
Serves: 6

SEAFOOD SALAD

1 package dry Italian dressing mix
1 pound fresh lump crabmeat
1 cup cooked shrimp
1 cup sliced ripe olives
1 cup thinly sliced fresh
  mushrooms
⅓ cup chopped celery

2 Tablespoons minced green
  onions
2 ounce jar diced pimientos
Bibb lettuce
Tomato wedges
Avocado slices

Prepare Italian dressing according to package directions, using wine vinegar. Set aside. Combine crabmeat, shrimp, olives, mushrooms, celery, green onions and pimientos. Pour prepared dressing over seafood mixture; toss gently to coat. Refrigerate 5 hours or overnight. Serve on Bibb lettuce with tomato wedges and avocado slices.
Serves: 6

Black peppercorns are harvested when the berries are slightly underripe and yellow-ish-red in color. Dried in the sun, they shrivel up and turn black. They have the most bite and most aromatic bouquet.

SHRIMP PASTA SALAD

7 ounces vermicelli, broken in half
5 hard-boiled eggs, chopped
5 ribs celery, chopped
6 medium size sweet pickles, chopped
¼ cup finely chopped onion

I cup mayonnaise
2 Tablespoons Dijon mustard
Salt to taste
½ pound fresh salad shrimp
Paprika

Cook vermicelli al dente. Drain and rinse with cold water to prevent sticking. In small bowl combine eggs, celery, pickles, onion, mayonnaise, mustard and salt. Blend well and add to pasta. Refrigerate. Just before serving, add shrimp and toss lightly. Sprinkle with paprika and serve.
Serves: 6 to 8

SHRIMP TORTELLINI SALAD

1 pound fresh asparagus, trimmed and blanched
½ pound fresh mushrooms, sliced
¾ cup black olives, sliced
1 medium tomato, cubed
9 ounces cheese tortellini, cooked and drained

9 ounces spinach tortellini, cooked and drained
2 pounds shrimp, cooked, peeled and deveined

Slice asparagus diagonally in 1-inch pieces. In large bowl combine asparagus, mushrooms, olives and tomato. Pour marinade over vegetables and refrigerate for 24 hours. Add tortellini and shrimp to marinated vegetables 2 hours before serving. Toss well.

Marinade
1½ cups walnut oil or olive oil
½ cup fresh lemon juice
3 cloves garlic, minced
2 Tablespoons minced fresh parsley
½ teaspoon oregano

½ teaspoon basil
¼ teaspoon Creole seasoning
Salt and freshly ground pepper to taste
¼ teaspoon cayenne pepper

Combine all marinade ingredients. Mix well.
Serves: 8 to 10

SHRIMP AND BEAN SALAD

2 (16 ounce) cans Blue Lake
  whole green beans, drained
14 ounce can artichoke hearts,
  drained and quartered
8 ounce can sliced water
  chestnuts, drained
¾ pound small shrimp, cooked
  and peeled

1 cup Green Goddess dressing
2-4 Tablespoons dry onion soup
  mix
2 Tablespoons chopped pimientos
Lettuce
Tomatoes for garnish

Toss beans, artichoke hearts and water chestnuts together. Add shrimp, salad dressing, onion soup mix and pimientos. Mix well. Cover and chill. Best made the day before serving. Serve on lettuce and garnish with tomatoes.
Serves: 8

SEAFOOD AND RICE SALAD

4 cups cooked wild rice mix,
  chilled
1 cup chopped crab, lobster,
  shrimp or crawfish
½ cup slivered Smithfield ham
1 cup finely chopped celery
3 hard-boiled eggs, finely
  chopped
2 Tablespoons chopped chives
⅓ cup chopped fresh parsley

2 Tablespoons olive oil
2 Tablespoons wine vinegar
½ cup mayonnaise
Salt and freshly ground pepper
  to taste
Cantaloupe
Honeydew

In a large bowl combine first 7 ingredients. Toss lightly. Sprinkle with oil and vinegar. Stir in mayonnaise, salt and pepper. Cover and refrigerate several hours before serving. Serve with sliced cantaloupe and honeydew melon.
Serves: 8

White peppercorns are picked when fully matured, at which time they are pink or red. Once dried, the pale inner seed becomes the white peppercorn as we know it. These are most often used in "pale" dishes to add flavor without adding color.

WHITE BEAN SALAD

2 cups canned white beans
¼ cup olive oil
1 Tablespoon fresh lemon juice
¼ teaspoon pepper
2 Tablespoons chopped onion

2 sprigs parsley, chopped
6½ ounce can tuna, drained
1 clove garlic, minced
Salt to taste

Drain beans well. Place in a serving bowl. Add olive oil, lemon juice, pepper, onion, parsley, tuna, garlic and salt. Toss gently. Refrigerate until ready to serve.
Serves: 4

Good and different!

LOBSTER TERRINE WITH SAUCE VERTE

1½ Tablespoons unflavored
  gelatin
½ cup cold water
½ cup fresh lemon juice
2 cups cooked chopped lobster
2 green onions, finely chopped

2 Tablespoons capers
2 Tablespoons Worcestershire
  sauce
1 cup mayonnaise
Tabasco sauce to taste

Soften gelatin in water. Heat, stirring until dissolved. Add lemon juice and set aside. Combine remaining ingredients. Fold in gelatin mixture and pour into chilled 8X4-inch loaf pan. Refrigerate until set.

Sauce Verte
1 cup mayonnaise
1 cup sour cream
1 teaspoon dry mustard

2 cucumbers, seeded and finely
  chopped
1-2 Tablespoons chopped chives

Mix sauce ingredients together and spoon over lobster terrine.
Serves: 6 to 8

Green peppercorns are the soft, green berries taken from the vine when unripe. They are usually canned in brine and are mild and fresh but pungent.

ORIENTAL CRABMEAT SALAD

½ pound crabmeat
8 ounce can sliced water
  chestnuts, drained
⅓ cup slivered almonds
1 cup chopped celery
1 teaspoon dry onion flakes

1 teaspoon lemon juice
½ cup sour cream
½ cup mayonnaise
Salt and pepper to taste
3 ounce can Chinese noodles

Combine all ingredients, except noodles, in serving bowl. Chill. Add noodles just before serving and toss gently.
Serves: 8

MARINATED PASTA WITH FETA

1 cup orzo pasta
4 ounces feta cheese, crumbled
3 Tablespoons chopped fresh
  parsley
3 Tablespoons minced fresh basil,
  or I Tablespoon dried basil

1 large tomato, seeded and
  coarsely chopped
⅓ cup olive oil
¼ cup fresh lemon juice
½ teaspoon salt
¼ teaspoon pepper

Cook and drain pasta. Add cheese, parsley, basil and tomato. Mix gently. For dressing combine olive oil, lemon juice, salt and pepper. Mix thoroughly. Pour dressing over pasta mixture. Toss gently. Refrigerate. Toss again before serving.
Serves: 8

SPAGHETTI SALAD

4 tomatoes, peeled, seeded and
  chopped
16 ounces mozzarella cheese,
  shredded
2 Tablespoons minced fresh basil
  or 2 teaspoons dried basil

2 cloves garlic, crushed
1⅓ cups olive oil
Salt and pepper
1 pound spaghetti
Freshly grated Parmesan cheese

Toss tomatoes, cheese, basil, garlic, olive oil, salt and pepper. Let mixture stand covered at room temperature for 30 minutes. Cook and drain spaghetti. Toss with oil mixture. Serve with Parmesan cheese. Serve at room temperature. Do not heat. May be used as a main dish or a side dish.
Serves: 10-12

TORTELLINI SALAD

18 ounces cheese tortellini
¼ ounces Gorgonzola cheese,
　divided
¼ cup olive oil
1 Tablespoon fresh lemon juice

½ medium red onion, chopped
½ red bell pepper, chopped
Salt and pepper to taste
½ cup mayonnaise
¼ cup sour cream

Cook tortellini al dente and drain. Crumble half the cheese and add to warm pasta. Toss gently. Combine oil, lemon juice, onion and pepper. Mix well. Add to pasta mixture. Cool. Mash remaining cheese, and mix with mayonnaise and sour cream. Add to cooled noodles. Refrigerate several hours before serving.
Serves: 10 to 12

A nice and easy luncheon dish that can be done ahead.

ITALIAN POTATO SALAD

4-5 medium potatoes
1 cup Italian dressing
1 green bell pepper, chopped
1 cup celery, chopped
1 medium onion, finely chopped

3 hard-boiled eggs, chopped
1 cup mayonnaise
½ cup sliced green olives
Paprika

Boil potatoes until just tender. Cool slightly, peel and cube. Pour Italian dressing over potatoes. Refrigerate overnight. The next day, add bell pepper, celery, onion, eggs and mayonnaise. Mix well. Place olives on top, and sprinkle with paprika before serving. Variation: Add 2 cups cooked and peeled shrimp for a great shrimp salad.
Serves: 6 to 8

Forget about freezing cooked, uncooked or partially cooked potatoes. They do not get along well with freezers. They become mealy, mushy, soggy and flavorless!

SALADS

DAY-AHEAD SPINACH SALAD

8-12 ounces fresh spinach, rinsed, stemmed and torn into pieces
½ medium cucumber, thinly sliced
½ cup thinly sliced radishes
¼ cup thinly sliced green onions
2 hard-boiled eggs, sliced
¾ cup Bleu cheese dressing
5 slices bacon, fried crisp and crumbled
½ cup salted peanuts

Arrange spinach evenly in a shallow salad bowl. Layer cucumber slices, radishes, green onions and eggs. Spread dressing over top. Cover and chill for 24 hours. Just before serving, sprinkle with bacon and peanuts.
Serves: 6

POLYNESIAN SPINACH

16 ounces fresh spinach, rinsed, stemmed and torn into pieces
1 head Bibb lettuce, torn into pieces
3 seedless naval oranges, peeled, sliced and quartered
⅔ cup flaked coconut
½ cup peanuts

In salad bowl combine spinach, lettuce, oranges, coconut and peanuts. Drizzle dressing over salad and serve immediately.

Dressing
½ cup white vinegar
½ cup vegetable oil
1 Tablespoon powdered sugar
½ teaspoon salt
¼ teaspoon dried basil

In mixing bowl combine all dressing ingredients.
Serves: 8 to 10

Pretreat any wooden kitchen equipment, i.e. salad bowls, cutting boards, etc., with mineral oil. It is odorless and tasteless, will not turn rancid and helps prevent food from being absorbed into the wood's finish.

SPICY SPINACH SALAD

8 ounces Monterey Jack cheese
   with jalapeño peppers,
   shredded
7 ounce jar baby corn ears,
   drained
1 large tomato, cut into chunks
1 cup zesty Italian dressing

2 Tablespoons chopped shallots
¼ teaspoon chili powder
Salt and pepper to taste
16 ounces fresh spinach, torn into
   pieces
1 small head romaine lettuce,
   torn into pieces

Place shredded cheese into medium bowl. Cut corn into ½-inch pieces. Add corn, tomato, salad dressing, shallots, chili powder, salt and pepper. Mix gently and let stand at room temperature for 30 minutes. In large salad bowl arrange greens. Add dressing mixture and toss. Variation: May add sliced avocado, chopped celery and shredded carrots. Also, broken pieces of corn chips may be sprinkled on top.
Serves: 8 to 10

This is a favorite of teenagers—even the ones who don't like spinach!

GREEN BEANS GLORIOUS

2 (14½ ounce) cans green beans,
   drained
1 medium onion, sliced
1 teaspoon vegetable oil

1 teaspoon white vinegar
3 Tablespoons Italian dressing
Salt and pepper to taste

Drain beans. Add onions, oil, vinegar, Italian dressing, salt and pepper. Marinate for several hours in refrigerator. Pour sour cream dressing over beans before serving. This recipe may be served hot or cold. If served hot, bake at 350 degrees for 35 minutes or until bubbly.

Sour Cream Dressing
1 cup sour cream
1 cup mayonnaise
1 teaspoon fresh lemon juice
1 teaspoon dry mustard

1 Tablespoon horseradish
1 teaspoon onion juice
2 teaspoons chives
1 teaspoon anchovy paste

Combine all ingredients. Mix well.
Serves: 8 to 10

BROCCOLI SURPRISE SALAD

2 bunches fresh broccoli
1 small onion, chopped
½ cup seedless raisins

10 slices bacon, fried crisp and crumbled
½ cup sunflower nuts, optional

Cut broccoli into small flowerets. In bowl combine broccoli, onion, raisins, bacon and nuts. Toss with dressing. Cover and refrigerate for 3-4 hours before serving.

Dressing:
1 cup mayonnaise
⅓ cup sugar

2 Tablespoons wine vinegar
⅓ cup grated Parmesan cheese

Combine all ingredients and mix well.
Serves: 8

CHINESE COLESLAW

2 Tablespoons vegetable oil
¼ cup sesame seeds
¼ cup slivered almonds
¼ cup sugar
1 teaspoon pepper
1 teaspoon salt
6 Tablespoons vinegar

½ cup vegetable oil
1 head cabbage, shredded or chopped
8 green onions, chopped
3 ounces Ramen Chinese noodles, broken, do not use seasoning mix

Heat oil in skillet. Toast sesame seeds and almonds. Remove from heat. Add sugar, pepper, salt, vinegar and oil. Stir well; pour into a container. Cover and refrigerate. This part may be made one day ahead. Mix shredded cabbage and onion together. Shake dressing and pour over coleslaw. Add noodles just before serving. Toss well. Serve immediately.
Serves: 8

Hate the calories but love the taste of coleslaw or potato salad? Substitute low-fat yogurt for the mayonnaise for great tasting dishes with a fraction of the fat and calories.

TOMATO AND BANANA SURPRISE

½ cup finely chopped white
  onions
½ cup white vinegar
½ teaspoon salt

¼ teaspoon pepper
3 Tablespoons sugar
3 tomatoes, peeled and cubed
4 bananas, sliced

In a 1-quart container mix together onion, vinegar, salt, pepper and sugar. Refrigerate. Just before serving, combine tomatoes and sliced bananas. Pour dressing over salad and toss well. Use slotted spoon to serve. Serve immediately.
Serves: 6 to 8

Try it to believe it!

VEGETABLE MEDLEY SALAD

2 bunches fresh broccoli, cut into
  flowerets
1 head cauliflower, cut into
  flowerets
1 cup grated carrots
1 cup black olives, sliced

½ cup green olives, sliced
1 ounce package dry ranch
  dressing mix
4 Tablespoons sunflower nuts
4 Tablespoons bacon bits
1 cup mayonnaise

In a large bowl combine broccoli, cauliflower, carrots and olives with dry dressing mix. When ready to serve, add sunflower nuts and bacon bits. Blend in mayonnaise.
Serves: 10-12

ASPARAGUS LUNCHEON SPECIAL

2 (15 ounce) cans asparagus tips,
  drain and reserve liquid
¼ cup cold water
1 Tablespoon unflavored gelatin
½ cup mayonnaise

½ cup whipping cream, whipped
1 teaspoon salt
2 Tablespoons fresh lemon juice
1 cup slivered almonds

Measure liquid from asparagus and add water to make 1 cup. Heat liquid. Soften unflavored gelatin in cold water. Add to hot liquid, stir until dissolved. Chill until partially set. Fold in mayonnaise, whipped cream, salt and lemon juice. Add asparagus and almonds. Pour into individual molds that have been lightly oiled.
Serves: 8

AVOCADO SMOOTH SALAD

3 ounces lime gelatin
1 cup boiling water
3 Tablespoons fresh lemon juice
¼ teaspoon onion juice
Salt to taste

1 cup whipping cream, whipped
½ cup mayonnaise
2 medium avocados, peeled and mashed

Dissolve gelatin in boiling water. Add lemon juice, onion juice, salt and pepper. Chill. When partially set, add remaining ingredients. Pour into oiled 4-cup mold. Chill until set.
Serves: 8

MYSTERY SALAD

3 ounces raspberry gelatin
⅓ cup plus 2 Tablespoons very hot water
14½ ounce can stewed tomatoes with onions, celery and green peppers

4 drops Tabasco sauce
1 cup sour cream
Sugar to taste
Salt to taste
Horseradish to taste

Dissolve gelatin in hot water. Cut tomatoes into small pieces and add to gelatin with Tabasco. Pour into lightly oiled mold and chill until firm. Unmold on salad greens. Serve with sour cream mixed with sugar, salt and horseradish.
Serves: 6

TOMATO MOUSSE SALAD

10¾ ounce can cream of tomato soup
3 ounces cream cheese, softened
1 Tablespoon unflavored gelatin
½ cup cold water

½ cup chopped celery
¼ cup chopped ripe olives
1 green bell pepper, chopped
1 teaspoon grated onion
3 Tablespoons sweet pickle relish

Heat soup to boiling point. Add cheese and stir until dissolved. Add gelatin to cold water and dissolve. Combine gelatin and remaining ingredients into soup mixture. Mix well. Pour into a chilled and oiled 1-quart mold or 8 individual molds. Chill until set.
Serves: 8

APRICOT DELIGHT

6 ounces apricot gelatin
2 cups boiling water
1¼ cups ginger ale
8 ounce can crushed pineapple,
  undrained

1 rib celery, diced
1 carrot, grated

Dissolve gelatin in boiling water. Add ginger ale, pineapple with juice, celery and carrot. Mix well and pour into oiled 2-quart mold. Refrigerate until congealed.
Serves: 8

ARTICHOKE STUFFED TOMATOES

2 cups canned artichoke hearts,
  drained and chopped
½ cup chopped celery
½ cup chopped green onions
¾ cup mayonnaise

Salt and pepper
6 tomatoes, peeled and hollowed
  out
10-12 slices bacon, fried crisp and
  crumbled

Combine first 4 ingredients. Chill. Salt and pepper inside of hollowed tomatoes, and allow to drain upside down. When ready to serve, fill tomatoes with artichoke mixture and top with crumbled bacon. Artichoke mixture may be stuffed into cherry tomatoes as an appetizer.
Serves: 6

CONGEALED VEGETABLE SALAD

3 ounces lemon gelatin
2 cups water, divided
2 teaspoons sugar
½ cup shredded cabbage
¼ cup chopped celery

¼ cup chopped green bell
  pepper
½ cup chopped pecans
16 ounce can tomatoes, drained
  and coarsely chopped

Dissolve gelatin in 1 cup boiling water. Pour in remaining 1 cup water. Add sugar. Let gelatin gel slightly, and add remaining ingredients. Pour into oiled 1-quart shallow dish. Refrigerate until congealed and serve with homemade mayonnaise.
Serves: 8

Great substitute for tomato aspic.

CRANBERRY SOUFFLÉ

**2 cups fresh whole cranberries,
reserving 18
1½ cups cranberry juice
1½ cups sugar, divided**

**3 Tablespoons unflavored gelatin
4 egg whites, room temperature
¼ teaspoon salt
1 cup whipping cream**

In a 2-quart saucepan add cranberries, cranberry juice and 1 cup sugar. Sprinkle with gelatin. Cook over medium heat, stirring constantly, until gelatin dissolves and berries pop, about 7 minutes. Refrigerate until mixture is partially set, approximately 1-2 hours. Make a collar for 1-quart soufflé dish using foil. Extend about 3 inches above rim. In a large bowl with mixer on high beat egg whites and salt to soft peaks. While beating, gradually add ½ cup sugar, 2 Tablespoons at a time, until sugar is dissolved. Egg whites should stand in stiff peaks. In a small bowl whip cream until soft peaks form. Gently fold cranberry mixture and whipped cream into egg whites until well blended. Pour into soufflé dish. Cover and refrigerate. Before serving, carefully remove foil and garnish with sugared cranberries.

Sugared Cranberries
**18 fresh cranberries
1 egg white**

Sugar

Beat egg white until frothy. Dip cranberries into egg white and roll in sugar to coat. Dry on a rack.
Serves: 8

GOOSEBERRY SALAD

**15 ounce can gooseberries, drain
and reserve juice
2 Tablespoons fresh lemon juice
6 ounces lemon gelatin**

**Pinch of salt
1 cup finely chopped celery
1 cup finely chopped almonds**

Measure liquid from gooseberries and add water to make 3 cups. Bring to boil. Add lemon juice and gelatin, stirring until gelatin has dissolved. Refrigerate until almost set. Combine salt, celery, almonds and gooseberries. Add to gelatin mixture. Pour into a 2-quart mold. Chill until firm.
Serves: 8

MINCEMEAT SALAD

6 ounces lemon gelatin
1½ cups hot water

2 cups orange juice
2 cups mincemeat

Dissolve gelatin in hot water. Add orange juice and chill until slightly thickened. Stir in mincemeat. Pour into an oiled 8-inch ring mold. Chill until firm.
Serves: 10 to 12

Delicious salad to serve at Christmas.

FRESH CRANBERRY SALAD

1 pound fresh cranberries
2 large apples, cored and
  unpeeled
1 large orange, seeded and
  peeled

2 cups sugar
6 ounces lemon gelatin
1 cup hot water
½ cup chopped pecans

Grind together cranberries, apples and orange. Add sugar. Dissolve gelatin in hot water. Cool. Combine fruit, gelatin mixture and pecans. Pour into lightly oiled fluted tube pan. Refrigerate for 8 hours or overnight. Unmold on a lettuce lined serving dish.
Serves: 10

FROZEN CHERRY SALAD

8 ounces cream cheese, softened
1 cup sour cream
¼ cup sugar
¼ teaspoon salt
2 cups miniature marshmallows
½ cup chopped pecans

16 ounce can pitted dark sweet
  cherries, drained
8 ounce can crushed pineapple,
  drained
11 ounce can mandarin oranges,
  drained

Beat cream cheese until smooth. Add sour cream, sugar and salt. Mix well. Fold in marshmallows and pecans. Add fruits, reserving a few cherries for garnish, if desired. Spoon mixture into 8X4-inch pan. Freeze at least 6 hours, or until firm. To serve, let stand at room temperature 5 minutes and cut into 1 inch slices.
Serves: 8

DELICIOUS SALAD

3 ounces lemon gelatin
1 cup boiling water
Juice of 1 lemon
20 ounce can crushed pineapple,
  undrained

1 cup chopped sweet gherkin
  pickles
1 cup chopped pecans
Pimiento, optional

Dissolve gelatin in boiling water. Add lemon juice, pineapple, pickles, pecans and pimiento. Pour into individual molds or an 8X8-inch pan. Refrigerate until firm. Serves: 8

Wonderful accompaniment for ham.

CINNAMON APPLE SALAD

⅓ cup red cinnamon candies
1 cup hot water
6 ounces lemon gelatin
2 cups unsweetened applesauce

6 ounces cream cheese, softened
⅓ cup mayonnaise
½ cup chopped pecans
½ cup chopped celery

In a saucepan melt cinnamon candy in hot water, stirring over low heat for 5 minutes. Remove from heat and add lemon gelatin, stirring until completely dissolved. Stir in applesauce. Pour half of gelatin mixture into an 8X8-inch pan. Chill until firm, about 30 minutes, letting remaining gelatin stand at room temperature. Beat cream cheese and mayonnaise together until fluffy. Fold in pecans and celery. When first mixture is firm, spread top with cream cheese mixture. Pour remaining gelatin on top of cream cheese, and return to refrigerator until set. To serve, cut into squares and serve on lettuce leaf.
Serves: 8

Kiwi fruit (Chinese gooseberry) cannot be successfully used in recipes using gelatin.

PEACH YOGURT SALAD

8 ounces peach yogurt
1 cup sour cream or plain yogurt
¾ cup sugar
Juice of a large lemon
2 bananas, sliced

8 ounce can crushed pineapple, drained
¼ cup maraschino cherries, chopped
¼ cup chopped pecans

Mix yogurt, sour cream and sugar. Add lemon juice, bananas, pineapple, cherries and pecans. Pour into lightly oiled individual molds. Freeze.
Serves: 8 to 10

Delicious salad.

SEPTEMBER TO CHRISTMAS SALAD

29 ounce can spiced peaches, drain and reserve juice
8 ounce can crushed pineapple, drain and reserve juice
6 ounce jar maraschino cherries, drain and reserve juice

2 Tablespoons unflavored gelatin
½ cup cold water
1 cup watermelon pickles, drain and reserve juice
1 Tablespoon grenadine syrup

Measure juices and add enough water to make 4 cups liquid. Place liquids in saucepan and bring to boil. Soften gelatin in cold water; add to hot juices. Stir until dissolved. Cool. Cut peaches, cherries and pickles into small pieces. Add all fruit, pickles and grenadine syrup to mixture. Mix well. Pour into a 2-quart dish. Chill until set.
Serves: 10 to 12

Excellent with game, duck, turkey and chicken.

ORANGE EASY

2 Tablespoons sugar
20 ounce can crushed pineapple, undrained
6 ounces orange gelatin

8 ounces frozen whipped topping, thawed
2 cups buttermilk
1 cup chopped pecans

Combine sugar and pineapple in small saucepan. Bring to a boil. Remove from heat and add gelatin. Stir until dissolved. Cool. Add whipped topping, buttermilk and pecans. Mix well. Pour into a 3-quart dish. Refrigerate overnight. Cut into squares for serving.
Serves: 10 to 12

SUMMER SURPRISE SALAD

**20 ounce can crushed
  unsweetened pineapple,
  drained and reserve juice
Water**

**6 ounces strawberry gelatin
4 cups watermelon balls, seeded
Peach for garnish**

Add water to reserved juice to make 2 cups. Bring to a boil. Pour over gelatin and dissolve completely. Cool to room temperature. Add pineapple to watermelon balls and mix well. (Do not drain this mixture.) Pour cooled gelatin over fruit and stir gently. Pour mixture into a very lightly greased 9X13-inch pan. Refrigerate until set. Slice into squares and serve on lettuce leaf. Drizzle dressing over top. Garnish with a slice of peach.

Dressing
**3 ounces cream cheese
½ cup whipping cream
2 Tablespoons powdered sugar**

**1 peach, peeled and seeded
1 teaspoon lemon juice**

Soften cream cheese and beat until fluffy. Slowly add cream and beat until smooth. Add sugar and mix well. Chop peach and sprinkle with lemon juice. Blend peach into a smooth pulp and add to cream mixture. Chill.
Serves: 12

The crunchy watermelon adds a delightful surprise to this unusual salad.

Iceberg lettuce is the "head" of the lettuce family, and what most people mean by lettuce.

Curly endive lettuce or chicory has narrow twisted leaves and has rather a bitter taste. Mix it with other types for a more mellow taste.

Boston lettuce or butternut has a very smooth, yes, buttery taste and large velvety leaves. Deserves a lighter dressing.

Romaine lettuce has a very long head and long leaves, with a very pungent flavor. Caesar salad material!

Bibb lettuce has small, delicate leaves and a rich taste. The aristocrat of all lettuces. Keep the leaves whole!

HONEY-GRAPEFRUIT SALAD DRESSING

½ cup grapefruit juice
¼ cup vegetable oil
¼ cup honey
2 Tablespoons Dijon mustard

2 Tablespoons chopped onion
2 Tablespoons poppy seeds
¼ teaspoon salt
Dash of pepper

Combine all ingredients; refrigerate before serving.
Yield: 1 cup

Very good with spinach salad.

UNCLE JOHN'S FRENCH SALAD DRESSING

⅔ cup sugar
1 teaspoon salt
1 teaspoon pepper
1 teaspoon celery seed
½ teaspoon paprika

2 teaspoons onion flakes
⅔ cup vegetable oil
½ cup vinegar
½ cup ketchup

Combine all ingredients in tightly covered container. Refrigerate.
Yield: 2½ cups

Very good served on salad greens or shredded cabbage.

FAVORITE MAYONNAISE

2 cups Wesson Oil, (no
    substitute), divided
2 eggs, room temperature
1½ Tablespoons fresh lemon
    juice

1½ Tablespoons tarragon vinegar
1 teaspoon salt
½ teaspoon red pepper

In food processor combine ½ cup oil, eggs, lemon juice, tarragon vinegar, salt and
pepper. Process, counting to 5 slowly. With motor running, pour remaining oil into
the funnel in a slow steady stream. Process to desired thickness.
Yield: 2 cups

DRESSINGS

VINAIGRETTE DRESSING

1 green onion, chopped
2 sprigs parsley, minced
½ teaspoon salt
Dash of pepper

½ teaspoon dry mustard
3 Tablespoons white wine vinegar
6 Tablespoons vegetable oil
1 clove garlic

In blender process onion and parsley until finely chopped. Add remaining ingredients, except garlic, and blend a few seconds. Spear garlic with a wooden pick; place in a jar with sauce. Marinate overnight. Remove garlic before serving.
Yield: ⅔ cup

YUMMY DRESSING

2 cloves garlic, minced
2 teaspoons minced fresh parsley
5 Tablespoons red wine vinegar
6 Tablespoons sour cream
1½ teaspoons salt

½ teaspoon dry mustard
2 Tablespoons sugar
Pepper to taste
1 cup vegetable oil, chilled

In blender or food processor combine garlic, parsley, vinegar, sour cream, salt, mustard, sugar and pepper. With motor running, add oil in slow stream. Blend until smooth. Store covered in refrigerator. Serve over spinach salad or fresh vegetables.
Yield: 1½ cups

THOUSAND ISLAND DRESSING

2 cups mayonnaise
½ cup chili sauce
2 hard-boiled eggs, chopped
2 Tablespoons chopped pimientos
¼ teaspoon Worcestershire sauce

1 Tablespoon chopped green
olives
3 Tablespoons chopped sweet
pickles

Combine all ingredients. Mix well. Refrigerate before serving. Serve on lettuce wedges.
Yield: 3 cups

MINT DRESSING FOR FRUIT

3 Tablespoons apple mint jelly,
  melted
2 Tablespoons honey

Juice and grated peel of 1 lime
Juice of 1 lemon
2 fresh mint leaves, chopped

Combine all ingredients and pour over fresh fruit .
Yield: ½ cup

ROQUEFORT DRESSING

3 ounces Roquefort cheese
1 cup sour cream
¼ cup vegetable oil
2 Tablespoons mayonnaise

1 Tablespoon white vinegar
2 Tablespoons water
½ teaspoon garlic salt

Place Roquefort cheese and sour cream in blender and process until smooth. Add remaining ingredients and blend. Refrigerate. Will keep in refrigerator approximately 2 weeks.
Yield: 2 cups

CELERY SEED DRESSING

⅓ cup sugar
1 teaspoon celery seed
1 teaspoon salt
1 teaspoon dry mustard
1 teaspoon grated onion

1 teaspoon paprika
4 Tablespoons white vinegar,
  divided
1 cup ice cold vegetable oil

In blender mix all dry ingredients with 1 Tablespoon vinegar. On high speed, gradually add alternately the remaining vinegar and oil. Blend until smooth. Keeps refrigerated 3-4 weeks.
Yield: 1½ cups

Good served over avocado, grapefruit or fruit salad.

DRESSINGS

BLEU CHEESE DRESSING

1 cup mayonnaise
¼ cup plus 2 Tablespoons
   buttermilk
1½ teaspoons white wine or
   vermouth
½ teaspoon Tabasco sauce

¾ teaspoon Parmesan cheese
¼ teaspoon celery salt
¼ teaspoon onion salt
¼ teaspoon seasoned salt
¼ teaspoon Worcestershire sauce
4 ounces Bleu cheese, crumbled

Combine all ingredients in a bowl and mix thoroughly. If a heavier texture is desired, fold in Bleu cheese after mixing other ingredients. Best served within 3 days.
Yield: 1½ cups

HONEY DRESSING

1 cup vegetable oil
½ cup ketchup
⅓ cup garlic wine vinegar
⅓ cup honey

1 teaspoon salt
1 teaspoon paprika
1 teaspoon grated onion

Combine all ingredients in jar with tight-fitting lid. Refrigerate. Bring to room temperature and shake well before serving.
Yield: 2 cups

Great served on salad greens or citrus fruit.

Corn oil is best for baking because its flavor is most like butter.

Sesame oil should be used for light tasting salad dressings and marinades.

Olive oil makes a hearty salad dressing because it is a robust oil. Best in pasta and tomato dishes.

Safflower and Sunflower oil are light in color and almost tasteless. Acceptable for most recipes.

Peanut oil can withstand high heat without smoking, which makes it best for stir-frying and deep frying.

VEGETABLES

STUFFED ARTICHOKE BOTTOMS

3 Tablespoons butter
¼ cup minced onions
10 ounces frozen chopped
   spinach, cooked and
   drained
¼ cup sour cream

2 Tablespoons grated Parmesan
   cheese
¼ teaspoon Worcestershire sauce
Salt and pepper to taste
7½ ounce can artichoke bottoms,
   drained

In saucepan melt butter; add onions and sauté until tender. Combine onions, spinach, sour cream, Parmesan cheese, Worcestershire sauce, salt and pepper. Blend well. Stuff mixture into artichoke bottoms. Sprinkle additional Parmesan cheese on top. Place in a flat baking dish with small amount of water in the bottom. Bake at 350 degrees for 15-20 minutes.
Serves: 4 to 6

ASPARAGUS ARTICHOKE BAKE

1 cup margarine
1 cup all-purpose flour
2 (15 ounce) cans asparagus
   pieces, drain and reserve liquid
2 (14 ounce) cans artichoke
   hearts, quartered, drain and
   reserve liquid

8 ounce can sliced water
   chestnuts, drain and reserve
   liquid
½ cup dry sherry
2 cups shredded New York sharp
   Cheddar cheese
Salt and pepper to taste

In a large saucepan melt margarine; add flour. Stir until blended. Slowly add reserved liquids and sherry. Continue stirring until smooth and creamy. Fold in cheese, salt and pepper. Combine sauce with vegetables and place in a greased 3-quart casserole dish. Bake at 350 degrees for 30 minutes. Recipe may be halved.
Serves: 10 to 12

When fresh asparagus stalks are large and the bottom portions are woody, use a knife to trim away the white portions, then lightly peel the remaining bottoms. Snapping removes and wastes too much stem, which can be salvaged by peeling.

BARBECUED BEANS

3 (15 ounce) cans whole green
  beans, drained
5 slices bacon, uncooked and
  chopped

1 medium onion, chopped
1 cup packed brown sugar
1 cup ketchup

Mix all ingredients together. Bake uncovered at 225 degrees for 4 hours, stirring occasionally.
Serves: 4 to 6

A nice change from pork and beans.

LEMON GREEN BEANS

1½ pounds fresh young green
  beans, string and trim
3 Tablespoons butter, melted
Salt and pepper to taste

1 Tablespoon chopped fresh
  parsley
Juice of 1 lemon

Steam beans until tender-crisp, but still a nice green color. Drain and place in bowl. Melt butter; add salt, pepper, parsley and lemon juice. Pour over beans. Serve hot.
Serves: 6

CRAN-ORANGE BEETS

1 cup cranberry juice
1 Tablespoon cornstarch
1 teaspoon salt

4 Tablespoons orange marmalade
2 pounds beets, peeled and
  cooked

In a medium saucepan combine cranberry juice, cornstarch and salt. Cook over medium heat, stirring constantly until thickened. Add marmalade and mix well. Cut beets into strips to resemble French fries. Add beets to sauce and cook for 10 minutes. Serve hot.
Serves: 6 to 8

To prevent lumps in cornstarch or flour-thickened sauces, stir constantly over low to medium heat. If lumps do form, beat the sauce briskly with a wire whisk or rotary beater.

LIMA BEAN CASSEROLE

20 ounces frozen Fordhook
   lima beans
4 Tablespoons butter, melted
4 Tablespoons all-purpose flour
2 cups milk
Salt and pepper to taste
1 cup shredded sharp Cheddar
   cheese

16 ounce can small onions, drain
   and reserve liquid
4 ounce can sliced mushrooms,
   drained
Buttered bread crumbs

Cook beans according to package directions. Drain; set aside. Combine butter, flour, milk, salt and pepper to make a thick white sauce. Add cheese and 2 Tablespoons reserved onion juice. Stir until blended. Add lima beans, onions and mushrooms. Mix well. Pour into greased 1½-quart casserole dish. Bake at 350 degrees until bubbly. Top with extra grated cheese or buttered bread crumbs.
Serves: 6 to 8

Best made 24 hours before serving.

BROCCOLI PUFF

20 ounces frozen chopped
   broccoli, thawed and drained
½ cup sliced water chestnuts
10¾ ounce can cream of
   mushroom soup
½ cup shredded American or
   Cheddar cheese
¼ cup milk

½ cup mayonnaise
2 Tablespoons cooking sherry
1 egg, beaten
½ teaspoon salt
Dash of pepper
1 Tablespoon margarine, melted
¼ cup dry bread crumbs
½ cup sliced almonds

Place broccoli and water chestnuts in a 10X6-inch baking dish. Combine next eight ingredients and mix well. Pour over broccoli and water chestnuts. Combine margarine and bread crumbs. Sprinkle on top. Place almonds over crumb mixture. Bake at 350 degrees for 45 minutes, or until crumbs and almonds are lightly browned.
Serves: 6 to 8

CARROTS EN CASSEROLE

1 pound carrots, sliced
½ cup finely chopped onion
1 cup shredded Cheddar cheese
1 teaspoon salt

1 teaspoon sugar
½ cup mayonnaise
Herb-seasoned stuffing

Cook carrots until just crisp. Drain. Combine next five ingredients and mix with carrots. Place in a 9X6-inch baking dish. Top with stuffing mix. Bake at 350 degrees for 20 minutes. This recipe may be prepared a day ahead.
Serves: 6

TAHITIAN CARROTS

12-14 carrots, sliced ½ inch thick
16 ounce can mandarin oranges, drained
16 ounce can pineapple chunks, drained
1 cup packed light brown sugar

1-2 Tablespoons cornstarch
1 teaspoon cinnamon
1 teaspoon nutmeg
½ cup butter
5 slices bread, crust removed
1 cup chopped pecans

Cook carrots until tender; drain. Mix together carrots, oranges and pineapple. Pour into a greased casserole. Combine brown sugar, cornstarch, cinnamon and nutmeg. Sprinkle over carrot mixture. Melt butter. Cut bread into bite size pieces. Add to melted butter and stir to coat. Add pecans and mix well. Sprinkle over top. Bake at 325 degrees for 30-40 minutes.
Serves: 8 to 10

Vegetables that grow above the ground, i.e. corn, beans, peas, etc., should be added to boiling water. Vegetables that grow under the ground, i.e. carrots, potatoes, etc., should be started in cold water.

CAULIFLOWER MUSHROOM BAKE

1 medium head cauliflower, cut into flowerets
8 ounce can sliced mushrooms, drained
½ cup diced green bell pepper
¼ cup butter

⅓ cup all-purpose flour
2 cups milk
1 teaspoon salt
6 ounces shredded American or Cheddar cheese
3 Tablespoons chopped pimiento

Cook cauliflower in boiling water 10 minutes or until tender. Drain and set aside. Sauté mushrooms and green pepper in butter. Add flour, milk and salt. Stir until thickened. In a separate bowl combine cheese and pimiento. In a 1½-quart casserole dish layer half of cauliflower, sauce, and top with cheese mixture. Repeat layers. Bake at 350 degrees for 15 minutes.
Serves: 6 to 8

CELERY ALMONDINE

4 Tablespoons butter
4 cups sliced celery
Salt and pepper
1 Tablespoon grated onion

1½ Tablespoons all-purpose flour
1 cup half-and-half cream
1 cup chicken broth
1 cup sliced almonds, toasted

In medium saucepan melt butter. Add celery and season lightly with salt and pepper. Cover and cook on medium heat for 15 minutes. Add grated onion, flour, half-and-half cream and chicken broth. Stir until thickened. Add almonds just before serving.
Serves: 6 to 8

This is a different and delicious holiday side dish.

Place a slice of bread on top of cabbage slices when boiling. This keeps the strong smell of the vegetable in the pot. Cook uncovered.

CELERY FRITTERS

**5 ribs celery, with leaves, cut into
  chunks**
1 cup all-purpose flour
2 eggs
Salt to taste
Pepper to taste

Oregano to taste
1 clove garlic
¼ cup water
¼ cup grated Parmesan cheese
1 cup olive oil

In food processor mince celery. Add remaining ingredients except oil. Process until consistency of pancake batter. Heat oil in skillet. When hot, drop batter from Tablespoon into oil and fry until golden brown. Drain on paper towels. Variation: Substitute 2 medium zucchini, unpeeled and sliced paper-thin, instead of celery.
Serves: 4

CORN WITH GREEN CHILIES

3 cups fresh yellow or white corn
2 Tablespoons butter, melted
⅓ cup yellow cornmeal
¾ teaspoon salt

2 teaspoons sugar
4 ounce can chopped green chilies
**1 cup shredded sharp Cheddar
  cheese**

Combine corn, butter, cornmeal, salt and sugar in food processor. Process until blended. Butter a 1-quart baking dish and layer half of the corn mixture, chilies and cheese. Repeat layers, ending with cheese on top. Cover and bake at 350 degrees for 1 hour.
Serves: 4 to 6

This is a real taste treat with barbecue or Mexican food!

Celery keeps longer refrigerated if stored in a paper bag.

BAKED EGGPLANT SLICES

1 cup mayonnaise
¼ cup finely chopped onion
1 eggplant, peeled

20 saltine crackers, finely
  crumbled
Salt to taste

Mix mayonnaise and onion. Slice eggplant into 12 (½-inch) thick slices. Spread mayonnaise on both sides of eggplant. Dip slices into crumbs and place on ungreased cookie sheet. Bake at 375 degrees for 15 minutes on each side. Season with salt. Serve immediately.
Serves: 6 to 8

EGGPLANT PARMESAN

1 medium onion, chopped
1 medium green bell pepper,
  chopped
2-3 Tablespoons vegetable oil
1 clove garlic, minced
1 medium eggplant, peeled and
  cubed
1 teaspoon salt

¼ teaspoon oregano
½ teaspoon basil
8 ounce can tomato sauce
½ cup grated Parmesan cheese,
  divided
8 ounces mozzarella cheese,
  shredded or sliced, divided

Sauté onion and green pepper in oil until soft. Add garlic and eggplant. On low heat, cook until eggplant is tender. Stir occasionally and add more oil if needed. Add salt, oregano, basil, tomato sauce, and ¼ cup Parmesan cheese, stirring to combine. Place half of mixture in a greased 1½-quart baking dish and cover with half of mozzarella cheese. Add remaining eggplant mixture and mozzarella cheese. Sprinkle with remaining Parmesan cheese. Bake uncovered at 325 degrees for 45 minutes. Freezes well.
Serves: 6

EGGPLANT AND OYSTERS

2 large eggplants, peeled, cut into
  small pieces
1 teaspoon salt
½ teaspoon pepper
½ cup butter, melted and divided
4 eggs, beaten
7 slices bread, cut into 1-inch
  pieces

1 pint fresh oysters, undrained
10¾ ounce can cream of
  mushroom soup
1½ cups shredded sharp Cheddar
  cheese, divided
1½ cups cracker crumbs

Cook eggplant in water until tender, about 10 minutes; drain and mash. Season with salt and pepper. Add ¼ cup butter and eggs. Mix well. Add bread pieces, oysters, soup and ¾ cup cheese. Pour mixture into a greased 9x13-inch baking dish. Bake uncovered at 350 degrees for 35-45 minutes or until almost firm. Remove from oven. Top with cracker crumbs which have been mixed with remaining butter. Sprinkle with remaining cheese. Return to oven and brown. Freezes well.
Serves: 8

KRAUT AND APPLES

5 Tablespoons bacon drippings
3 apples, chopped
1 large onion, chopped
16 ounce can sauerkraut, drained

2 Tablespoons packed dark brown
  sugar
½ cup water

In a skillet sauté apples and onion in drippings over low heat for 15 minutes or until tender. Add sauerkraut, brown sugar and water. Cook uncovered for an additional 15 minutes.
Serves: 4

Serve with pork and a fresh baked sweet potato. This combination of fruit and vegetables is a sure warm-up on a cold day.

CHAMPAGNE MUSHROOMS

¼ cup unsalted butter
2 cloves garlic, minced
1 teaspoon nutmeg
3 Tablespoons chopped green
 onions
2 Tablespoons chopped parsley
1 teaspoon salt
½ teaspoon freshly ground
 pepper

2 pounds fresh mushrooms,
 sliced
½ cup dry champagne
2 Tablespoons Pernod, optional
1 cup whipping cream, room
 temperature
Puff pastry shells or toast points

In a large skillet melt butter. Add garlic, nutmeg, green onions, parsley, salt and pepper. Cook for 2 minutes. Stir in mushrooms and cook until liquid is absorbed and mushrooms are browned. Remove mushrooms from pan. Add champagne to pan and boil uncovered over high heat until reduced by half. Stir in Pernod and cream. Continue boiling until cream thickens. Return mushrooms to liquid. Serve in pastry shells or on toast points.
Serves: 8

MUSHROOM PIE

2 pounds whole fresh mushrooms
¼ cup + 2 Tablespoons butter,
 divided
Salt and pepper to taste
Juice of ½ fresh lemon

3 Tablespoons all-purpose flour
¼ to ½ cup Madeira wine
½ cup whipping cream, heated
1 pastry crust
Melted butter

Sauté mushrooms in ¼ cup butter. Add salt, pepper and lemon juice. Cover and cook over low heat for 10 minutes, stirring frequently until mushrooms are tender. Arrange mushrooms in a buttered deep-round baking dish or an 8X8-inch baking dish. To liquids remaining in skillet, melt 2 Tablespoons butter; stir in flour. Add wine, warm cream and additional salt and pepper, if needed. Stir until thickened. Pour sauce over mushrooms. Cover with pastry crust. Brush with melted butter. Make several slits on top of crust. Bake at 450 degrees for 15 minutes; reduce heat to 350 degrees and bake for 10-15 minutes.
Serves: 8

Slice fresh mushrooms with a stainless steel knife to keep mushrooms from turning dark.

BAKED ONION CASSEROLE

4 large onions, thinly sliced
1½ cups crushed potato chips
1 cup shredded Cheddar cheese
10¾ ounce can cream of
   mushroom soup

¼ cup milk
Red pepper

Grease a 9X13-inch baking dish. Alternate layers of onion, potato chips, and cheese. Spoon soup over last layer and pour milk on top. Sprinkle with red pepper. Bake at 300 degrees for 1 hour.
Serves: 6 to 8

PHILADELPHIA BLACK-EYED PEAS

1 pound dried black-eyed peas
½ pound Canadian bacon,
   cooked crisp and chopped
2 medium onions, chopped
2 ribs celery, chopped
1 bay leaf

1 clove garlic, chopped
1 red pepper pod
6 ounce can tomato paste
2 teaspoons salt
¼ teaspoon pepper

Wash peas. Cover with water and soak for 1 hour. Drain. Add fresh water to cover peas. Add remaining ingredients. Bring to a boil. Reduce heat. Cover and simmer until tender, approximately 3-4 hours. Add additional water if needed.
Serves: 10 to 12

These are a must served to friends for good luck on New Year's Day!

To remove cabbage leaves without tearing them, immerse the cabbage in, or hold it under warm water. The leaves will separate from the core with ease, undamaged.

FRENCH EPICUREAN PEAS

**4 large lettuce leaves, cleaned,
  pat dry**
4 Tablespoons white wine
**30 ounces frozen English peas,
  thawed**

Dash of Accent
3 green onions, chopped

Moisten 2 lettuce leaves with half of wine and place in bottom of a saucepan. Fill each half with peas. Add seasoning and onions. Cover peas with remaining 2 lettuce leaves which have been moistened with wine. Simmer on very low heat until peas are tender.
Serves: 8

ITALIAN STYLE NEW POTATOES

8 new potatoes
¼ cup olive oil
1 teaspoon salt
1 teaspoon pepper
¼ teaspoon oregano

1 clove garlic, minced
¼ cup grated Parmesan cheese
**1 Tablespoon chopped fresh
  parsley**

Boil potatoes until tender. Cool in cold water, then peel. Place whole potatoes in a bowl. Add oil, salt, pepper, oregano and garlic. Toss together gently. Sprinkle with cheese and parsley. Serve at room temperature.
Serves: 4

Removing a thin strip of peel from around the center of new potatoes before boiling prevents the very thin, fragile skin from bursting.

RANCH POTATOES

6 medium red potatoes, peeled
   and sliced ¼-inch thick
1 medium onion, sliced
1 package dry ranch dressing mix

1 cup mayonnaise
1 cup buttermilk
1 cup shredded Cheddar cheese

Boil potato and onion slices together until tender. Drain. Combine dressing mix with mayonnaise and buttermilk. In a lightly greased 9X13-inch baking dish, layer half of potatoes, onions, dressing mixture and cheese. Repeat with a second layer ending with cheese on top. Bake at 350 degrees for 30 minutes.
Serves: 8

This is very tasty. Very good served with beef.

ROSEMARY POTATOES

10 small red potatoes, unpeeled
3 ounce bag shrimp and crab boil
¼ cup olive oil

2 teaspoons dried rosemary
2 teaspoons salt
Pepper to taste

In large saucepan combine potatoes with shrimp and crab boil bag and enough water to cover. Boil until potatoes are tender. Drain and cut into halves or quarters. In a large skillet add olive oil, rosemary, salt and pepper. Arrange potatoes in a single layer, being careful not to crowd potatoes. Cover and cook over low-medium heat, shaking skillet occasionally to keep potatoes from sticking. Cook until potatoes are crusty.
Serves: 6 to 8

A pat of chive or watercress butter can add color and flavor to a plain baked potato, steamed vegetables or a broiled steak.

APPLE-MAPLE SWEET POTATOES

**6 medium baking apples, peeled
and sliced
½ cup maple syrup
½ cup packed dark brown sugar
½ cup butter or margarine**

**Salt to taste
4 medium sweet potatoes,
unpeeled and baked
1 cup chopped pecans**

Place apples in saucepan and cover with maple syrup; add brown sugar and butter. Cook until tender. Add salt to taste. Remove apples; reserve liquid. Peel and slice sweet potatoes. Layer potatoes and apples in a greased 2-quart casserole. Pour maple syrup liquid over apples and potatoes. Top with pecans. Bake at 350 degrees for 30-45 minutes.
Serves: 6 to 8

Start a wonderful holiday tradition!

SWEET POTATO SOUFFLÉ

**3 cups cooked mashed sweet
potatoes
1 cup sugar
½ teaspoon salt**

**2 eggs, beaten
3 Tablespoons margarine, melted
½ cup milk
1 teaspoon vanilla extract**

Combine potatoes and sugar while potatoes are hot. Add salt, eggs, margarine, milk and vanilla. Pour into a greased baking dish.

Topping
**½ cup packed dark brown sugar
3 Tablespoons self-rising flour**

**½ cup chopped pecans
3 Tablespoons margarine, melted**

Mix all ingredients well. Sprinkle on top of potatoes. Bake at 300 degrees for 45 minutes.
Serves: 8

PRALINE YAMS WITH ORANGE SAUCE

**4-5 medium sweet potatoes,
  peeled and quartered
½ cup packed dark brown sugar,
  divided**

**2 eggs
½ cup butter, melted and divided
1 teaspoon salt
Pecan halves**

Cook potatoes in water to cover until tender. Drain. Add ¼ cup sugar to hot potatoes. Add eggs, 3 Tablespoons butter and salt. Beat until smooth. Pour into a greased 1½-quart casserole dish. Lay pecan halves end to end, covering the entire casserole. Sprinkle with remaining brown sugar. Drizzle remaining melted butter over top. Ladle orange sauce over individual servings.

Orange Sauce
**⅓ cup sugar
1 Tablespoon cornstarch
⅛ teaspoon salt
1 teaspoon grated orange rind**

**1 cup orange juice
1 Tablespoon lemon juice
2 Tablespoons butter
3 dashes Angostura bitters**

In saucepan combine sugar, cornstarch, salt, orange rind, orange juice and lemon juice. Bring to a boil over medium heat. Cook until thickened. Remove from heat. Stir in butter and bitters.
Serves: 8 to 10

Herbed and spiced butters are an excellent way to add interest to a dish or meal and can be made ahead and frozen. Spiced butters are simple to make. Add 1 Tablespoon powdered spice to ½ cup butter. Herbed butters may be made with fresh or dried herbs. Simply add 2 Tablespoons dried dill, tarragon, chives, etc., and 2 teaspoons lemon juice to ½ cup butter.

ALMOND WILD RICE

1¼ cups wild rice
½ cup butter
½ pound fresh mushrooms, sliced
½ cup chopped onion
½ cup chopped celery
2 Tablespoons chopped green bell pepper, optional
1 teaspoon salt
½ cup sliced almonds, toasted
2 Tablespoons dry sherry
3 cups chicken broth

Pour boiling water over rice and let sit for 15 minutes. Drain and rinse well. Melt butter in large skillet. Sauté mushrooms, onion, celery and bell pepper. Add the rice, salt and almonds. Stir until well mixed. Sauté a few more minutes. Add sherry and mix well. Place in a lightly buttered casserole dish and pour chicken broth over rice mixture. At this point casserole may be frozen or placed in refrigerator for 24 hours. Bake covered at 350 degrees for 1¼ hours. Uncover and bake additional 15 minutes.
Serves: 10 to 12

CAJUN RICE DRESSING

2 cups cooked rice
½ cup butter
2 large onions, finely chopped
4 ribs celery, finely chopped
1 green bell pepper, finely chopped
4 whole chicken livers, cut into pieces
1 Tablespoon salt
1 Tablespoon poultry seasoning
2 eggs, beaten until foamy
1 cup chopped pecans
½ cup chopped fresh mushrooms

In large skillet melt butter. Sauté onions, celery, bell pepper and chicken livers until tender. Add seasonings and mix well. Add chicken liver mixture to cooked rice. Fold in eggs, mixing thoroughly. Add pecans and mushrooms. Pour into a greased casserole dish and bake at 350 degrees for 25 minutes.
Serves: 6 to 8

Delicious served with quail or chicken.

DINNER PARTY SPINACH

1 pound whole fresh mushrooms
8 ounce can sliced water
    chestnuts, drained
14 ounce can artichoke hearts,
    drained and quartered
8 ounces cream cheese, softened
½ cup butter

40 ounces frozen chopped
    spinach, cooked and well
    drained
Juice of 1 lemon
Salt and pepper to taste
Seasoned bread crumbs

Line bottom of 3-quart casserole with mushrooms, water chestnuts and artichoke hearts. In a saucepan melt cheese and butter. Stir in spinach, lemon juice, salt and pepper. Pour spinach mixture over vegetable mixture in casserole. Top with seasoned bread crumbs. Bake at 350 degrees for 25-30 minutes.
Serves: 12

JEFFERSON PLACE SPINACH

6 large eggs
6 Tablespoons butter, melted
6 Tablespoons all-purpose flour
1 teaspoon salt
Pepper to taste
2-3 Tablespoons Worcestershire
    sauce

48 ounces cottage cheese
2 pounds shredded sharp Cheddar
    cheese
20 ounces frozen chopped
    spinach, thawed and squeezed
    dry

Beat eggs until light and thick. Make a roux with butter and flour. Blend until smooth. Add to eggs. Add remaining ingredients and mix well. In a 9X13-inch casserole dish pour in spinach mixture. Bake at 350 degrees for 45 minutes or until knife inserted in center comes out clean. May be baked in 3 greased 9-inch pie plates.
Serves: 12

For a real Southern twist, use chopped turnip greens rather than spinach. Delicious!

Stir cream sauces with a spatula to move a large amount at one time.

SPINACH ROLL

1 onion, chopped
¼ cup vegetable oil
20 ounces frozen chopped
    spinach, thawed and well
    drained
2 eggs, beaten
¼ cup chopped fresh parsley

¼ cup cottage cheese
Pepper to taste
½ pound butter, melted
6 phyllo pastry sheets
1 Tablespoon Cream of Wheat
Melted butter

In skillet sauté onion in oil. In a large bowl combine the spinach and eggs; add onion, parsley, cheese and pepper. Mix well. Brush melted butter generously on each phyllo sheet. Stack phyllo sheets on top of each other. On narrow ends of phyllo sheets sprinkle Cream of Wheat. Spread spinach mixture evenly over top phyllo sheet to within 1 inch of edge. Fold in long sides of pastry 1 inch. From narrow ends of pastry, roll pastry up jelly-roll style. Seal seam with melted butter. Place seam side down on ungreased baking sheet. Brush top of roll with melted butter. Bake at 350 degrees for 35 minutes; or bake for 15 minutes and freeze. Thaw for a few minutes if frozen and bake at 350 degrees for 30-40 minutes.
Serves: 8

SPINACH SQUARES

4 Tablespoons butter
3 eggs
1 cup all-purpose flour
1 cup milk
1 teaspoon salt
1 teaspoon baking powder

16 ounces Cheddar cheese,
    shredded
10 ounces frozen chopped
    spinach, thawed and drained
¼ cup chopped onion
½ cup chopped mushrooms

Melt butter in 9X13-inch casserole. In a large bowl mix remaining ingredients together. Pour into casserole. Bake at 350 degrees for 35 minutes. Cool slightly before cutting into squares. Can be served hot or at room temperature.
Serves: 12

This dish may be served as an appetizer if cut into small squares.

CORNBREAD SQUASH

2 cups sliced yellow squash
1 small onion, chopped
2 Tablespoons margarine
1½ cups crumbled cornbread

1 egg, beaten
1¼ cups shredded Cheddar
   cheese, divided
⅓ cup milk

Place squash in saucepan with water to cover. Cook until tender. Drain. Sauté onion in margarine. Mix squash, cornbread crumbs and onion. Add egg, 1 cup cheese and milk. Pour into a 1-quart baking dish and top with remaining cheese. Bake at 350 degrees for 30 minutes.
Serves: 4 to 6

GARDEN STUFFED YELLOW SQUASH

8-10 medium yellow squash
½ cup chopped green bell
   pepper
1 medium tomato, chopped
1 medium onion, chopped
4 slices bacon, fried crisp and
   crumbled

1 cup shredded sharp Cheddar
   cheese
½ teaspoon salt
Dash of pepper
Butter

Simmer whole squash in water for 8 minutes, or until just fork tender. Drain and cool slightly. Halve squash lengthwise and remove seeds. Combine remaining ingredients, except butter. Mix well and spoon into squash shells. Dot each shell with butter. Place on baking sheet and bake at 400 degrees for 20 minutes.
Serves 6 to 8

Freeze fresh parsley packed tightly in a freezer container. When needed remove desired amount and chop while frozen.

TOMATO PIE

1 unbaked 10-inch pie crust
3 large tomatoes
5 green onions, sliced
1 teaspoon basil
1 teaspoon chopped chives
½ teaspoon leaf oregano
½ teaspoon Italian or Greek
  seasoning
Salt and pepper to taste
1 cup mayonnaise
1 cup shredded sharp Cheddar
  cheese

Bake pie crust at 375 degrees for 10-12 minutes. Slice unpeeled tomatoes 1-inch thick. Fill pie crust with sliced tomatoes. Sprinkle green onions and seasonings over tomatoes. Mix mayonnaise and cheese together. Spread over tomatoes, sealing to edge of crust. Bake at 350 degrees for 30 minutes. Cool 10-15 minutes before slicing. May be served hot or at room temperature.
Serves: 8

Great for Fourth of July picnic!

TOMATO ONION CASSEROLE

28 ounce can plum tomatoes,
  undrained
2 red Bermuda onions, sliced
1 cup cracker crumbs
¼ cup shredded Cheddar cheese
¼ cup shredded Monterey Jack
  cheese
Salt and pepper to taste

Pour tomatoes into a bowl. Mash tomatoes with liquid until thoroughly mixed. In a 1½-quart casserole layer tomatoes, onions, cracker crumbs and cheeses. Repeat layers. Salt and pepper. Bake at 350 degrees for 45 minutes.
Serves: 4 to 6

To remove the seeds from tomatoes, peel and halve the tomato, and then squeeze! Hold the tomato half in the palm of the hand, gently squeeze, extracting juice and seeds. The juice isn't from the flesh of the tomato, just from the inside seedy sections.

WINT...

2 (28 ounce) cans tomat...
undrained
8 cloves
8 peppercorns
1 bay leaf

...ed
...wn sugar
...nto small

Place tomatoes in a la... ...nd bay leaf in cloth
bag. Add to tomatoes ... ...ice bag. Add onion,
brown sugar, bread p... ...-quart casserole and
bake at 400 degrees ...
Serves: 6

Makes a great ... ...oes are not available.

3 cups zucchini...
coarsely cho...
1 large onion...
½ green bell...
1 egg, beate...
½ cup mayo...

...d Cheddar cheese
...o sugar
...alt
...pepper

In medium s... ...pper in water until just tender.
Be careful not to le... ...Mix remaining ingredients and
add to cooked vegetables. Pou... ...erole and bake at 300 degrees
for 30 minutes. Remove from oven and s... ... paprika.
Serves: 6

A family favorite.

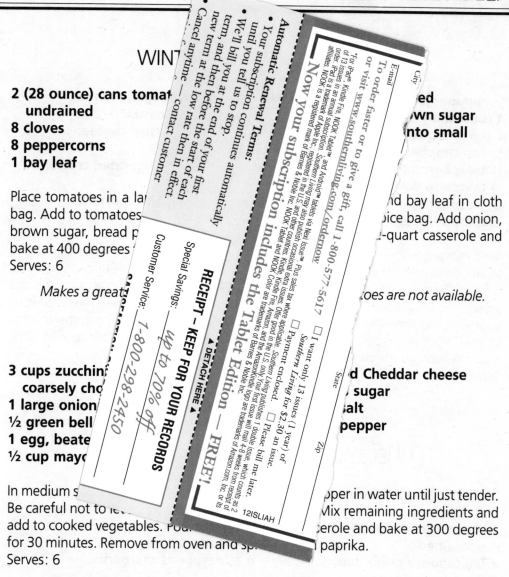

Try chopped pecans with carrots, zucchini, creamed onions, sweet potatoes or wild rice.

ZUCCHINI PIE

¼ cup margarine
4 cups thinly sliced zucchini
1 cup chopped onion
½ cup chopped fresh parsley
½ teaspoon salt
½ teaspoon pepper
¼ teaspoon garlic powder
¼ teaspoon basil

¼ teaspoon oregano leaves
2 eggs, well beaten
8 ounces Muenster cheese, shredded
8 ounce can refrigerated crescent rolls
2 teaspoons Dijon mustard

Melt margarine in large skillet. Sauté zucchini and onion for 10 minutes or until tender. Stir in parsley and seasonings. Combine eggs and cheese. Stir into vegetable mixture. Separate dough into rectangle; roll out to fit over the bottom and up the sides of an ungreased 8X12-inch baking dish. Spread the crust with mustard. Pour vegetable mixture evenly into crust. Bake at 375 degrees for 18-20 minutes or until knife inserted in middle comes out clean. Let stand 10 minutes before serving. Variation: Yellow squash may be substituted for zucchini.
Serves: 6 to 8

CHEEZY ZUCCHINI AND TOMATOES

1 cup peeled and chopped zucchini
16 ounce can stewed tomatoes, undrained
2 Tablespoons onion flakes
⅛ teaspoon oregano

Salt and pepper to taste
3 slices bread, toasted and cubed
8 ounces mozzarella cheese, cubed
4 Tablespoons margarine

Steam zucchini until tender. Place zucchini in a baking dish. Add stewed tomatoes, onion flakes, oregano, salt and pepper. Mix until well blended. Stir in bread cubes and cheese. Dot with margarine. Bake at 350 degrees for 20 minutes.
Serves: 4

SWISS VEGETABLE CUSTARD

¼ cup butter
1½ cups sliced yellow squash
1½ cups diagonally sliced
   broccoli
1 egg, beaten
¼ cup milk

1 teaspoon salt
¼ teaspoon dry mustard
Dash of red pepper
½ cup shredded Gruyère or baby
   Swiss cheese
¼ cup grated Parmesan cheese

In a large skillet sauté vegetables in butter until fork-tender. Set aside. Combine egg, milk, salt, mustard and red pepper. Add Gruyère cheese to egg mixture. Place vegetables in a shallow 1-quart greased dish. Pour egg mixture over vegetables, and sprinkle with Parmesan cheese. Bake at 375 degrees for 15-20 minutes.
Serves: 6

Everyone will like this dish.

RATATOUILLE CASSEROLE

1 cup slivered almonds
¼ pound bacon, cut into 1-inch
   pieces
1 pound zucchini, sliced
1 pound eggplant, peeled and
   diced
1 large onion, cut into wedges

1 Tablespoon all-purpose flour
2 cups chopped tomatoes
1 teaspoon minced garlic
1½ teaspoon salt
¼ teaspoon pepper
1 teaspoon basil
6 ounces Swiss cheese, sliced

In a large skillet sauté almonds with bacon. When almonds are lightly roasted and bacon crisp, remove with slotted spoon. Add zucchini, eggplant and onion to skillet. Cover and cook over medium heat for 15 minutes, shaking pan, or stirring often. Stir in flour. Add tomatoes, garlic, salt, pepper and basil. Mix well. Layer vegetables, cheese and almond mixture in a 2-quart baking dish, ending with almond mixture on top. Bake uncovered at 400 degrees for 20-25 minutes.
Serves: 8

COLD VEGETABLE MEDLEY

1 bunch fresh broccoli, cut into
   flowerets
8 large mushrooms, sliced
1 medium green bell pepper,
   chopped

3 ribs celery, chopped
1 small head of cauliflower, cut
   into flowerets

In a large bowl combine all vegetables. Pour marinade over vegetables. Cover and refrigerate. Chill for 3 hours, stirring occasionally.

Marinade
1 cup sugar
2 teaspoons dry mustard
1 teaspoon salt
½ cup vinegar

¾ cup oil
1 small onion, grated
2 teaspoons poppy seeds

Combine all ingredients.
Serves: 6

Excellent for a "tailgate" picnic.

BEST BAKED APPLES

6 small baking apples, York or
   Rome
½ cup Red Hot candies
¼-½ cup sugar

¼ teaspoon salt
⅜ cup light corn syrup
¼ cup water

Cut apples in half and core. Do not peel apples. In a baking dish arrange apples, cut side up, in a single layer. Fill each apple cavity with Red Hot candies, using all of candy. Sprinkle with sugar and salt. Pour syrup and water over apples. Bake at 300 degrees for 30 minutes. Turn apples cut side down. Cook an additional 20 minutes, or until apples are tender and liquid is thickened. Remove from oven. Leave apples in syrup mixture until ready to serve. May be served hot or cold.
Serves: 6

CRANBERRY APPLES

3 cups peeled and chopped
apples
2 cups fresh cranberries, washed
and drained
½ cup + 2 Tablespoons
all-purpose flour, divided
1 cup sugar

3 (1⅛ ounce) packages instant
oatmeal with cinnamon
and spice
¾ cup chopped pecans
½ cup packed dark brown sugar
½ cup melted butter

Combine the apples, cranberries, 2 Tablespoons flour, sugar and instant oatmeal. Mix well. In a small bowl combine the pecans, ½ cup flour, brown sugar and butter. Add to fruit mixture. Pour into a 2-quart baking dish. Bake at 350 degrees for 45 minutes. Garnish with cranberries and pecans.
Serves: 6

A delicious brunch dish.

AMBRE FRUIT

2 unpeeled oranges, sliced and
seeded
20 ounce can pineapple chunks
29 ounce can pear halves
16 ounce can sliced peaches
16 ounce can apricot halves

1 cup sugar
½ cup + 1 Tablespoon cider
vinegar
3 cinnamon sticks
3 whole cloves
3 ounces cherry gelatin

Cut orange slices in half and place in pan with water to cover. Simmer until rind is tender. Drain and set aside. Drain all fruit well, reserving all of the pineapple juice and half of the peach and apricot juices. Combine reserved juices, sugar, vinegar, cinnamon, cloves and gelatin in a saucepan. Simmer for 30 minutes. Combine fruits, except for oranges, in a 9-cup container. Pour hot liquid over all. Add oranges and refrigerate at least 24 hours. Drain and serve cold, or at room temperature. Will keep in refrigerator for up to 1 week.
Serves: 12 to 15

A complement to any meal.

BRANDIED FALL FRUIT

20 ounce can sliced pineapple, drained
16 ounce can peach halves, drained
29 ounce can pear halves, drained
16 ounce can apricot halves, drained
½ cup butter

½ cup packed light brown sugar
2 Tablespoons all-purpose flour
¼ cup frozen orange juice, thawed
½ cup apricot brandy
6 ounces maraschino cherries, optional

Cut pineapple slices, peach and pear halves in half. Arrange fruit in alternate layers in a buttered casserole. In top of double boiler combine butter, brown sugar, flour and orange juice. Cook, stirring until smooth and thickened. Add brandy and pour over fruit. Garnish with cherries. Cover and refrigerate overnight. Remove 1 hour before baking. Bake at 350 degrees for 20 minutes.
Serves: 8 to 10

HOT SPICED FRUIT

29 ounce can sliced peaches
29 ounce can pear halves
20 ounce can pineapple chunks
½ cup orange marmalade
2 Tablespoons margarine

1 cinnamon stick
¼ teaspoon nutmeg
¼ teaspoon cloves
Maraschino cherries, optional

Drain fruit, reserving ½ cup liquid from each. Combine juices, marmalade, margarine and spices in a large saucepan. Bring to a boil and cook for 3 minutes. Reduce heat and add fruit. Simmer for 20 minutes.
Serves: 10

Better each time it is reheated.

MEAT
AND
GAME

MARINATED EYE OF ROUND

3 pound eye of round roast
1 heaping teaspoon pepper
1 heaping teaspoon garlic and parsley salt
1 heaping teaspoon onion flakes or powder

1 heaping teaspoon ginger
1 heaping teaspoon paprika
1 heaping teaspoon meat tenderizer

On a large sheet of aluminum foil prepare marinade mixture. Mix thoroughly. Roll roast in mixture to coat evenly. Seal foil tightly and refrigerate overnight. Unwrap and roast uncovered in a Dutch oven in a 300 degree oven for 3 hours for well done or 1 hour for medium rare. Remove from oven and cover at once to let the meat juices form gravy. Gravy can be thinned by adding water.
Serves: 8

MARINATED BEEF BRISKET

5 pound beef brisket
1 Tablespoon meat tenderizer
2-4 Tablespoons Liquid Smoke
2 teaspoons salt
1 teaspoon celery salt
1 teaspoon onion salt

1 teaspoon garlic salt
1 teaspoon nutmeg
1 teaspoon paprika
¼ cup packed dark brown sugar
1-2 Tablespoons Worcestershire sauce

Pierce meat with a fork and place on large piece of heavy duty aluminum foil. Sprinkle with next 6 ingredients. Wrap securely and refrigerate for at least 12 hours. Approximately 4-5 hours before cooking, open foil and add nutmeg, paprika, brown sugar and Worcestershire sauce. Rewrap securely until ready to cook. Cook at 275 degrees for 4-5 hours. Remove from oven and let cool. Refrigerate until cold so meat will slice easily. Can be returned to drippings and frozen. When ready to serve, heat and serve in juice.
Serves: 25-30 for a cocktail buffet

When using fresh garlic, remember the larger the bulb, the stronger the flavor with the exception of elephant garlic, the largest of all, which is mild in flavor.

KANSAS BRISKET

4½-6 pound beef brisket
Salt and pepper
½ teaspoon garlic powder
½ teaspoon onion powder
½ teaspoon celery salt
3 Tablespoons Liquid Smoke

3 Tablespoons Worcestershire sauce
2¼ cups good quality barbecue sauce
1½ cups beer

Rub meat with dry spices on both sides. Line a 9X12-inch baking dish with foil, place brisket in dish. Punch holes in brisket with a fork and rub in Liquid Smoke. Pour Worcestershire sauce and barbecue sauce over meat. Cover with foil. Marinate overnight. Next day, open foil, add beer, and tightly close foil. Bake at 250 degrees for 5-6 hours. Slice very thin. Serve with pan gravy.
Serves: 10 to 12

BARBECUED BRISKET WITH SUPER SAUCE

2 (3-4 pound) beef briskets, pork spare ribs or chicken quarters

Brush briskets with super sauce. Place at one end of a large, covered charcoal grill. Use wet hickory chips with charcoal. Meat should cook slowly 4-5 hours. Add additional wet hickory chips and brush meat with sauce every 30 minutes. When cooked, slice or chop brisket and serve with additional sauce. Pork ribs will cook in approximately 3 hours, turning and basting every 30 minutes. Grill chicken approximately 1 hour, turning and basting every 15 minutes.

Super Sauce
1 small onion, grated
2½ cups ketchup
1½ cups water
1½ cups vinegar

3 Tablespoons chili powder
3 Tablespoons pepper
3 Tablespoons sugar
2 Tablespoons salt

Combine all ingredients in a 2-quart saucepan. Bring to a slow boil; simmer for 30 minutes.
Serves: 8 to 10

GRILLED FLANK STEAK

2-3 pound flank steak   **2 teaspoons ginger**

Rub a teaspoon of ginger into each side of steak. Pour marinade over steak and marinate for 12-24 hours. Cook on hot grill 5 minutes on each side for medium to medium rare.

Marinade
1 cup oil
3 Tablespoons soy sauce   **1 clove garlic, chopped**
1 Tablespoon Worcestershire   **Fresh herbs to taste: basil,**
** sauce**   ** parsley, oregano (dried herbs**
½ teaspoon garlic powder   ** may be substituted)**

Combine all ingredients; mix well.
Serves: 4 to 6

LOUISIANA POT ROAST

3-4 pound roast, bottom round or   **1 Tablespoon vinegar**
** sirloin tip**   **½ cup vegetable oil, divided**
½ teaspoon pepper   **All-purpose flour**
½ teaspoon cloves   **1½ cups tomato juice**
½ teaspoon mace   **2-3 bay leaves**
½ teaspoon allspice   **6 medium carrots, peeled**
1 Tablespoon salt   ** and sliced**
1 large onion, chopped   **3 medium potatoes, peeled**
1 clove garlic, minced   ** and halved**
½ cup fresh lemon juice

Combine dry ingredients. Score meat and rub with dry ingredients. Combine onion, garlic, lemon juice, vinegar and ¼ cup oil. Pour over roast. Cover and marinate in refrigerator 5-6 hours or overnight. Remove from marinade and roll in flour to cover. Add remaining oil to a Dutch oven and brown meat on all sides. Add marinade liquid, tomato juice and bay leaves. Cover and cook at 300 degrees for 2½ hours or until tender. Add carrots and potatoes during the last hour of cooking. Remove bay leaves. Thicken pan juices for gravy. Season to taste.
Serves: 6 to 8

BEEF BURGUNDY

3 pound boneless chuck steak
3 Tablespoons vegetable oil
½ clove garlic, minced
1 shallot or green onion, chopped
1 bay leaf
Pinch of thyme

3 sprigs parsley
1½ cups red wine
½ cup beef stock
1 Tablespoon tomato sauce
2 Tablespoons beurre manié

Cut meat into 2-inch cubes, removing fat. Heat oil in heavy skillet; add meat and brown. Add remaining ingredients, except beurre manie. Bring to a boil, cover and reduce heat. Simmer 1½-2 hours until tender. Remove bay leaf and parsley. Add beurre manié, stir and simmer for a few minutes until slightly thickened. Can be served with warm rice or noodles.

Beurre Manié
½ pound butter   **1 cup all-purpose flour**

Cut butter into 1-2 Tablespoon pieces. Place in food processor with flour and process until thoroughly blended. Refrigerate. Can be frozen in Tablespoon amounts. 1 Tablespoon will thicken about ¾ cup liquid.
Serves: 6

KOREAN BEEF

1 Tablespoon sesame seeds
2 pounds lean beef (round or
  flank steak about 1-inch thick)
3 scallions, finely chopped
3-4 cloves garlic, minced
5 Tablespoons soy sauce

2 Tablespoons vegetable oil
¼ cup sugar
2 Tablespoons dry sherry
¼ teaspoon MSG, optional
⅛ teaspoon pepper

Lightly brown sesame seeds over low heat; set aside. Slice steak on the diagonal in very thin slices. Combine remaining ingredients, mix well. Pour over steak slices and let marinate 30 minutes or longer. Drain meat, reserving marinade. Stir fry half of the meat in a very hot 10-inch skillet until very little pink can be seen in meat. Remove to serving dish. Repeat with remaining meat. Heat reserved marinade in skillet. Sprinkle sesame seeds over meat. Serve immediately with cooked rice and marinade.
Serves: 4 to 6

CHI CHOW SIRLOIN

1½ pound sirloin steak, cubed
2 Tablespoons vegetable oil
½ cup chopped green onions
1 small onion, chopped
2 cups sliced fresh mushrooms
2 teaspoons cornstarch
1 Tablespoon sugar

½ cup soy sauce
½ cup beef broth
8 ounce can bamboo shoots, drained
8 ounce can sliced water chestnuts, drained

In a large skillet sauté meat quickly a few pieces at a time in oil. Drain. Add onions and mushrooms to meat and sauté until tender. Add bamboo shoots and water chestnuts. Stir well. In a bowl combine cornstarch, sugar, soy sauce and broth. Pour over meat and vegetables. Cook uncovered on low heat stirring constantly to prevent sticking. Cook 20-30 minutes. Serve over cooked rice.
Serves: 6

Simple but good.

BEEF, PEPPERS AND TOMATOES

1 pound sirloin steak, sliced very thin
2 Tablespoons vegetable oil
2 beef bouillon cubes
1 cup water
2 Tablespoons cornstarch
2 Tablespoons water
3 cloves garlic, minced

⅓ cup packed dark brown sugar
⅓ cup soy sauce
¼ cup vinegar
1 teaspoon ginger
3 small tomatoes, sliced
2 small green bell peppers, sliced
2½ cups sliced fresh mushrooms

In large skillet brown steak in hot oil. Dissolve bouillon cubes in water. Pour over steak and simmer until tender. Combine cornstarch and water. Mix well; pour into skillet. Add garlic, brown sugar, soy sauce, vinegar and ginger. Cook on medium heat until thickened. Add peppers, tomatoes and mushrooms. Simmer until vegetables are just tender.
Serves: 6

Store garlic in a cool, well-ventilated place.

BEEF SURPRISE STIR FRY

2 cups potato sticks
3 Tablespoons butter, divided
6 ounces beef tenderloin, cubed
Soy sauce
8 frozen small white onions
½ cup frozen corn

2 Tablespoons capers
6 Tablespoons beef stock
1 Tablespoon all-purpose flour
2 teaspoons tomato paste
Fresh spinach leaves

Stir fry potato sticks in 2 Tablespoons butter (yes, you can!) in a wok or heavy pan until lightly browned. Remove from pan and set aside. Toss beef with enough soy sauce to coat. Melt remaining butter; add beef and stir fry until browned. Add onions, corn and capers; stir fry until heated through. Mix stock with flour; add to vegetables and stir until liquid comes to a boil. Stir in tomato paste and remove from heat. Place spinach leaves on plate and top with steak and vegetables. Arrange potato sticks around edge.
Serves 2

OVEN STEW

1½ pounds stew meat
2 onions, peeled and sliced
6 carrots, sliced
3 potatoes, peeled and cubed
16 ounce can tomatoes
1 Tablespoon tapioca
1 Tablespoon sugar

1 cup chopped celery
1 clove garlic, minced
¼ teaspoon oregano
¾ cup claret wine
Bay leaf
Salt and pepper
Fresh parsley or parsley flakes

Place all ingredients in a heavy pot; cover tightly. Bake in a 250 degree oven for 5½ hours.
Serves: 6

Great to put into the oven early in the day for a good family meal.

Combination dishes that have among their ingredients foods that started out as a frozen product, may safely be frozen. However, the dish in question must already have been thoroughly cooked.

ITALIAN MEAT ROLL

2 eggs, beaten
¾ cup Italian bread crumbs
½ cup V-8 juice
2 Tablespoons minced fresh
   parsley
½ teaspoon oregano
¼ teaspoon salt

¼ teaspoon pepper
1 clove garlic, minced
2 pounds lean ground beef
8 thin slices ham
1½ cups shredded mozzarella
   cheese
3 slices mozzarella cheese

Combine eggs, bread crumbs, juice, parsley and seasonings. Stir in ground beef. On a large piece of aluminum foil pat meat mixture to a 12X10-inch rectangle. Arrange ham slices on meat. Sprinkle with shredded cheese. Using foil to help lift meat, roll meat up jelly roll style. Pinch ends and put seam side down on cooking sheet. Bake at 350 degrees for 1 hour and 15 minutes. Place sliced cheese on top and return loaf to oven until cheese is melted.
Serves: 8

May be prepared ahead and refrigerated.

PENNSYLVANIA DUTCH MEATLOAF

1 pound ground beef
1 egg, beaten
1 teaspoon salt
½ teaspoon pepper

1 small onion, chopped
1 teaspoon Worcestershire sauce
1 cup fresh soft bread crumbs
½ cup tomato sauce

Mix ground beef, egg, salt and pepper. Add chopped onion, Worcestershire sauce, bread crumbs and tomato sauce. Mix together and shape into a loaf and place in baking dish. Pour ½ of sauce over loaf. Bake at 350 degrees for 30 minutes. Pour remaining sauce over loaf and continue baking for an additional 30 minutes.

Sauce
2 Tablespoons prepared mustard
2 Tablespoons light brown sugar

2 Tablespoons apple cider vinegar
½ cup tomato sauce

Combine all ingredients.
Serves: 4 to 5

GROUND BEEF AND NOODLES

4 ounces medium egg noodles, cooked al dente and drained
½ cup chopped green onions, divided
2 Tablespoons butter
1½ pounds ground beef
1 teaspoon salt
2 (8 ounce) cans tomato sauce
1 cup creamed cottage cheese
1 cup sour cream
1 cup grated Cheddar cheese

Sauté half the green onions in butter. Add ground beef and cook until meat is no longer pink; drain. Add salt and tomato sauce; simmer 5-10 minutes. Combine cottage cheese, sour cream and remaining onions. In a greased 2-quart casserole layer noodles, cottage cheese mixture and meat sauce. Cover with grated cheese. Bake at 350 degrees for 25 minutes.
Serves 6

MORE-MORE BEEF

16 ounces medium egg noodles, cooked al dente and drained
1 cup chopped onions
1½ Tablespoons margarine or butter
3½ pounds ground chuck
1½ cups chopped green bell pepper
5 (8 ounce) cans tomato sauce
12 ounce or 17 ounce can whole kernel corn, drained
2 Tablespoons chili powder
Small bottle stuffed green olives, drained and sliced
Salt and pepper to taste
16 ounces Cheddar cheese, grated

In a large skillet sauté onions in butter. Add meat; brown and drain. Add pepper, tomato sauce, corn, chili powder, salt, pepper and olives. Add noodles and stir well. Pour into 2 greased 9X13-inch casseroles and top with cheese. Bake at 350 degrees for 45 minutes. May be frozen before baking.
Serves: 18

Men and boys love this. They will want more and more!

Substitute ⅛ teaspoon garlic powder for 1 clove fresh garlic.

MEAT

SONATA SALAMI

5 pounds ground beef
2½ teaspoons mustard seed
2½ teaspoons coarsely ground
  pepper
2½ teaspoons garlic powder

1 teaspoon hickory smoke salt or
  Liquid Smoke
1 teaspoon fennel seeds, optional
5 teaspoons Morton Tenderquick

Mix all ingredients together. Cover and refrigerate for 3 days, mixing well once a day. On 4th day, mix and shape into 5 rolls. Bake on a broiler pan for 11 hours at 140 degrees or 9 hours at 150 degrees. Turn rolls every 2 hours. Cool. Seal in plastic wrap and refrigerate. Freezes well.
Yield: 2 rolls

GLORIFIED DRIED BEEF

2 Tablespoons butter
1 cup sour cream
14 ounce can artichoke hearts,
  drained and thinly sliced
1 heaping Tablespoon grated
  Parmesan cheese

½ cup dry white wine
5 ounces dried beef, lightly rinsed
  and shredded
English muffins or toast
Paprika

Melt butter in skillet over low heat. Add sour cream; stir until smooth. Add artichoke hearts, Parmesan cheese, wine and shredded beef. Heat thoroughly on low heat. Serve on English muffins or toast. Sprinkle with paprika.
Serves: 6

PORK CHOPS ON AMBER RICE

6 pork chops, 1½-inches thick
Margarine
10¾ ounce can cream of chicken
  soup
1½ cup orange juice

½ cup water
1½ cups uncooked rice
Salt and pepper
2 Tablespoons Worcestershire
  sauce

Brown pork chops in skillet in small amount of margarine. Combine remaining ingredients and pour into a 9X13-inch casserole dish. Place pork chops on top of mixture. Cover and bake at 350 degrees for 45 minutes. Uncover and bake an additional 10 minutes.
Serves: 6

JULIA'S PORK

1 pound green bell peppers, cut
  in l-inch strips
2 cups cherry tomatoes
12 cloves garlic, peeled
3 Tablespoons olive oil, divided
1 Tablespoon rosemary, divided

1 Tablespoon lemon peel, divided
½ teaspoon salt, divided
¼ teaspoon pepper, divided
2 pound pork tenderloin
3 Tablespoons lemon juice

Preheat oven to 400 degrees. In a bowl combine peppers, tomatoes, garlic, 1½ Tablespoons olive oil, ½ Tablespoon rosemary, ½ Tablespoon lemon peel, ¼ teaspoon salt and ⅛ teaspoon pepper. Rub pork with remaining 1½ Tablespoon olive oil, ½ Tablespoon rosemary, ½ Tablespoon lemon peel, ¼ teaspoon salt and ⅛ teaspoon pepper. Place pork in a shallow roasting pan and roast 25 minutes. Turn pork and add vegetable mixture. Roast for an additional 35 minutes . Remove from oven and sprinkle with lemon juice. Let sit for 3 minutes. Slice and serve.
Serves: 4

DEVILED PORK CHOPS

4 Tablespoons butter, divided
1 medium cooking apple, cut into
  wedges
1 pound fresh mushrooms, sliced
¼ teaspoon pepper
½ teaspoon salt, divided
4 pork loin chops, ½ inch-thick,
  butterflied

½ cup mayonnaise
⅓ cup soft bread crumbs
1 Tablespoon chopped watercress
1 Tablespoon prepared mustard
⅛ teaspoon paprika
Watercress sprigs for garnish

Melt 1 Tablespoon butter in a 12-inch skillet over medium heat. Cook apple wedges 5 minutes or until fork-tender, turning once. Remove to large platter; keep warm. In same skillet over medium heat melt 3 Tablespoons butter. Add mushrooms, pepper, and ¼ teaspoon salt. Cook until mushrooms are tender, stirring occasionally. Remove mushrooms to platter with apple wedges; keep warm. Preheat broiler. Place pork chops on rack of broiler pan; broil 5 minutes on each side, turning once. In small bowl mix mayonnaise, bread crumbs, watercress, mustard, paprika and ¼ teaspoon salt. When chops are done, spread mayonnaise mixture over tops. Broil 1 minute longer or until topping is hot and bubbly. To serve, arrange pork chops on platter with apples and mushrooms. Garnish each chop with a watercress sprig.
Serves: 4

PORK TENDERLOIN WITH SOUR CREAM
AND MUSHROOMS

2 (1½-2 pounds) whole pork
  tenderloins
Butter
10¾ ounce can cream of
  mushroom soup
2 cups white wine
1 teaspoon crushed rosemary

1 Tablespoon onion salt
½ teaspoon garlic powder
1 Tablespoon freshly ground
  black pepper
1 pound fresh mushrooms,
  quartered
2 cups sour cream

Brown whole tenderloins in butter over high heat. Add soup, wine, rosemary, onion salt, garlic powder and pepper. Bake 1½ hours in a 325 degree oven. While meat is baking, sauté mushrooms in small amount of butter. During last 15 minutes of baking, add sour cream and sautéed mushrooms.
Serves: 8 to 10

PORK ROAST RIVIERA

4-5 pound pork loin roast
2 Tablespoons dry mustard
2 teaspoons thyme
¼ teaspoons ground cloves

½ cup dry sherry
¼ cup soy sauce
1 teaspoon ginger

Trim excess fat from roast and place in a shallow baking dish. Combine remaining ingredients and pour over roast. Marinate 12 hours, turning frequently. Drain and reserve marinade. Roast at 325 degrees for 2½-3 hours or to an internal temperature of 160 degrees, basting every 30 minutes with reserved marinade. Serve with Currant Sauce poured over sliced meat.

Currant Sauce
¾ cup red currant jelly
1 teaspoon soy sauce

2 Tablespoons sherry

Melt jelly in saucepan. Add soy sauce and sherry. Mix well. Heat thoroughly. May be made ahead and reheated.
Serves: 8 to 10

PORK AND CABBAGE

4 pork chops
1 head cabbage, shredded
¼ cup all-purpose flour
½ teaspoon salt

¼ teaspoon pepper
¼ teaspoon paprika
2 Tablespoons vegetable oil
1-2 Tablespoons water

Remove fat from chops. Combine flour, salt, pepper and paprika. Dust chops lightly. In a 10-inch skillet brown meat in oil. Remove chops and keep warm. Drain fat leaving 1 Tablespoon in skillet. Add cabbage, salt and pepper to taste. Place chops over cabbage and add water. Cover and simmer until cabbage is cooked, approximately 45 minutes. May add small potatoes and peeled small onions when adding meat.
Serves: 4

SHREDDED PORK BARBECUE

6-8 pound pork roast, picnic ham
  or pork shoulder
Rosemary
½ teaspoon salt
¼ teaspoon pepper
½ cup chopped celery
1 onion, chopped
2 Tablespoons vegetable oil
2 Tablespoons vinegar
2 Tablespoons brown sugar
3 Tablespoons Worcestershire
  sauce

1 Tablespoon Liquid Smoke
Dash of Tabasco sauce
¼ cup fresh lemon juice
1 cup tomato juice, chili sauce, or
  ketchup or a mixture of 2
Dash of garlic salt
½ teaspoon prepared mustard
1 Tablespoon horseradish
½ cup meat drippings or water

Preheat oven to 500 degrees. Rub roast with rosemary, salt and pepper. Place in a roasting pan and cook 15 minutes. Reduce heat to 300 degrees and cook covered for several hours, or until meat is falling off bone. Cool, remove bone and fat; shred meat. In skillet add oil and sauté celery and onions until tender. Add remaining ingredients and bring to a boil. Pour over shredded meat. Cover and bake 1 hour at 275 degrees. Stir occasionally. Sauce can be made ahead, poured over meat, refrigerated and heated when ready to serve.
Serves 10

Good served on cornbread with slaw and sliced tomatoes.

GRILLED PORK TENDERLOIN

2-4 pound pork tenderloin
1 cup apple juice
⅓ cup soy sauce
1 teaspoon garlic powder

1 teaspoon ginger
1 teaspoon pepper
Commercial barbecue sauce
Mesquite wood, optional

Pour apple juice, soy sauce, garlic powder, ginger and pepper into a large zip-lock bag. Place tenderloin in bag. Marinate at least 3 hours, turning every 20 minutes if possible. Just before cooking, mix barbecue sauce in equal portion with marinade. Cook tenderloin on grill using mesquite wood. Turn meat basting frequently until well seared on all sides. Finish cooking on grill for an additional 45 minutes or wrap in foil and complete cooking at a later time in a 350 degree oven, basting with sauce.
Serves: 6-8

OVEN BARBECUED SPARERIBS

2 slabs lean spareribs, 4 pounds each

Salt and pepper to taste

Preheat oven to 400 degrees. Sprinkle ribs with salt and pepper. Arrange ribs in 2 large baking dishes. Bake 1 hour. Turn ribs and bake 10 minutes longer; pour off fat. Brush ribs with sauce and return to oven. Bake 30 minutes, brushing on sauce every 10 minutes. Turn the ribs and brush on remaining sauce. Bake an additional 30 minutes. Cut ribs into wide individual pieces to serve.

Sauce
8 Tablespoons unsalted butter
2 cups chopped onions
2 teaspoons minced garlic
2 cups ketchup
¼ cup soy sauce

1½ Tablespoons chili powder
1 teaspoon Tabasco sauce, or to taste
¼ cup sherry wine vinegar or red wine vinegar
3 Tablespoons dark brown sugar

Melt butter in large saucepan; add onion and garlic. Cook, stirring, until onions are transparent. Add remaining ingredients. Bring to boil and let simmer about 5 minutes.
Serves: 8

ITALIAN SPAGHETTI FOR A CROWD

3 pounds loin butt pork, ground
4 Tablespoons olive oil
3 cloves garlic, chopped
4 (6 ounce) cans tomato paste
4 (8 ounce) cans tomato sauce
6 (14 ounce) cans whole tomatoes
2 cups chopped green bell pepper
2 cups chopped onion
6 ounce can sliced mushrooms
10 fennel seeds
2 teaspoons oregano
2 teaspoons basil

2 teaspoons rosemary
2 teaspoons salt
1 teaspoon pepper
¼ teaspoon red pepper flakes
¾ pound pepperoni, thickly
  sliced
1 cup grated Romano cheese
1 cup dry red wine
32 ounces spaghetti, cooked al
  dente and drained
Freshly grated Parmesan cheese

In a large Dutch oven brown pork in 2 Tablespoons oil. Remove meat and set aside. Drain fat. Add remaining oil; sauté garlic until browned. Add tomato paste and cook 15 minutes, stirring until it becomes dark in color. Add tomato sauce, tomatoes, green pepper, onions and mushrooms. Cook 1 hour. Add spices, pork and pepperoni. Cover and cook 2 hours on low heat. Add Romano cheese. Cook 2 more hours. Add wine. Serve sauce over spaghetti. Sprinkle with Parmesan cheese, if desired. Serves 18-20

HAM ROLL-UPS

12 slices lean boiled ham
10 ounces frozen chopped
  spinach, cooked and squeezed
  dry
1 cup herb stuffing mix
1 cup sour cream
4 Tablespoons butter

4 Tablespoons all-purpose flour
2 cups milk, heated
¾ cup grated sharp Cheddar
  cheese
Salt and pepper to taste
Grated Parmesan cheese
Paprika

Combine spinach, stuffing mix and sour cream. Spread approximately ¼-inch thick on ham slices. Roll up and place in a 3-quart baking dish. Place in a single layer, seam side down. In top of double boiler melt butter. Add flour; stir to blend. Gradually add milk and cook until thickened. Add cheese, salt and pepper, stirring until smooth. Pour over ham rolls. Sprinkle with Parmesan cheese and paprika. Cover and bake at 375 degrees for 15 minutes. Uncover and continue baking for an additional 15 minutes.
Serves: 6

VEAL CHOPS WITH CREAM AND CHIVES

6 Tablespoons unsalted butter, divided
4 veal chops
Salt and pepper
⅔ cup vermouth

1½ cups heavy cream
2 Tablespoons chopped chives, or finely chopped green onion tops

Place 4 Tablespoons butter in skillet and heat. Sprinkle chops with salt and pepper. Cook in butter over medium heat until slightly pink in color, approximately 4-5 minutes per side. Remove to serving plate and cover. Deglaze pan with wine, reducing to approximately 3 Tablespoons. Add cream and cook until slightly thickened. Salt and pepper to taste; stir in remaining 2 Tablespoons butter and chives. Cover chops with sauce. Serve immediately.
Serves: 4

HAM LOAF WITH MUSTARD SAUCE

1 pound ground ham
½ pound fresh ground pork
1 egg
1 cup milk
2 cups Rice Krispies, crushed

2 Tablespoons ketchup
1 Tablespoon Worcestershire sauce
2 Tablespoons dark brown sugar

Combine ham, pork, egg, milk, Rice Krispies, ketchup and Worcestershire sauce. Place in a 9X5-inch loaf pan. Sprinkle with 2 Tablespoons brown sugar. Bake at 350 degrees for 1 hour.

Mustard Sauce
½ cup butter
1 Tablespoon all-purpose flour
½ cup sugar
2 teaspoons instant chicken bouillon

½ cup hot water
1 Tablespoon dry mustard
¼ cup vinegar
3 egg yolks, beaten

In top of double boiler melt butter. Stir in flour and sugar. Dissolve bouillon in hot water and add to flour mixture. Stir until smooth. Add mustard and vinegar. Whisk in egg yolks and cook until thickened. Serve hot over sliced ham loaf.
Serves: 8

SENSATIONAL "SLIM" VEAL

**1 heaping teaspoon instant beef
bouillon**
½ cup very hot water
1 Tablespoon lemon juice
**3 Tablespoons fresh chopped
parsley**

¼ cup dry white wine
⅓ cup fine dry bread crumbs
2 Tablespoons butter
1-1½ pounds veal scallopini

In a small bowl combine bouillon, water, lemon juice, parsley and wine. On a piece of waxed paper spread bread crumbs. Press veal into crumbs, coating both sides. Melt butter in a large non-stick skillet. Brown meat on both sides over moderate heat. Add liquid, cover and simmer for 30 minutes or until tender. Remove veal and place on a warm platter. Reduce pan juices and pour over veal.
Serves: 4

BAKED HAM BALLS

1½ pounds cooked ham, ground
1½ pounds fresh pork, ground
1¼ cups cracker crumbs

1 cup milk
Salt and pepper to taste

Combine ham, pork, cracker crumbs, milk, salt and pepper. Shape mixture into 1½-inch balls. Bake uncovered at 450 degrees for 15 minutes, turning to keep balls round. Reduce heat to 325 degrees. Pour off fat and bake for 1 hour basting with sauce every 15-20 minutes, turning ham balls each basting time.

Sauce
½ cup water
½ cup vinegar

1½ cups packed dark brown sugar
1 Tablespoon dry mustard

In a saucepan combine all ingredients. Bring to a boil and simmer over low heat for 5 minutes.
Serves: 6 to 8

PEPPERED LAMB CHOPS

1 teaspoon onion powder
½ teaspoon freshly ground
   black pepper
½ teaspoon white pepper
¾ teaspoon garlic powder
1 teaspoon cayenne pepper

½ teaspoon thyme
½ teaspoon salt
½ teaspoon dry mustard
½ cup butter, melted
4 lamb chops, 1 inch thick
Mint jalapeño jelly

Heat a cast iron skillet over a high flame for 15-20 minutes or until white in color. Best to do this outside on a propane gas grill. Combine seasonings in a flat dish. Brush each side of chops with melted butter. Put chops in seasoning mixture, pressing chops so spices will adhere. Fry chops for 1-2 minutes on each side, or until charred, turning once. Serve with mint jelly.
Serves: 2

BRAISED LEG OF LAMB

3 pound leg of lamb
1 Tablespoon butter
3 Tablespoon Cognac
3 Tablespoons sherry
1 cup water
⅛ cup rosemary
⅛ cup basil

1 medium onion, sliced
1 large clove garlic, crushed
1 Tablespoon mint jelly
4 fresh mushrooms, sliced
⅛ cup oregano
Salt and pepper

Trim fat from lamb. Brown on all sides in a heavy 5-quart pot in hot butter over high heat. When browned, add remaining ingredients in order given. Cover tightly and cook over low heat until tender, approximately 1 hour. Transfer to large platter to serve.
Serves 6

For added flavor, blend garlic and herbs—fresh or dried—into a dish early on...then at the last moment add a bit more. This gives an extra dimension in taste.

MARINATED LEG OF LAMB

3 pound leg of lamb
¼ cup vegetable oil
¼ cup olive oil
2 teaspoons salt
1 teaspoon pepper
Juice of 2 lemons
1 clove garlic, minced

1 teaspoon thyme
2 Tablespoon minced fresh parsley
1½ teaspoons oregano
1 small onion, chopped
1 bay leaf
2 cups dry red wine

In a bowl combine all ingredients in order given. Mix well and pour over lamb. Marinate for 24 hours, turning several times. Bake at 300 degrees, uncovered, in marinade for 1½ hours. Baste with marinade during cooking.
Serves: 6

MISSISSIPPI SAUSAGE CORNBREAD

½ pound smoked sausage links
1½ cups yellow self-rising
  cornmeal
⅔ cup vegetable oil
2 large eggs

1 cup sour cream
1 cup cream style corn
3-4 green onions, chopped
1½ cups grated hot pepper
  cheese

Brown sausage links, drain on paper towels and slice ½-inch thick. In a bowl combine cornmeal, oil, eggs, sour cream, corn and onions. Mix well. Pour half of batter into a greased 8-inch skillet. Place sausage slices on top and sprinkle with half of cheese. Pour remaining batter on top and sprinkle with remaining cheese. Bake at 450 degrees for 30 minutes or until golden brown.
Serves: 6 to 8

Add a green salad and lots of ice tea and you have a terrific meal after a busy days.

To make a bouquet garni, the little bunch of herbs traditionally used in many meat, game and poultry dishes, place a mixed teaspoon of dried basil, thyme, majoram, savory and parsley with a bay leaf on a 4-inch square of cheesecloth. If desired, a clove of peeled garlic and 3 or 4 black peppercorns may be added. Several juniper berries also added will enhance pork or game dishes. Secure bundle with thread.

BRANDIED DUCK BREASTS WITH WILD RICE

1 cup uncooked wild rice
4 duck breasts
½ cup butter
⅓ cup brandy
⅓ cup sherry

1 Tablespoon Worcestershire
  sauce
4 Tablespoons grape jelly
2 teaspoons cornstarch
2 teaspoons cold water

Cook rice according to package directions. Melt butter in skillet; brown duck breasts quickly. Remove duck breasts from skillet. Stir in brandy, sherry, Worcestershire sauce and grape jelly. Bring to a boil, stirring to dissolve the jelly. Add the duck breasts. Cover; reduce heat to low. Simmer 20 minutes, turning duck breasts once. Remove duck breasts from pan. Blend cornstarch in cold water and stir until smooth; add to liquid in skillet. Stir until thickened. To serve, spoon sauce over duck breasts and wild rice.
Serves 4

ROAST DUCK WITH COINTREAU

2 (3-4 pound) ducks
2 ribs celery, cut in 2-inch pieces
1 small onion, quartered
2 carrots, peeled and quartered
2 oranges
⅔ cup water, divided
½ cup vermouth
¼ cup dry sherry

½ cup sugar
1 Tablespoon fresh lemon juice
1 Tablespoon vinegar
1 Tablespoon Cointreau liqueur
1 Tablespoon cornstarch
⅛ teaspoon salt
Dash of pepper

Place ducks on rack in roasting pan. Stuff with celery, onions, carrots and 1 orange, quartered. Roast uncovered at 375 degrees for 1½ hours. Remove ducks to platter; keep warm. Skim fat from juices in pan. To juices add ⅓ cup water, vermouth and sherry. Bring to a boil, boil until reduced to ¾ cup. Squeeze remaining orange, reserving juice. Scrape membrane from rind of ½ the orange skin. Cut this rind into very thin strips. In heavy saucepan caramelize sugar; stir in remaining ⅓ cup water, reserved orange juice, lemon juice and vinegar, stirring until caramel melts. Add orange rind strips and reduced wine mixture. Blend cornstarch into Cointreau; add salt and pepper. Add to sauce. Cook and stir until thickened and bubbly. Remove breast meat and legs from ducks; spoon sauce over meat to serve.
Serves 6

DUCKS BURGUNDY

1 large or 2 small ducks
Salt and pepper
2 Tablespoons dark brown sugar
2 Tablespoons ketchup
2 Tablespoons vinegar

2 Tablespoons Worcestershire
 sauce
1 teaspoon paprika
⅔ cup Burgundy wine

Salt and pepper duck. In a saucepan combine all ingredients. Place duck on aluminum foil and bring sides up. Pour sauce over ducks. Wrap tightly. Place in a baking pan. Bake 3-4 hours at 375 degrees.
Serves: 2

WILD DUCK PIE

2 large or 4 small ducks
Water
1 Tablespoon salt
1 teaspoon pepper
1 large onion, chopped
1 bay leaf
5 Tablespoons all-purpose flour
5 Tablespoons vegetable
 shortening
8-10 green onions, chopped

1 large yellow onion, finely
 chopped
1 cup chopped fresh parsley
1 green bell pepper, finely
 chopped
2 ribs celery, chopped
Salt and pepper to taste
Pinch of thyme
2 (9-inch) unbaked pie crusts with
 top crusts

Wash ducks inside and out thoroughly. Cut off tails, being sure to remove oil gland. In a large pot place ducks, onions, bay leaf, salt and pepper. Add water to cover. Cook until tender and meat comes off the bone easily. Discard skin and chop cooked ducks. Reserve broth. In a large skillet make a dark roux with flour and shortening. Add next 7 ingredients and cook until wilted. Slowly add enough duck broth to make a medium gravy. Stir in chopped duck. Adjust seasoning. Pour into unbaked pie crusts. Cover with top crusts. Make slits in top. Bake at 350 degrees for approximately 45 minutes or until browned. Can be frozen at this point and reheated. This recipe is not exact, depending on how meaty the ducks are. You should have about 4 cups chopped duck.
Yield: 2 pies

QUAIL IN WINE WITH WILD RICE

12 quail
Salt
All-purpose flour
4 Tablespoons butter or
  margarine
½ cup chopped fresh mushrooms

¼ cup chopped onion
½ cup white wine
1 Tablespoon parsley
½ cup heavy cream
3 cups cooked long grain and
  wild rice

Wash and dry birds. Rub with salt and flour. Sauté lightly in butter in skillet. Remove to a 1½-quart casserole. Sauté mushrooms and onion in butter remaining in skillet. Pour over the birds. Add wine and parsley. Cover and bake at 350 degrees for 45-55 minutes, basting frequently. Remove quail and keep warm. To make a sauce, heat cream and add to juices in baking dish. Stir until well blended. Serve quail on rice topped with sauce.
Serves: 6

24 QUAIL OR DOVE

½ cup chopped shallots
2 slices bacon, cooked and
  crumbled
½ cup sliced fresh mushrooms
1 cup butter
24 quail or dove
Salt and pepper

All-purpose flour
3 Tablespoons all-purpose flour
1 cup white wine
2 cups chicken stock
¼ teaspoon tarragon
¼ teaspoon basil
¼ teaspoon chervil

In a Dutch oven sauté shallots, bacon and mushrooms in butter. Remove with a slotted spoon and set aside. Very lightly flour, salt and pepper birds. To Dutch oven add remaining butter. Brown birds a few at a time. Remove birds from pan as they are browned. Add 3 Tablespoons flour, wine and stock; stirring until smooth. Add shallot mixture and spices. Mix well. Return birds. Cover and bake at 350 degrees for 30 minutes.
Serves: 10 to 12

DOVE DELIGHT

1½ cups Italian salad dressing
4 Tablespoons Worcestershire
   sauce

1 teaspoon lemon pepper
2 dozen doves
1 pound bacon

Combine Italian dressing, Worcestershire sauce and lemon pepper. Pour over doves. Let sit at least 1 hour. Wrap each dove with ½ slice of bacon and secure with a wooden pick. Place on grill, cover and cook for 30-45 minutes or until tender. Variation: Use duck breasts using additional bacon and cooking longer.
Serves: 6

STUFFED VENISON

1 venison hindquarter, deboned
Sage leaves, thyme and rosemary,
   preferably fresh
1 clove garlic, cut
All-purpose flour
2 Tablespoons olive oil
2 Tablespoons chopped onion
2 cups soft bread crumbs
3 cups chopped tart apples
½ cup chopped celery

White wine
Salt
Paprika
1 pound bacon
4-8 sweet potatoes, peeled and
   sliced
8-10 small onions
2 Tablespoons all-purpose flour
½ cup water

Open up hind quarter by cutting meat at intervals for stuffing, being careful not to cut all the way through meat. Rub inside with cut garlic clove and herbs. Dredge in flour. Sauté onion in olive oil until soft and transparent. Combine onions with bread crumbs, apples and celery; moisten with wine and season with salt and paprika to make stuffing mixture. Stuff venison by filling cavities. Roll meat and tie with string at intervals. Place in a roaster, seam side down. Completely cover with bacon strips, sliding bacon under string to hold in place. Bake uncovered at 325 degrees for 30 minutes per pound, basting every 30 minutes with wine. Roast will form rich, brown juices. During last hour of cooking place potatoes and onions around meat and baste with juices. To serve, remove roast and vegetables to serving dish; keep warm. Mix flour with water until dissolved. Add to juices in pan and stir over low heat until thickened; adjust seasoning. Pour over potatoes and onions.
Serves: 16 to 18

Wonderful served with boiled cabbage and cornbread.

COUNTRY FRIED GAME

Choice of game:
1 rabbit, cup up
2 squirrel, cup up
1 venison tenderloin, butterflied
1 cup buttermilk
1½ cups all-purpose flour

Salt and pepper
½ teaspoon nutmeg
2 cups vegetable shortening or
vegetable oil
3 cups water, divided
1 large onion, finely chopped

Place cut-up meat in buttermilk. Shake flour, salt, pepper and nutmeg together in a paper bag. Heat oil in a deep skillet. Shake pieces of meat in sack of flour. Fry in hot oil for 10-15 minutes on each side, or until browned. Drain on paper towels. Place in baking dish; add 1 cup water and cover with aluminum foil. Bake at 350 degrees for 30 minutes to 1 hour or until tender. While meat is baking, pour oil from skillet leaving just enough to cover bottom. Heat oil, add onion and sauté. Add seasoned flour from bag and stir constantly until golden brown; reduce heat. Add 2 cups water slowly, stirring constantly. Add salt and pepper to taste. Serve with rice and hot biscuits.
Serves: 4

WILD DUCK

4 wild ducks
Butter
Salt and pepper
Accent
1 onion, chopped
1 apple, chopped

1 potato, chopped
2 ribs celery, chopped
2 oranges, unpeeled and chopped
Bacon
1 cup Burgundy wine

Preheat oven to 500 degrees. Wash and pat ducks dry. Season inside and out with butter, salt, pepper and Accent. Combine vegetables and fruits and stuff each duck. Place ducks in a heavy roaster. Cover each with strips of bacon. Bake uncovered for 30-40 minutes until browned. Reduce oven to 275 degrees and add wine to each duck. Cover and bake until tender, about 4 hours basting every 20-30 minutes. When done, remove stuffing and discard. Thicken the gravy to serve with ducks.
Serves: 8 to 10

POULTRY

PECAN CHICKEN BREASTS

**6 chicken breasts, skinned and
    boned**
Salt and pepper to taste
½ cup + 3 Tablespoons butter

3 Tablespoons Dijon mustard
1 cup finely chopped pecans
1 Tablespoon vegetable oil

Flatten chicken breasts and season with salt and pepper. Melt ½ cup butter and add mustard. Dip chicken into mixture to coat well. Roll chicken in chopped pecans. Melt together 3 Tablespoons butter and oil. Sauté chicken until brown. Place chicken in 11X14-inch baking dish. Bake uncovered at 350 degrees for 15-20 minutes.

Sauce
1 Tablespoon butter, melted
⅔ cup sour cream
1 Tablespoon Dijon mustard

Salt and pepper to taste
Whole, toasted pecans for garnish

Combine butter, sour cream, mustard, and seasonings. Pour 1-2 Tablespoons of sauce on each serving plate; top with chicken breast and garnish with whole toasted pecans.
Serves: 6

A different taste!

CHICKEN, HAM AND SHRIMP DIVAN

20 ounces frozen broccoli spears
2 cups cooked, cubed chicken
2 cups cooked, cubed ham
2 cups cooked and peeled shrimp
**2 (10¾ ounce) cans cream of
    chicken soup**
1 cup mayonnaise

2 cups grated Cheddar cheese
1 teaspoon lemon juice
**¼ cup dry white wine or
    vermouth**
½ cup grated Parmesan cheese
Paprika

Cook broccoli for 1 minute and drain well. Place broccoli in bottom of 9X13-inch greased casserole. Layer chicken, ham and shrimp on top of broccoli. Mix together soup, mayonnaise, Cheddar cheese, lemon juice and wine. Pour over broccoli mixture. Sprinkle with Parmesan cheese and paprika. Bake uncovered at 350 degrees for 20-30 minutes.
Serves: 10 to 12

CHICKEN CROQUETTES

5½ pound hen
2 cups chopped pecans
2 Tablespoons grated onion
2 Tablespoons chopped parsley
2 Tablespoons margarine
2 Tablespoons all-purpose flour

2 cups milk
Salt
1 egg
2 Tablespoons milk
1-2 cups bread crumbs
Cooking oil

Boil hen in seasoned water until tender. Cool. Debone hen and cut meat into small pieces. Add nuts, onions, and parsley to chicken. Mix in a food processor until well-blended. Make a white sauce using margarine, flour and milk. Cook until thickened. Add salt to taste. Cool. Add chicken mixture to white sauce and shape into croquettes. Beat egg and milk. Dip chicken croquettes into egg mixture and roll in bread crumbs. Chill. Fry in hot oil until lightly browned.
Yield: 12 to 14 croquettes

CHICKEN CRESCENT DELIGHTS

6 ounces cream cheese
½ cup margarine, divided
4 cups cooked chopped chicken
¼ cup milk
½ teaspoon salt
2 Tablespoons chopped onion

2 Tablespoons chopped pimiento
2 (8 ounce) cans refrigerated
  crescent rolls
¾ cup crumbled seasoned
  croutons

Preheat oven to 350 degrees. In a medium bowl blend cream cheese and 5 Tablespoons of margarine. Add the chicken, milk, salt, onion and pimiento. Mix well. Separate dough into 8-rectangles. Press perforations firmly to seal. Spoon ½ cup of chicken mixture into center of rectangle. Pull four corners of dough to top center of filling. Twist firmly and press any openings in dough together. Place on cookie sheet and drizzle with remaining margarine and crumbled croutons. Bake 30 minutes or until golden brown.
Serves: 8

Wonderful for a ladies' luncheon.

Substitute 3 parts fresh herbs to 1 part dried herbs.

LEISURE CHICKEN

6 chicken breasts
½ cup butter

½ cup sherry
½ cup soy sauce

Wash and pat dry chicken. In a saucepan melt butter. Add sherry and soy sauce. Pour butter mixture over chicken and marinate for 15 minutes. Broil for 30-40 minutes. Turn chicken occasionally and baste with marinade. May be served hot or cold. Variation: grill chicken instead of broiling.
Serves: 4 to 6

ITALIAN CHICKEN

8 chicken breasts, boned
1-2 eggs
Italian bread crumbs
½ cup vegetable oil
3 (8 ounce) cans tomato sauce

Salt, pepper and garlic to taste
1 Tablespoon basil
1 Tablespoon butter
Grated Parmesan cheese
Mozzarella cheese, thinly sliced

Dip chicken into beaten egg. Coat well, then roll in bread crumbs. Brown in oil. Drain chicken and place in casserole in a single layer. To oil left in skillet add tomato sauce, seasonings, and butter. Simmer and pour over chicken. Sprinkle with Parmesan cheese. Cover casserole and bake at 350 degrees for 30 minutes. Remove from oven; uncover and top with sliced mozzarella cheese. Return to oven for 10 minutes.
Serves: 8

Easy to prepare and delicious.

CHICKEN AND HERBS

2½ pound chicken, cut up
½ cup sliced onion
½ cup sliced green bell pepper
2 cloves garlic, minced
1 bay leaf
2 Tablespoons chopped parsley
½ teaspoon oregano
¼ teaspoon cayenne pepper

1¾ cups tomato purée
2 Tablespoons mustard
2 Tablespoons sugar
1 teaspoon salt
¼ teaspoon pepper
¼ cup vinegar
1 Tablespoon Worcestershire
  sauce

Place chicken in baking dish. Combine remaining ingredients and pour over chicken. Cover and bake at 350 degrees for 2 hours. Serve with buttered noodles.
Serves: 6 to 8

LIME ROASTED CHICKEN

1 frying chicken
¼ cup lime juice
¼ cup salad oil
½ teaspoon salt
⅛ teaspoon pepper

1 Tablespoon chopped parsley
1 Tablespoon chopped capers
Vegetable garni: cooked carrots, potatoes, leeks and raw mushrooms

Prepare marinade using lime juice, oil, salt, pepper, parsley and capers. Place chicken in baking dish. Pour marinade over chicken and into cavity. Marinate for 1 hour, turning frequently. Bake uncovered at 400 degrees for 1 hour, basting and turning every 20 minutes. Add vegetables during last 20 minutes of cooking time.
Serves: 4

CHICKEN BREASTS ALFREDO

6 chicken breasts, skinned and boned
½ cup all-purpose flour
3 eggs, beaten
3 Tablespoons water
½ cup grated Romano cheese

¼ cup chopped fresh parsley
½ teaspoon salt
1 cup seasoned bread crumbs
3 Tablespoons butter
2 Tablespoons vegetable oil
6 slices mozzarella cheese

Coat chicken breasts with flour. Combine egg, water, Romano cheese, parsley and salt. Mix well. Dip flour-coated chicken into egg mixture. Roll chicken breasts in seasoned bread crumbs. Heat butter and oil in large skillet and fry chicken until golden brown. Cook slowly 15-20 minutes. Remove to baking dish. This may be done a day ahead of serving. When ready to bake, top each piece of chicken with mozzarella cheese. Pour cheese sauce over chicken. Bake uncovered at 425 degrees for 10-15 minutes. Serve immediately.

Sauce

1 cup whipping cream
¼ cup water
¼ cup margarine

½ cup grated Romano cheese
¼ cup chopped fresh parsley

Heat cream, water and margarine until margarine is melted. Add cheese and parsley. Heat until cheese melts.
Serves: 6

A very delicious and moist dish.

RED CURRANT CHICKEN DIJON

6 chicken breast
1 cup bread crumbs
¼ cup grated Parmesan cheese
¼ cup sesame seeds
2 Tablespoons chopped parsley

½ teaspoon salt
¼ teaspoon pepper
¼ teaspoon paprika
4 Tablespoons melted butter

Combine bread crumbs, cheese, sesame seeds, parsley, salt, pepper and paprika. Dip chicken pieces into melted butter and then into bread crumb mixture. Place chicken in a 9X13 baking dish. Bake uncovered at 350 degrees for 50 minutes or until golden brown. Ladle sauce over chicken when ready to serve.

Sauce
1 Tablespoon cornstarch
¼ teaspoon ginger
Juice and grated rind of 1 orange
¾ cup red currant jelly

2 Tablespoons Dijon mustard
3 drops hot pepper sauce
Grated rind of 1 lemon

In a saucepan combine cornstarch, ginger, orange juice, jelly, mustard and pepper sauce. Cook and stir until well mixed. Add grated orange and lemon rinds. Serve sauce separately with chicken.

Serves: 6

A family favorite.

TURKEY ALMOND ORIENTAL

2 cups cooked cubed turkey
½ cup crushed pineapple, drain
  and reserve juice
2 Tablespoons butter
1½ Tablespoons cornstarch
½ cup pineapple juice
2 cups turkey stock

½ cup slivered almonds
½ cup sliced celery
1½ teaspoons salt
¾ cup grated coconut
½ cup seedless white raisins
Chow mein noodles

Sauté pineapple in butter for 5 minutes. Add cornstarch to pineapple juice. Add juice mixture and turkey stock to pineapple mixture. Stir over low heat until thickened. Add turkey, almonds, celery, salt, coconut and raisins. Heat thoroughly. Serve over chow mein noodles.

Serves: 8

Great for left-over turkey.

CHICKEN TARRAGON

8 chicken breasts
Salt and pepper
½ cup oil
½ cup honey
½ cup white wine tarragon
  vinegar

2 Tablespoons Worcestershire
  sauce
1 package dry onion soup mix

Season chicken with salt and pepper. In a jar place remaining ingredients. Shake well. Place chicken in a single layer in a shallow baking dish. Pour sauce over chicken and bake uncovered at 350 degrees for 1 hour or until tender.
Serves: 8

CHICKEN AND EGGPLANT CASSEROLE

4 chicken breasts
1 rib of celery
¼-½ teaspoon poultry
  seasoning
½ small onion
¼ teaspoon pepper
1 medium eggplant, peeled and
  quartered
1 clove garlic, minced
1 medium onion, chopped
1 green bell pepper, chopped

½ cup raw rice
10 ounce can Rotel tomatoes,
  diced
1 cup chicken broth
½ teaspoon salt
½ teaspoon pepper
¼ teaspoon basil
¼ teaspoon oregano
Tabasco sauce to taste
1 cup bread crumbs
1 cup grated Cheddar cheese

Cook chicken in water seasoned with celery, poultry seasoning, ½ small onion and pepper. When chicken is tender, remove from broth. Add eggplant to broth and cook until tender. Cut chicken into bite-size pieces. Set aside. Coat a skillet with vegetable cooking spray and olive oil. Add garlic, onion and bell pepper. Sauté until vegetables are tender. Add rice and sauté 5 minutes, stirring frequently. Add remaining ingredients, except bread crumbs and cheese. Pour into a greased 9X13-inch casserole. Top with bread crumbs. Bake uncovered at 350 degrees for 30 minutes. Top with cheese and bake 30 minutes more.
Serves: 6 to 8

A very good low cholesterol dish.

CHICKEN LOAF

2 cups cooked chopped chicken
1¼ cups bread crumbs
2 Tablespoons minced onion
2 Tablespoons chopped parsley
½ cup chopped celery
2 ounces diced pimiento, drained
  and divided

2 eggs
¾ cup milk
1½ teaspoon salt
10¾ ounce can cream of
  mushroom soup

Combine chicken, bread crumbs, onion, parsley, celery and half of the pimiento. Beat eggs. Add milk and salt to eggs. Pour into chicken mixture. Mix thoroughly. Place in a greased 9X5-inch loaf pan. Bake at 350 degrees for 40-50 minutes. Make a sauce with remaining pimiento and soup. Heat sauce and serve over chicken loaf. Serves: 6 to 8

A good change from meat loaf.

SWEET AND SOUR CHICKEN WITH VEGETABLES

4 cups cooked cubed chicken
16 ounce can Blue Lake green
  beans
⅔ cup packed dark brown sugar
4 Tablespoons cornstarch
⅔ cup vinegar

16 ounce can pineapple chunks,
  drain and reserve juice
4 Tablespoons margarine
1 cup cherry tomato halves
2 cups cooked rice

Heat green beans for 15 minutes while combining other ingredients. In a medium saucepan, combine brown sugar and cornstarch. Stir in vinegar, ⅔ cup pineapple juice and margarine. Bring to a boil, stirring constantly, until sauce is thickened and bubbly. Stir in pineapple chunks, chicken and tomatoes. Drain beans and add to mixture. Continue to cook over medium heat until thoroughly heated. Serve over rice. Serves: 6

This is a low-fat, low cholesterol dish.

Removing the skin from poultry will cut the calories and cholesterol almost in half.

COUNTRY CHICKEN PIE

6 chicken breasts, cooked and diced
10¾ ounce can cream of mushroom soup
10¾ ounce can chicken broth
½ cup + 1 Tablespoon sour cream, divided
8½ ounce can English peas, drained

4 ounce can chopped mushrooms, drained
3 hard-boiled eggs, sliced
1 cup self-rising flour
1 cup milk
½ cup butter
1 Tablespoon sugar

Place chicken in a greased 2-quart casserole. Combine soup, broth and ½ cup sour cream. Pour over chicken. Layer peas, mushrooms and eggs over chicken. In separate bowl mix flour, milk, butter, 1 Tablespoon sour cream and sugar. Pour evenly over chicken and vegetables. Bake uncovered at 375 degrees for 1 hour.
Serves: 6 to 8

All hearts will be happy after this hearty dish.

EASY CHICKEN TETRAZINNI

1 large hen
3 Tablespoons butter
6 ribs of celery, chopped
2 medium onions, chopped
3 cups chicken stock
8 ounces spaghetti
10¾ ounce can cream of mushroom soup

8 ounces sharp Cheddar cheese, grated
1 Tablespoon Worcestershire sauce
1 small jar stuffed olives, drained and sliced
Salt and pepper to taste
1 cup chopped pecans, optional

Cook hen in seasoned water. Cool. When cool, remove meat from bones and cut into bite-size pieces. Sauté celery and onion in butter. Add chicken stock and simmer 15 minutes. Add uncooked spaghetti to chicken stock and cook 6-8 minutes. Add soup and cheese. Stir until cheese melts. Let stand for 1 hour. Add chicken, olives and Worcestershire sauce. Place in a greased 9X13-inch casserole. Sprinkle with chopped pecans. Bake uncovered at 350 degrees for 20-30 minutes or until thoroughly heated.
Serves: 12-15

MEXICAN CHICKEN FIESTA

1 whole chicken, cooked
Chicken broth
1 cup chopped onion
½ pound grated Cheddar cheese
½ cup chopped green bell
  pepper
1 teaspoon chili powder

10¾ ounce can cream of chicken
  soup
10¾ ounce can cream of
  mushroom soup
10 ounce can Rotel tomatoes,
  drained and diced
1 bag tortilla chips

After cooking chicken, debone and shred meat. Make sauce combining onion, cheese, bell pepper, chili powder, soups and tomatoes. Place tortilla chips into a greased 9X13-inch casserole. Mash the chips down and moisten with some of the broth. Add the chicken. Pour sauce over chicken. Bake uncovered at 375 degrees for 45 minutes.
Serves: 6 to 8

One of the best.

CHICKEN GRUYÈRE

½ cup flour
1½ teaspoons salt
2 teaspoons paprika
10 chicken breasts, skinned
½ cup butter
½ cup water
2 teaspoons cornstarch
1½ cups half-and-half cream

¼ cup sherry
1 Tablespoon granular chicken
  bouillon
1 Tablespoon lemon juice
1 teaspoon grated lemon peel
1 cup grated Gruyère cheese
½ cup chopped fresh parsley

Mix flour, salt and paprika. Coat chicken with flour mixture. In a large skillet brown chicken in butter on both sides. Add water, cover and simmer chicken for 30 minutes or until almost tender. Remove and arrange in a 9X13-inch baking dish. Mix cornstarch with ½ cup half-and-half cream. Stir into pan drippings. Cook over low heat. Gradually add remaining cream, sherry, bouillon, lemon juice and peel. Cook until thick. Pour over chicken. At this point the dish may be refrigerated or frozen until cooking time. If frozen allow to thaw 4 hours before baking. To cook, cover and bake at 350 degrees for 1 hour. Uncover, sprinkle with cheese, and return to oven until cheese melts.
Serves: 10

An outstanding dish.

OVEN BARBECUED CHICKEN

8-10 chicken breasts or 3 pounds
  cut-up chicken
3 Tablespoons ketchup
2 Tablespoons vinegar
1 Tablespoon lemon juice
2 Tablespoons Worcestershire
  sauce
4 Tablespoons water

2 Tablespoons butter
3 Tablespoons dark brown sugar
1 teaspoon salt
1 teaspoon prepared mustard
1 teaspoon chili powder
1 teaspoon paprika
½ teaspoon cayenne pepper

Preheat oven to 500 degrees. Salt and pepper chicken. Mix all ingredients, except chicken, to make a sauce. Dip chicken in sauce and place in large iron skillet or baking dish. Pour remaining sauce over chicken. Cover and cook for 15 minutes in hot oven. Lower oven temperature to 350 degrees. Bake 1¼ hours. Do not uncover until cooking time is completed.
Serves: 8 to 10

This chicken is easy, tasty and tender.

CHICKEN AND VEGETABLE SAUTÉRNE

¼ cup butter
2 Tablespoons olive oil
8 chicken breasts
½ cup all-purpose flour
1 teaspoon salt
¼ teaspoon white pepper
1 cup sliced green onions
1 clove garlic, crushed

1 cup sliced fresh mushrooms
1 cup dry sautérne
1 cup chicken stock
1 cup diced fresh tomatoes,
  peeled and seeded
¼ cup chopped fresh parsley
Salt and pepper to taste

In a large skillet melt butter and add olive oil. Remove skin from chicken. Dust chicken lightly with flour, salt and pepper. Shake off any excess flour. Brown chicken lightly in the butter and oil. Remove. In the same pan sauté the onions, garlic and mushrooms until soft. Add remaining ingredients and mix well. Add chicken. Simmer until sauce is thickened. Correct seasonings. Place in casserole. Bake covered at 350 degrees for 45 minutes.
Serves: 8

Freezes well.

STIR-FRIED CHICKEN AND BROCCOLI

1 pound chicken breasts, skinned and boned
1-1½ cups broccoli flowerets
3 Tablespoons vegetable oil
¼ teaspoon pepper
½ cup water

3 teaspoons cornstarch
1 Tablespoon chicken bouillon granules
1 Tablespoon cooking sherry
1 Tablespoon soy sauce

Cut chicken into 1-inch cubes. Cut broccoli into small bite-size pieces. Heat oil in wok or skillet to 375 degrees. Do not allow to smoke. Make sure entire cooking surface is coated with oil. Sprinkle pepper on heated oil. Add chicken and stir fry 1½ minutes. Remove chicken and set aside. Add a small amount of oil to skillet, if necessary. Add broccoli and stir fry 1-2 minutes until flowerets turn bright green. Add chicken and continue to stir fry together about 1 minute. Pour mixture of water, cornstarch, bouillon, sherry and soy sauce over chicken and broccoli. Stir fry another minute on low heat to coat meat and vegetables thoroughly . Serve over brown rice.

Brown Rice Plus
1 cup white rice
2 Tablespoons brown rice
2 Tablespoons chopped pimiento
½ cup fresh, sliced mushrooms
½ teaspoon oregano

1 teaspoon basil
1 Tablespoon chopped parsley
1 Tablespoon chicken bouillon granules
Pepper to taste

Cook white rice according to package directions. In a separate container cook brown rice as package directs. Halfway during cooking of brown rice add remaining ingredients, stirring once. When done, combine brown rice with cooked white rice. Serve with chicken and broccoli.
Serves: 4

Great dish!

Based on figures that one USDA chicken breast weighs 7½ ounces and yields 4½ ounces of edible cooked chicken, approximately 4 pounds 3½ ounces or 9 chicken breasts will yield 5 cups cooked chopped chicken.

MARSALA ARTICHOKE CHICKEN

4 chicken breasts, boned and skinned
2 Tablespoons butter
14 ounce can artichoke hearts, drained and chopped
4 ounce can mushrooms, drained

½ cup Marsala wine
⅛ teaspoon salt
Dash of pepper
1 teaspoon lemon juice
2 teaspoons chopped parsley

Flatten chicken breasts to ¼ inch thickness by placing each piece between two sheets of waxed paper and pounding with a meat mallet. In a medium skillet melt butter and add chicken. Cook over low heat 4-5 minutes on each side until golden brown. Remove chicken. Place artichokes, mushrooms, wine, salt, pepper, and lemon juice in skillet and mix well. When wine mixture is heated, return chicken to skillet and simmer for 3 minutes. Serve sprinkled with fresh parsley.
Serves: 2

CHICKEN AND CRAB ELEGANTE

½ pound Alaskan King Crab
3 chicken breasts, cooked and sliced
½ cup sliced fresh mushrooms
¼ cup chopped onion
3 Tablespoons butter
3 Tablespoons all-purpose flour
½ teaspoon salt

⅛ teaspoon white pepper
1½ cups chicken broth
½ cup dry white wine
2 egg yolks, beaten
1½ cups artichoke hearts, cut in halves
½ cup whipping cream, whipped
¼ cup grated Parmesan cheese

Drain and slice crab. Set aside. Place chicken, overlapping slices, in 9X13-inch shallow baking dish or individual dishes. Sauté mushrooms and onion in butter until tender. Blend in flour, salt and pepper. Gradually add broth and wine. Cook, stirring until thickened. Add small amount of hot mixture to egg yolks and blend thoroughly. Return egg yolks to hot mixture and cook 2 minutes. Remove from heat. Stir in artichoke hearts and crab. Gently fold in whipped cream. Pour sauce over chicken in baking dish. Sprinkle with Parmesan cheese. Bake uncovered at 325 degrees for 15-20 minutes or until golden brown. This recipe may be doubled easily.
Serves: 6

CHICKEN RONDELÉ

6 chicken breasts, boned
¼ cup flour
8 ounces Rondele or herbed
   cheese, softened
6 slices dried beef
3 Tablespoons butter
1 Tablespoon oil

½ pound fresh mushrooms,
   sliced
3 green onions, chopped
2 Tablespoons brandy
1 cup chicken broth
½ cup dry vermouth
¼ cup chopped fresh parsley

Pound each breast until thin. Season with salt and pepper, dust with flour. Spread 2 Tablespoons cheese on each breast and cover each with 1 slice dried beef. Roll up each breast, secured with wooden pick, and brown in butter and oil. Sauté mushrooms and onions until tender. Add brandy to pan and ignite, tipping pan until flame dies down. Add broth, vermouth and parsley. Cover and simmer about 30 minutes until chicken is tender. Season to taste. Remove wooden picks and serve over rice.
Serves: 6

A dish that would appeal to men.

CHICKEN DUXELLES

8 chicken breasts, boned and
   skinned
2 Tablespoons butter
½ pound fresh mushrooms
2 Tablespoons butter
3 Tablespoons chopped green
   onions, divided

Juice of ½ lemon
Salt and white pepper to taste
8 slices Swiss cheese
¼ cup sherry
¾ cup whipping cream

Brown chicken breasts over medium heat in 2 Tablespoons butter for 2 minutes on each side. Season with salt and pepper. Place in shallow baking dish. To make duxelles, chop mushrooms and squeeze out all the liquid by placing in a cloth bag. Sauté 2 Tablespoons green onions in butter. Add mushrooms, lemon juice, salt and pepper. Cook until liquid has evaporated but do not let mushrooms brown. Cover each breast with 2 Tablespoons duxelles. Place a slice of Swiss cheese over duxelles mixture. Add remaining Tablespoon of onion and sherry to skillet and stir. Add cream and cook for 1 minute until smooth. Pour sauce over chicken. Bake uncovered at 350 degrees for 30 minutes.
Serves: 8

CURRIED CHICKEN AND RICE SQUARES

2 Tablespoons all-purpose flour
2 Tablespoons butter
2 cups milk
½ teaspoon salt
¼ teaspoon pepper
½ teaspoon curry powder

½ teaspoon sugar
¼ teaspoon ginger
2 teaspoons lemon juice
2½-3 cups cooked chopped
   chicken
Seedless raisins

Melt butter over low heat. Add flour and blend. Cook for 5 minutes. Stir in milk slowly and cook sauce until it thickens. Add salt, pepper, curry, sugar and ginger. Add lemon juice and chicken. Serve over rice squares. Sprinkle raisins on top.

Rice Squares
3 cups cooked rice
¼ cup finely chopped onion
½ cup chopped fresh parsley
¼ cup chopped green bell
   pepper
¼ cup chopped pimiento
1 cup grated sharp Cheddar
   cheese

2 large eggs, beaten
1½ teaspoons Worcestershire
   sauce
2 cups milk
1 teaspoon salt

Combine first 6 ingredients and toss to mix. Add eggs, Worcestershire sauce, milk and salt to rice mixture. Pour into a greased 8X13-inch pan. Bake uncovered at 325 degrees for 40 minutes or until set. Serve immediately.
Serves: 8

AUNT DALE'S CREAMED CHICKEN

½ cup butter
½ cup all-purpose flour
2 cups hot chicken broth
½ cup whipping cream
¼ cup milk, scalded

1 teaspoon salt
1 teaspoon paprika
4 ounce can sliced mushrooms,
   drained
2 cups cooked, diced chicken

Melt butter and slowly add flour. Stir in broth, whipping cream and scalded milk, stirring constantly. Cook until smooth. Season with salt and paprika. Add mushrooms and diced chicken. Serve in a puff pastry shell or over waffles.
Serves: 6 to 8

CHICKEN TORTELLINI

4 chicken breasts
9 ounces cheese tortellini
½ cup butter
2 zucchini, peeled and diced
4 green onions, chopped,
  including tops
10-12 fresh mushrooms, sliced
½-1 Tablespoon garlic powder

14 ounce can artichoke hearts,
  quartered
1 cup whipping cream
½ cup half-and-half cream
2 Tablespoons all-purpose flour
Salt to taste
Freshly ground black pepper to
  taste

Place chicken breasts in medium pot and cover with water. Bring to a boil and simmer 20-30 minutes. Remove chicken from pot and cool. Remove meat from bones and cut into bite-size pieces. Cook tortellini al dente. Drain and set aside. In a large skillet melt butter. Add sliced zucchini and onions. Saut until limp. Add mushrooms, garlic powder and artichoke hearts. Simmer 5 minutes. Blend flour with whipping cream and half-and-half cream in blender until smooth. Slowly add cream mixture to skillet, stirring constantly until thickened and creamy. Add cheese tortellini and chicken. Season with salt and pepper. Toss to blend. Serve with freshly grated Parmesan cheese.
Serves: 8

TANKED TURKEY

4-6 pound turkey breast or small
  whole turkey
1 teaspoon salt
1 teaspoon basil
1½ teaspoon black pepper
3 Tablespoons curry, divided
1 teaspoon paprika

1 unpeeled orange, cut in half
4 carrots, peeled and sliced
1 large or 2 small onions,
  quartered
1½ cups gin
1 cup water

Wash turkey. Pat dry. Mix salt, basil, pepper, 1½ Tablespoons curry and paprika. Pat herb mixture inside and on outside of turkey. Place in roasting pan with vegetables and orange. Mix gin and water. Place 1 cup of the mixture in roaster. Bake at 350 degrees for 2½ hours. Baste turkey at intervals with remaining gin mixture and pan juices. Occasionally, sprinkle remaining curry over turkey for stronger flavor and color. Slice as thinly as possible and serve with pan juices. Good with yellow or saffron rice.
Serves: 10 to 12

FISH
AND
SEAFOOD

BAKED CATFISH PARMESAN

6 catfish fillets
⅔ cup grated Parmesan cheese
¼ cup all-purpose flour
½ teaspoon salt
¼ teaspoon pepper

1 teaspoon paprika
¼ cup milk
1 egg, beaten
¼ cup melted butter
⅓ cup sliced almonds

Combine cheese, flour, salt, pepper and paprika; set aside. Combine milk and egg. Dip fillets in egg-milk mixture and then dredge in flour mixture. Arrange in 9X13-inch baking dish. Drizzle with melted butter. Sprinkle with sliced almonds. Bake at 350 degrees for 35-40 minutes.
Serves: 6

SHRIMP STUFFED FILLET OF FLOUNDER

12 flounder fillets, divided
½ pound fresh mushrooms, divided
1 medium onion, finely chopped
6 Tablespoons butter, divided
1 Tablespoon fresh parsley, minced
¼ teaspoon salt

¼ pound cooked shrimp, finely chopped
½ cup boiling water
6 Tablespoons all-purpose flour
3 Tablespoons fresh lemon juice
1 cup fish stock
1 egg yolk, well beaten
Freshly ground pepper to taste

Chop 3 flounder fillets and ¼ pound mushrooms. Sauté onion and chopped mushrooms together in 1 Tablespoon butter. Add parsley, ¼ teaspoon salt, chopped flounder and shrimp. Make a white sauce by combining water and 1 Tablespoon butter with 4 Tablespoons flour, stirring until smooth. Remove from heat and add shrimp and flounder mixture. Place 2 Tablespoons of flounder and shrimp mixture on remaining fillets. Roll up fillets from the tail to the wide end. Secure with wooden picks. Place fillets in buttered 2-quart baking dish and drizzle with 4 Tablespoons melted butter and 2 Tablespoons lemon juice. Cover dish with aluminum foil and bake at 375 degrees for 20 minutes. Make a sauce by combining 2 Tablespoons flour with pan juices. Add fish stock and stir until thickened. Slice remaining ¼ pound mushrooms and add salt and pepper to taste. Add 1 Tablespoon lemon juice and egg yolk and beat well. Garnish fillets with pimiento and serve with sauce.
Serves: 8 to 9

BAKED FLOUNDER IN COQUILLE SHELLS

1 pound flounder fillets
1 small onion, quartered
3 lemon slices
10¾ ounce can cream of shrimp soup
3 Tablespoons all-purpose flour
¼ cup milk
¼ cup dry white wine
¼ cup shredded Monterey Jack cheese

2 Tablespoons chopped fresh parsley
½ cup soft bread crumbs
2 Tablespoons grated Parmesan cheese
2 teaspoons butter
½ teaspoon paprika

Cut fish into ½-inch cubes. Place fish, onion and lemon slices in a greased skillet and add water to cover. Bring water to boil; then reduce heat, cover, and poach the fish for 5 minutes. In a saucepan blend soup and flour, gradually adding milk and wine. Cook, stirring until thickened. Add Monterey Jack cheese and parsley. Heat thoroughly. Carefully drain fish and fold into sauce mixture. Spoon mixture into 4 coquille shells. Combine crumbs, Parmesan cheese, butter and paprika. Sprinkle over fish mixture. Broil 1-2 minutes until browned and bubbly. Variation: 1 pound cooked shrimp can be substituted for flounder.
Serves: 4

GRILLED CATFISH

1 Tablespoon garlic powder
1 Tablespoon seasoned salt
1 Tablespoon chili seasoning
1 Tablespoon onion powder
1 Tablespoon paprika
1 Tablespoon chili powder

1 Tablespoon coarsely ground black pepper
Catfish fillets, one for each person
Margarine

Mix all seasonings and put in shaker jar. This is more than needed for one cooking. Wash fillets and pat dry. Place fillets on plate and sprinkle with seasoning mix. Dot top of each fillet with margarine. Heat gas grill on high until very hot. Turn grill off and spray grill with no-stick cooking spray. Place fillets on grill and close top. Leave for 15-20 minutes. Check for doneness. Fish turns white and flakes easily. If fish needs to cook more, move all fillets to one side of grill. On empty side of grill, turn heat on low. Close top and cook until done. The secret of this fish not sticking to the grill is to get the grill very hot and then turn the grill off and spray with no-stick cooking spray. Fillets will stay in solid pieces.

GRILLED SALMON STEAKS WITH HERBED BEURRE BLANC SAUCE

4 salmon steaks
¼ cup soy sauce
Juice of 1 lemon

1 teaspoon pepper
½ cup Italian salad dressing

Marinate salmon steaks in soy sauce, lemon juice, pepper and Italian dressing for 1 hour. Grill over hot coals until fish flakes easily. Serve with Herbed Beurre Blanc sauce.

Herbed Beurre Blanc Sauce

1 Tablespoon shallots
2 Tablespoons white wine vinegar
1½ Tablespoons dry white wine
1½ Tablespoons lemon juice
½ cup whipping cream

1 cup unsalted butter
Salt
Pepper
Herbs of choice: chives, tarragon
  or basil

Cook shallots, vinegar, wine and lemon juice and reduce by half. Add cream and cook 1-2 minutes. Place in double boiler and add butter, salt, pepper and herbs. Cook until butter melts completely. Serve hot.
Serves: 4

THE CAPTAIN'S SPECKLED TROUT

4 speckled trout fillets
1 cup buttermilk
1 package dry onion soup mix

All-purpose flour
2-3 Tablespoons vegetable oil

Mix buttermilk and dry onion soup mix. Soak fillets in buttermilk mixture for 15 minutes. Lightly flour fillets and pan sauté in hot oil until browned and crisp.
Serves: 4

To get a thin, even and unbroken coating that will adhere to foods when sautéeing, the food should be room temperature, dry and lightly floured before adding food to coating mixture. Then, after the food is breaded, chill for half an hour or more.

FLOUNDER THERMIDOR

Vermouth or other dry white
  wine
Water
1 pound flounder or sole
½ cup butter, divided
¼ cup all-purpose flour

1 teaspoon salt
2 cups half-and-half cream
¼ cup dry sherry
½ pound fresh mushrooms,
  sliced
½ cup grated Parmesan cheese

In a 10-inch skillet bring a mixture of half vermouth and half water, 1½-inches deep, to a boil. Add fish. Return to boil and simmer covered approximately 5 minutes, or until fish flakes easily. Remove from heat; drain and place fish in buttered casserole. In a saucepan melt ¼ cup butter and whisk in flour and salt, stirring constantly until smooth and bubbly. Add half-and-half cream and sherry. Simmer over low heat until thickened. Sauté mushrooms in ¼ cup butter and pour over flounder. Pour the wine sauce over fish and sprinkle cheese on top. Bake at 375 degrees for 20 minutes or until browned and bubbly.
Serves: 2

POMPANO IN PAPILLOTE

1 cup white wine
2 Tablespoons brandy
4 bay leaves
½ onion, chopped
2 fresh tomatoes, diced
2 carrots, peeled, chopped
  and cooked
1 rib celery, chopped
½ green bell pepper, chopped
10¾ ounce can cream of
  mushroom soup

4 ounce can mushrooms, chopped
6 ounces crabmeat
6 ounces cooked shrimp
Salt
Pepper
Paprika
Garlic
6 pompano fillets, or any mild
  white fish
1 Tablespoon vegetable oil
1 Tablespoon lemon juice

Place the first eight ingredients in a saucepan and simmer for 20 minutes. Add the soup, mushrooms, crabmeat and shrimp. Season with salt, pepper, paprika and garlic to taste. Place fish fillets in baking dish. Sprinkle with oil, lemon juice, salt, pepper and paprika. Bake at 350 degrees for 10 minutes. Remove from oven. Place each fillet on a piece of aluminum foil and spoon sauce on top. Close foil tightly and bake at 350 degrees for 30 minutes.
Serves: 6 to 8

SHRIMP CROQUE MONSIEUR

1 pound shrimp, boiled and
  peeled
4 (1½ inches thick) slices French
  bread
1 egg, beaten
⅓ cup milk
2 Tablespoons oil, more if needed
2 Tablespoons butter

2 Tablespoons all-purpose flour
3 Tablespoons sherry
1 cup half-and-half cream
6 ounces Swiss cheese, grated
1 teaspoon chopped fresh parsley
4 teaspoons salt
White pepper, to taste

Boil shrimp and peel. Trim crust from bread slices and cut a circle ¾-inch deep half way through the bread and ¾-inch from the sides of each slice, making a hole in the bread. Pull out loose bread to make a shell. Combine egg with milk and beat slightly. Dip both sides of bread quickly into the egg mixture. Fry in 2 Tablespoons of hot oil until brown on both sides. Drain bread and keep warm. To make sauce, melt butter and add flour, cooking until smooth. Slowly blend in sherry and cream, stirring until thick and smooth. Add cheese and seasonings, stirring to melt the cheese. Fill the warm bread shell with shrimp and pour the sauce over each.
Serves: 4

SHRIMP PILAU

1 pound bacon, cooked crisp and
  crumbled
1 pound raw medium shrimp,
  peeled and cleaned
1 pound uncooked smoked
  sausage, cut in chunks
10½ ounce can beef bouillon
10½ ounce can French onion
  soup
8 ounce can tomato sauce
½ cup butter or margarine
1½ cups chopped green bell
  pepper

½ cup chopped fresh parsley
½ cup chopped green onions
½ cup chopped celery
8 ounce can sliced water
  chestnuts, drained
4 ounce can sliced mushrooms,
  drained
2 cups raw rice
1 garlic clove, crushed or 1
  teaspoon garlic powder
1 Tablespoon Creole seasoning,
  more for spicier taste

Mix all ingredients in a large bowl or pan. Pour into a 9X13-inch baking dish. Cover and bake at 350 degrees for 1 hour, stirring occasionally. Test to see if rice is tender.
Serves: 10

SHRIMP CURRY IN PATTY SHELLS

½ cup butter
½ cup all-purpose flour
2 cups hot chicken stock
¾ cup half-and-half cream
1 Tablespoon lemon juice
1 teaspoon salt

Paprika
¼-½ teaspoon curry powder
2½ cups shrimp, cooked and
   peeled
4 ounce can sliced mushrooms,
   drained

In top of double boiler combine butter, flour, chicken stock, cream, lemon juice and seasonings. Cook on medium heat, stirring until smooth. Add shrimp and mushrooms. Serve hot in patty shells or toast cups.
Serves: 6

SHRIMP FETTUCCINE PRIMAVERA

8 jumbo shrimp, peeled and
   deveined
1 cup whipping cream
2 egg yolks
½ teaspoon Tabasco sauce
4 Tablespoons butter
1 teaspoon fresh garlic, minced
2 cups broccoli flowerets
12 large snow peas
½ medium red bell pepper, cut
   into 12 julienne strips

1½ ounces dry vermouth, or
   other dry white wine
Dash of salt
Dash of pepper
8 ounces fettuccine, cooked al
   dente and drained
6 Tablespoons freshly grated
   Parmesan cheese

Mix cream, egg yolks and Tabasco; set aside. In a large skillet sauté shrimp in butter and garlic just until shrimp begins to color. Add vegetables and sauté until tender, but slightly crisp. Add wine, salt, pepper and fettuccine. Mix well. Add cream mixture and then cheese. Toss until cheese and cream have blended to make a rich sauce.
Serves: 2

SHRIMP RICHARD

7 ounces vermicelli, cooked
  al dente and drained
1 cup butter
1 teaspoon minced garlic
½ pound fresh mushrooms,
  sliced
1½ pounds peeled raw shrimp

1½ teaspoons oregano
½ teaspoon salt
½ teaspoon freshly ground
  pepper
¼ teaspoon Tabasco sauce
Freshly grated Parmesan cheese

Melt butter in a large skillet and sauté garlic, mushrooms and shrimp for 10 minutes.
Add seasonings, toss with vermicelli and top with Parmesan cheese.
Serves: 4 to 6

SHRIMP CROQUETTES

6 Tablespoons butter, divided
5 Tablespoons flour
½ cup whipping cream
½ cup milk
½ teaspoon salt
6 Tablespoons grated Parmesan
  cheese
¼ cup grated Gruyère cheese
2 egg yolks, lightly beaten
1 Tablespoon medium-dry sherry

2 Tablespoons butter
2 Tablespoons minced shallots
2 cups minced cooked shrimp
2 teaspoons Dijon mustard
Salt to taste
Pepper to taste
All-purpose flour
1 egg, slightly beaten
2 Tablespoons water
2-3 cups fine, dry bread crumbs

In a large saucepan melt 4 Tablespoons butter; stir in flour until smooth. Add cream
to milk and stir to blend. Gradually add milk mixture to butter and flour mixture,
stirring constantly. Cook over low heat until thickened. Add cheeses to sauce mixture
and cook, stirring until cheese is just melted, do not boil. Remove from heat. Cool
and add egg yolks and sherry. In a small skillet add 2 Tablespoons butter and sauté
shallots until soft but not browned. Add to cheese mixture with minced shrimp,
Dijon mustard, salt and pepper. Spread in an 8X8-inch pan and cover. Chill until firm.
When firm, shape into croquettes. Roll in flour; shake off excess. Beat egg with
water. Dip croquettes in egg mixture; roll in bread crumbs. Chill several hours. Fry in
deep fat fryer. Needs to be prepared well ahead and cooked just before serving.
Serves: 6 to 8

Serve with Summer Tomato Sauce

CRAB AND SHRIMP LASAGNA

3 Tablespoons butter
3 Tablespoons all-purpose flour
2 cups milk
2 (10¾ ounce) cans cream of
　shrimp soup
1⅓ cups grated Parmesan
　cheese, divided
¼ cup sherry
8 ounces lasagna noodles
1 Tablespoon olive oil
2 cups cottage cheese
8 ounces cream cheese
2 eggs, beaten

1 large white onion, chopped
4 Tablespoons fresh basil or 2
　Tablespoons dried basil
2 Tablespoons fresh chopped
　parsley or 1 Tablespoon dried
Salt and pepper to taste
1 pound fresh crabmeat
1 pound shrimp, cooked and
　peeled
Juice of 1 lemon
2 cups grated Swiss cheese,
　divided
3 tomatoes, sliced

Make a white sauce by melting butter in saucepan and stirring in flour. Cook until smooth, stirring constantly, over very low heat. Add milk slowly, stirring until thickened. Add soup, 6 Tablespoons of Parmesan cheese and sherry. Set aside. Cook lasagna noodles, adding 1 Tablespoon of olive oil to cooking water. Cook noodles to al dente stage and drain. Combine cottage cheese, cream cheese, eggs, onion, basil, parsley, salt and pepper. In another bowl combine shrimp, crabmeat, lemon juice and 1½ cups of the soup sauce. In a 9X13-inch casserole layer the lasagna in the following order: ½ cup soup sauce, lasagna noodles, ½ shrimp and crabmeat sauce, ½ cottage cheese mixture, ½ remaining soup sauce and 1 cup Swiss cheese. Repeat layers. Top with 1 cup Parmesan cheese. Bake at 350 degrees for 45 minutes. Place sliced tomatoes on top and bake an additional 10-15 minutes. Allow lasagna to sit 10 minutes before serving.
Serves: 10 to 12

A show stopper! Well worth the trouble.

SEASHELL SEAFOOD

½ cup butter
3 large cloves garlic
½ teaspoon salt
1 cup whipping cream
½ cup mayonnaise
½ teaspoon ground nutmeg
½ teaspoon white pepper

16 ounces fresh spinach, chopped
1 pound shrimp, boiled and peeled
½ pound crabmeat
8 ounces tiny seashell pasta, cooked al dente and drained
3 ounces grated Parmesan cheese

Melt butter and sauté garlic with salt until tender. Add cream and mayonnaise. Cook until reduced by half. Remove garlic and discard. Add nutmeg, pepper and spinach and heat thoroughly. Remove from heat and stir in seafood and pasta. Pour into a 9X13-inch baking dish. Bake at 325 degrees for 30 minutes. Sprinkle with Parmesan cheese just before serving.
Serves: 8

SHRIMP AND CRAB BLITZ

1 package long grain and wild rice mix
1 cup chopped onion
1 cup chopped celery
1 cup chopped green bell pepper
¼ cup margarine
6 ounce can shrimp, undrained
6 ounce can crabmeat, undrained
2 ounce jar diced pimientos, undrained
4 ounce can sliced mushrooms, undrained

8 ounce can sliced water chestnuts, drained
2 (10¾ ounce) cans cream of mushroom soup
1 teaspoon Cajun seasoning
Dash of Tabasco sauce
Bread crumbs
Grated Parmesan cheese
Lemon slices

Cook rice according to directions on package. Sauté vegetables in margarine until tender. Combine rice, vegetables, seafood, pimientos, mushrooms, water chestnuts, soup, Cajun seasoning and Tabasco in a greased 9X13-inch casserole. Cover with bread crumbs and cheese. Bake uncovered at 350 degrees for 1 hour. Garnish with lemon slices.
Serves: 8 to 10

When you are in a hurry for a quick and easy dish, try this one.

JAMBALAYA

½ pound hot smoked sausage,
   cut into ¼ inch rounds
½ pound ham, minced
3 Tablespoons bacon grease
1 cup chopped onion
1 cup chopped green bell pepper
1 cup chopped celery
3 cloves garlic, peeled and minced
1 bay leaf
½ teaspoon thyme

1 teaspoon basil
2 cups raw rice
2 cups chopped tomatoes
2 teaspoons salt
½ teaspoon freshly ground black
   pepper
½ teaspoon Tabasco sauce
3 cups chicken stock
1 pound boiled shrimp, peeled

In large Dutch oven sauté sausage and ham. Remove with slotted spoon and set aside. Add bacon grease to drippings and stir in onion, bell pepper, celery, garlic, bay leaf, thyme and basil. Sauté for 5 minutes, or until vegetables are tender. Add rice and sauté for 3 minutes, stirring constantly. Add tomatoes, salt, pepper, Tabasco, chicken stock and the reserved sausage and ham. Bring to a boil, reduce heat, and simmer slowly, covered for 12-15 minutes or until rice is almost tender. Add shrimp. Bake at 350 degrees until heated throughout. Add more liquid, if needed. Stir several times to fluff rice.
Serves: 6 to 8

May be made a day ahead.

SPICY OYSTERS FLORENTINE

1 pint oysters
20 ounces frozen chopped
   spinach
½ pound bulk sausage

¾ cup seasoned bread crumbs
¼ cup margarine, melted
Sliced bacon

Cook oysters in their own liquor until they curl. In separate pans cook spinach and sausage. Drain each well. Layer the ingredients in a shallow casserole in the following order: spinach, oysters, sausage, crumbs, margarine and bacon. Cook in oven at 325 degrees for 20 minutes or until bacon is cooked.
Serves: 6

Different and good.

DEVILED OYSTERS IN PATTY SHELLS

1½ Tablespoons chopped shallots
⅛ cup butter
1 pint oysters, drained
1 cup medium cream sauce

¼ cup beef broth
1 teaspoon chopped fresh parsley
1 teaspoon Worcestershire sauce

Sauté shallots in butter. Brown oysters in an iron skillet until they crust. Add shallots and sauté slowly for 5 minutes. Add remaining ingredients and simmer for 5 minutes. Serve hot in patty shells or on toast points.

Cream Sauce
¼ cup butter
¼ cup flour
¾ cup milk

Dash salt
⅛ teaspoon cayenne pepper

In a saucepan melt butter. Stir in flour and blend well. Gradually stir in milk. Add salt and cayenne, stirring constantly until thickened.
Serves: 4 to 6

OYSTERS CASINO

1 cup butter
2 green onions, finely chopped
1 Tablespoon grated Parmesan
   cheese
2 drops Tabasco sauce
¼ teaspoon garlic powder
2 Tablespoons vermouth

Juice of 1 large lemon
3 dozen oysters on the half shell
Bread crumbs
Paprika
Parsley flakes
3 slices bacon, cooked and
   crumbled

Soften butter in small mixing bowl. Add onions, cheese, Tabasco, garlic powder, vermouth and lemon juice. Blend well. Arrange oysters on the half shell in a pan lined with rock salt. Top each oyster with a heaping teaspoon of the butter sauce. Sprinkle generously with bread crumbs, paprika and parsley. Bake at 450 degrees for 10-15 minutes or until oyster edges curl. Sprinkle with crumbled bacon just before serving.
Serves: 4 to 6

CRAB CAKES RAMBIN

1 large rib celery, chopped
1 large green bell pepper,
 chopped
1 large white onion, chopped
3 cloves garlic, chopped
½ cup butter
6 slices stale French bread
4 eggs

2 Tablespoons Old Bay seasoning
1 teaspoon red pepper
1 pound lump crabmeat
All-purpose flour
Bread crumbs
½ cup milk
Vegetable oil

Sauté celery, bell pepper, onion and garlic in butter. Tear French bread into small pieces and soak in 3 well beaten eggs. Prepare and set aside a plate of flour, a plate of bread crumbs, and a bowl containing 1 egg and milk, beaten. In a large bowl combine vegetables, French bread mixture, Old Bay seasoning, red pepper and crabmeat. Mix well by hand. Form mixture into cakes or round patties. Coat each patty in flour, dip in egg-milk mixture, and then coat with bread crumbs. Best to refrigerate until frying. In approximately ½ inch hot oil, fry patties in skillet until golden brown and serve hot. Do not over cook.
Serves: 12

CRABMEAT WITH MORNAY SAUCE

¼ cup butter
¼ cup all-purpose flour
⅛ cup chopped onion
¼ cup chopped green onion
1 sprig parsley, chopped
1 cup hot milk
½ cup dry white wine
½ teaspoon salt

¼ teaspoon white pepper
⅛ teaspoon cayenne pepper
3 ounces Swiss cheese, grated
2 Tablespoons lemon juice
1 pound crabmeat
½ pound fresh mushrooms,
 thinly sliced
3 Tablespoons Romano cheese

Melt butter; stir in flour and cook 5 minutes, stirring often. Add onions and parsley. Gradually add milk, wine, salt, white pepper and cayenne. Blend well and simmer. Add Swiss cheese and continue to cook until cheese has melted. Remove from heat and cool. When sauce has cooled to lukewarm, add lemon juice. In a 3-quart casserole layer crabmeat and mushrooms using sauce between layers. Sprinkle Romano cheese over the top; cover and refrigerate. Before baking let casserole come to room temperature. Cook uncovered at 350 degrees for 30-45 minutes.
Serves: 8

CRAB NEWBURG

6 Tablespoons butter
6 Tablespoons flour
3 cups milk
¼ cup chopped fresh parsley
Grated rind of 2 lemons
4 Tablespoons lemon juice
2 Tablespoons Worcestershire
    sauce
Dash of Tabasco sauce

¼ cup Durkee's dressing
½ teaspoon salt
¼ teaspoon pepper
1 teaspoon nutmeg
½ cup sherry
2 pounds crabmeat
2 eggs, well-beaten
Bread crumbs

Melt butter in a heavy skillet. Add flour and stir until smooth. Gradually add milk and cook until thickened. Stir in parsley, lemon rind, lemon juice, Worcestershire, Tabasco, Durkee's, salt, pepper and nutmeg. Stir well. Remove from heat and add sherry and crabmeat. Stir a small amount of hot liquid into eggs. Then mix egg mixture with crab mixture. Pour into a buttered 9X13-inch casserole and top with buttered bread crumbs. Bake at 350 degrees for 20-30 minutes, or until browned and bubbly. Variation: Serve in patty shells or over toast points.
Serves: 8

FRIED CALAMARI WITH GARLIC SAUCE

2 pounds calamari, cleaned
All-purpose flour

Oil for deep frying

Slice calamari into ¼-inch slices. Slices will look like tiny onion rings because the squid is a hollow tube after cleaning. Roll in flour until coated well and deep fry until browned. Serve calamari with garlic sauce for dipping.

Garlic Sauce
5 slices white bread, crust
    removed and cubed
½ cup olive oil
¼ cup white vinegar

1 Tablespoon finely minced garlic
1 Tablespoon lemon juice
¼ teaspoon oregano

Soak bread in olive oil, vinegar and minced garlic for 1 hour. Add lemon juice and oregano. Purée in food processor until smooth and creamy.
Serves: 6

GRILLED SEAFOOD KABOBS

6 (12-inch) wooden skewers
2 pounds swordfish steaks
12 medium shrimp, shelled
    leaving the last joint and tail
    intact

12 sea scallops, rinsed and
    patted dry
Salt
Pepper

Cut swordfish steaks into 6 (1-inch thick) slices. Thread 1 of the shrimp and 1 of the scallops onto a skewer. Add 2 of the swordfish pieces and add another scallop and shrimp. Make 5 more of the kabobs in the same manner. Season with salt and pepper.

Marinade
½ cup white wine
1 cup Wishbone salad dressing

¼ cup soy sauce
Juice of 2 lemons

In a bowl combine marinade ingredients. Pour over kabobs, cover and refrigerate overnight. Reserve marinade for basting. Grill the kabobs over glowing coals, basting often, for 4-5 minutes on all sides or until the fish flakes and the shrimp are pink and firm.
Serves: 6

SCALLOP REMOULADE

1 pound cooked scallops
Vegetable oil
½ cup mayonnaise
3 green onions, chopped
1 Tablespoon chopped fresh
    parsley
1 Tablespoon Creole mustard
½ teaspoon celery seed

2 Tablespoons horseradish
2 teaspoons vinegar
½ teaspoon paprika
½ teaspoon salt
1 teaspoon Worcestershire sauce
¼ teaspoon Tabasco sauce
Spinach
Kiwi fruit

Sear scallops on both sides in a very hot non-stick pan with a little vegetable oil. Place scallops in flat dish and refrigerate. Make sauce by mixing together all ingredients except spinach and kiwi fruit. Pour sauce over scallops and let chill for several hours. Serve on a fresh spinach leaf and garnish with sliced kiwi fruit.
Serves: 4

An excellent remoulade.

SCALLOPS IN MARINARA SAUCE

1 pound scallops
4 Tablespoons olive oil
¼ cup butter
16 sprigs fresh parsley, chopped
3 large cloves garlic, chopped
3 (16 ounce) cans peeled
  tomatoes, drained and chopped
1 teaspoon basil leaves

½ teaspoon oregano leaves
1 Tablespoon Italian seasoning
½ teaspoon salt
½ teaspoon pepper
2 ounce can anchovies, mashed
2 Tablespoons heaping tomato
  paste

Heat olive oil and butter in a skillet. Sauté parsley and garlic 5 minutes. Add tomatoes, basil, oregano, Italian seasoning, salt and pepper. Cook slowly for 30 minutes. Add mashed anchovies and tomato paste. In a very hot non-stick skillet sear scallops on both sides until edges are browned and scallops are cooked, approximately 4 minutes. Keep warm. Divide warm sauce onto 4 plates and place 6 scallops on each. Serve with Italian bread.
Serves: 4

This sauce is good on vegetables, pasta and any seafood.

CRAWFISH ÉTOUFFÉE

½ cup margarine
2 cups chopped green bell pepper
4 medium onions, chopped
1 cup chopped fresh parsley
3 cloves garlic, chopped
½ Tablespoon Worcestershire
  sauce
½ Tablespoon Cajun hot sauce

Dash of paprika
Dash of celery salt
Salt
Pepper
16 ounce can tomato sauce
16 ounce can whole tomatoes
3 cups crawfish meat
Cooked rice

Use a well-seasoned cast iron pot, if possible. Melt margarine in pot. Add pepper, onion, parsley, garlic, Worcestershire sauce, hot sauce and seasonings. Cover and cook for 45 minutes, stirring occasionally. Add tomato sauce and tomatoes and cook 15-20 minutes. Add crawfish and cook 30-45 minutes. Spoon over cooked rice. Variation: Can substitute shrimp cut in half or quartered for crawfish.
Serves: 12

Good with garlic bread and cold beer.

EGGS,
CHEESE
AND
PASTA

TOMATO POACHED EGG SUPPER

10½ ounce can tomato bisque
  soup
1¼ cups milk
4 large eggs
4 slices cheese or sourdough
  bread, toasted

Salt and pepper to taste
1 avocado, peeled and sliced
Sour cream
4 Tablespoons chopped cilantro
4 teaspoons chopped green
  onion, optional

In a deep skillet pour soup and milk to a depth of 2 inches. Bring to a light simmer, stirring to avoid burning on bottom. Slip eggs, one at a time, into soup. Simmer 4-5 minutes or until firm. Remove eggs with a slotted spoon. Place on toasted bread slices. Season with salt and pepper. Place slices of avocado and a dollop of sour cream on top of each sandwich. Ladle soup into serving bowl. Sprinkle cilantro and green onions on top.
Serves: 4

A wholesome, filling and easy meal cooked in a skillet.

CREOLE EGGS

2 Tablespoons chopped onion
¼ cup chopped green bell
  pepper
1 clove garlic, minced
¼ cup butter
2 Tablespoons olive oil
2 Tablespoons all-purpose flour

½ cup beef stock
1 cup stewed tomatoes
1 Tablespoon chopped fresh
  parsley
Salt and pepper to taste
12 hard-boiled eggs, sliced

Sauté onions, bell pepper and garlic in butter and olive oil. Blend in flour. Add beef stock and tomatoes. Simmer 30 minutes over low heat, stirring occasionally. Add parsley and simmer 5 minutes more. Salt and pepper to taste. Place egg slices in a 9X13-inch baking dish. Pour sauce over eggs and bake at 350 degrees until bubbly.
Serves: 8

To poach eggs and remove them without breaking, use a small skillet filled with boiling water to which a little white vinegar has been added.

GUM TREE BRUNCH

12 slices sourdough bread, crusts
  removed
2-3 Tablespoons butter, softened
½ cup butter, melted
2½ cups sliced fresh mushrooms
1 cup thinly sliced yellow onion
Salt and pepper to taste
1 pound mild pork sausage
8 ounces Cheddar cheese,
  shredded
8 ounces Monterey Jack cheese,
  shredded

5 eggs
2½ cups milk
1 Tablespoon Dijon mustard
1 teaspoon dry mustard
1 teaspoon nutmeg
1 teaspoon salt
⅛ teaspoon black pepper
¼ teaspoon cayenne pepper
1 teaspoon Worcestershire sauce

Butter one side of bread with softened butter and set aside. In ½ cup melted butter brown mushrooms and onions over medium heat for 5-8 minutes, until tender. Season to taste with salt and pepper. Drain well. Crumble sausage and brown in skillet. Drain well. In a greased 7X11-inch baking dish layer half the bread with buttered side down, half the mushroom and onion mixture, and half the sausage and cheeses. Repeat layers. In a bowl mix eggs, milk, mustards, nutmeg, salt, pepper, cayenne and Worcestershire sauce. Pour over sausage and cheese. Cover casserole and refrigerate overnight. Let stand at room temperature 1 hour. Bake uncovered at 350 degrees for 1 hour, or until bubbly.
Serves: 6 to 8

If you enjoy scrambled eggs, use one whole egg plus two whites for two servings. Cook them in a non-stick skillet or use a no-stick spray coating to lower the cholesterol and fat intake.

Serve cereal in a cantaloupe half...then eat the bowl!

CHICKEN QUICHE

1 unbaked 9-inch deep pie crust
1 egg yolk, beaten
Dijon mustard
1 cup diced cooked chicken
4 ounce can sliced mushrooms,
   drained
3 green onions, chopped
½ cup shredded Swiss cheese

½ cup mayonnaise
3 eggs
2 Tablespoons all-purpose flour
½ cup whipping cream
¼ teaspoon garlic salt
Dash nutmeg
Grated Parmesan cheese

Brush inside of pie crust with beaten egg yolk. Bake at 350 degrees for 3 minutes. Spread bottom of crust with mustard. Place chicken in crust. Add mushrooms and onions. Sprinkle Swiss cheese over mixture. Beat mayonnaise, eggs, flour, cream, garlic salt and nutmeg together. Pour gently into crust. Sprinkle top with Parmesan cheese. Bake at 350 degrees for 30-35 minutes.
Serves: 6 to 8

BACON OR SEAFOOD QUICHE

1 unbaked 9-inch pie crust
1 Tablespoon butter or margarine,
   softened
12 slices bacon, fried and
   crumbled, or 1 cup shrimp or
   crabmeat

4 eggs
2 cups whipping cream
¾ teaspoon salt
⅛ teaspoon pepper
4 ounces Swiss cheese, shredded

Preheat oven to 425 degrees. Rub butter over surface of pie crust. Add bacon to crust. Combine eggs, cream, salt and pepper. Beat well. Sprinkle cheese over bacon, then pour in cream mixture. Bake at 425 degrees for 15 minutes. Reduce oven temperature to 300 degrees and bake an additional 40 minutes, or until a knife inserted in center comes out clean.
Serves: 6

Doesn't an apple, Swiss cheese and bacon omelet sound good?

SPINACH QUICHE

1 unbaked 9-inch pie crust
10 ounces frozen spinach
1 pound Velveeta cheese
2 Tablespoons margarine

2 eggs, beaten
¾ cup half-and-half cream or
  evaporated milk
Salt to taste

Thaw and drain spinach. In a saucepan cook spinach and cheese in margarine until cheese melts. Add remaining ingredients. Pour into pie crust and bake at 350 degrees 45 minutes or until set. Variation: For a thicker quiche, use 20 ounces frozen spinach and 3 eggs.
Serves: 6 to 8

HAM AND CHEESE QUICHE

1 unbaked 9-inch deep-dish pie
  crust
1-1½ cups chopped or cubed
  ham
¼ cup chopped green onion
1 cup shredded Swiss cheese

1 cup shredded Cheddar cheese
6 eggs, beaten
1 cup whipping cream
½ teaspoon salt
¼ teaspoon pepper
⅛ teaspoon ground nutmeg

Prick bottom and sides of pie crust with a fork; bake at 425 degrees for 6-8 minutes. Set aside. Sauté ham and onion in a skillet until slightly browned. Drain on paper towel and spread evenly in pie crust. Sprinkle with cheeses and set aside. Combine eggs, cream, salt, pepper and nutmeg. Mix well and pour over cheese. Sprinkle lightly with additional nutmeg. Bake at 350 degrees for 45-55 minutes or until set.
Serves: 6 to 8

PICANTE OMELET

1 cup picante sauce
1 cup shredded Monterey Jack
  cheese

1 cup shredded Cheddar cheese
1 cup sour cream
6 eggs

Spread picante sauce in an 8 or 9-inch quiche dish. Layer cheese over sauce. Whip sour cream into eggs and pour over cheeses. Bake at 350 degrees for 30-45 minutes.
Serves: 6 to 8

EGG CASSEROLE

½ cup chopped onion
3 Tablespoons butter
3 Tablespoons all-purpose flour
2 cups milk, scalded
1 cup shredded sharp Cheddar
  cheese

6 hard-boiled eggs, sliced
10-12 slices bacon, fried crisp and
  crumbled
1½ cups crushed potato chips

Cook onions in butter until tender, not browned. Blend in flour. Add scalded milk and stir until thickened. Add shredded cheese and stir until melted. Place layer of egg slices in 1½-quart casserole. Cover with half of the cheese sauce, half the bacon and half the potato chips. Repeat layers. Bake at 350 degrees for 20-30 minutes. Serves: 6 to 8

ROMAINE SOUFFLÉ

1 medium head Romaine lettuce
3 green onions, chopped
4 Tablespoons butter, divided
3 Tablespoons all-purpose flour
1 cup milk
4 eggs, separated

1 cup shredded Jarlsberg Swiss
  cheese
½ teaspoon Worcestershire sauce
1 teaspoon salt
2-3 dashes Tabasco sauce
¼ cup grated Parmesan cheese

Preheat oven to 400 degrees. Wash and drain lettuce. Chop lettuce and put in a saucepan. Cover lettuce with a small amount of water. Cook over medium heat until wilted. Drain well and chop fine in processor. Cook onions in 1 Tablespoon butter and add lettuce. Add 3 Tablespoons butter and melt. Add flour and milk. Beat in egg yolks, then add cheese, Worcestershire sauce, salt and Tabasco. Stir until cheese is melted. Butter a 6-cup soufflé dish and sprinkle Parmesan cheese on bottom. Beat egg whites until stiff, but not dry, and gently fold into the soufflé base. Pour into prepared soufflé dish. Place soufflé in oven and immediately turn oven to 375 degrees. Bake for 25-30 minutes, or until puffed and browned. Serve immediately. Serves: 6

Very different and delicious.

For baking a soufflé, preheat the oven, and don't open the oven door during the first 20 to 25 minutes of baking. A cool draft can deflate a partially baked soufflé.

HAM AND CHEESE SOUFFLÉ

16 slices white bread
1 pound ham, cubed
16 ounces Cheddar cheese,
shredded
1½ cups shredded Swiss cheese
6 eggs

3 cups milk
1½ teaspoons dried onions
½ teaspoon dry mustard
3 cups corn flakes, crushed
½ cup butter, melted

Grease a 9X13-inch baking dish. Trim crust from bread. Cut bread slices into cubes. Spread half of bread cubes evenly in baking dish. Add ham and both cheeses. Cover with remaining bread cubes. Mix eggs, milk, onions and mustard. Pour evenly over dish. Must refrigerate overnight. Before baking, combine corn flakes with butter and spread over casserole. Bake at 375 degrees for 40 minutes.
Serves: 8 to 10

CHEDDAR CHEESE SOUFFLÉ

6 eggs
½ cup whipping cream
¼ cup grated Parmesan cheese
8 ounces sharp Cheddar cheese,
cubed

11 ounces cream cheese, cubed
½ teaspoon prepared mustard
½ teaspoon salt
¼ teaspoon pepper

In a 6-8 cup food processor place eggs and cream. Blend quickly. Add cheeses and seasonings a little at a time. Blend just until mixed. Butter an 8-cup soufflé dish. Pour in mixture. Bake at 375 degrees for 45-50 minutes or until browned and jiggles slightly when dish is shaken. Serve immediately or crack the oven door and serve within 30 minutes. This soufflé may be prepared ahead. Prepare soufflé according to instructions and set aside at room temperature for up to 2 hours before baking. May also refrigerate for several hours before baking. If refrigerated, bring to room temperature before baking or allow an additional 5-10 minutes to bake.
Serves: 6 to 8

Never fails.

For a perfect soufflé, beat the egg whites until stiff peaks form. A little cream of tartar will stabilize the whites.

BREAKFAST ON A MUFFIN

8 ounces cream cheese
¼ cup mayonnaise
Garlic powder
Onion salt
Pepper
Worcestershire sauce
2-3 drops Tabasco sauce

8 hard-boiled eggs, grated
8-10 slices cooked bacon,
  crumbled
6 English muffins, split
Grated Parmesan cheese
Cheddar cheese, shredded

Soften cream cheese and stir in mayonnaise until easy to spread. Season mixture to taste with garlic powder, onion salt, pepper, Worcestershire sauce and Tabasco. Add the eggs and bacon to mixture and stir well. This will keep in the refrigerator for several days. When ready to serve, spread on English muffins. Top with Cheddar and Parmesan cheeses. Place under broiler until cheeses melt.
Serves: 12

FRITTATA OLÉ

2 small eggplants, peeled and
  thinly sliced
½ teaspoon salt
½ cup olive oil
2 baking potatoes, peeled and
  thinly sliced
2 small zucchinis, thinly sliced
2 red bell peppers, minced

4 ounce can chopped green chilies
12 eggs
2 cups shredded Monterey Jack
  cheese
Salt and pepper to taste
Sprigs of fresh thyme

Preheat oven to 450 degrees. Sprinkle eggplant with salt. Place in a colander and let stand for 10 minutes. Rinse with cold water and pat dry. Pour olive oil into a 12X12-inch baking dish. Heat in oven 5 minutes and remove. Arrange the potato slices in baking dish and bake for 20 minutes or until potatoes are tender. Arrange the zucchini and eggplant slices on top of potatoes and bake 5-10 minutes. Sprinkle peppers and chilies over other vegetables. Beat eggs and combine with Monterey Jack cheese; season with salt and pepper. Pour egg mixture over vegetables and arrange thyme on top. Bake until eggs are set and sides have puffed, approximately 20 minutes. Top should be golden brown and knife inserted in center should come out clean. Frittata should be firm but not dry.
Serves: 8 to 10

CRAB STRATA

12 slices white bread, crusts
  removed
10 ounces mild Cheddar cheese,
  shredded
2 cups crabmeat

4 eggs
3 cups milk
¾ teaspoon dry mustard
½ teaspoon salt
Dash pepper

Place bread, cheese and crabmeat in layers in a greased 9X13-inch baking dish. Beat eggs with milk and add mustard, salt and pepper. Pour the egg mixture over the layers in dish and refrigerate overnight. Bake at 350 degrees for 1 hour.
Serves: 10

SPINACH LASAGNA

10 ounces frozen chopped
  spinach, thawed and drained
2½ cups cottage cheese
3 cups shredded mozzarella
  cheese, divided
1 egg, lightly beaten
1 teaspoon salt

⅛ teaspoon pepper
1 teaspoon oregano
32 ounces prepared spaghetti
  sauce, divided
8 ounces lasagna noodles,
  uncooked
1 cup water

Squeeze excess liquid from spinach. Combine cottage cheese, 1 cup mozzarella cheese, egg, spinach, salt, pepper and oregano. Grease a 3-quart casserole. Pour ½ cup spaghetti sauce in bottom of casserole. Place 3 lasagna noodles over sauce. Pour half of cottage cheese mixture over noodles. Sprinkle half of remaining mozzarella cheese over cottage cheese mixture. Add more layers in this order: noodles, spaghetti sauce, noodles, cottage cheese mixture, mozzarella cheese and spaghetti sauce. Pour water around edge of casserole. Cover tightly with aluminum foil. Bake at 350 degrees for 1 hour and 15 minutes. Let stand 10 minutes, uncovered, before serving.
Serves: 8 to 10

An excellent recipe.

Four ounces of any natural or process cheese equals one cup shredded.

MEXICAN PASTA

8 ounces elbow macaroni
½ cup butter
2 heaping Tablespoons all-
  purpose flour
½ cup milk
1 cup whipping cream
6 ounces jalapeño cheese

4 ounces Monterey Jack cheese
10 ounces frozen chopped
  spinach, thawed and drained
4 ounce can green chili peppers,
  chopped
Dash Worcestershire sauce
Salt and pepper to taste

Cook macaroni, drain and set aside. Melt butter in a saucepan. Add flour and stir.
Add milk and cream to make a sauce. Melt cheeses into sauce. Stir well. Add spinach,
peppers, Worcestershire sauce, salt and pepper. Combine with cooked macaroni.
Pour into a 2-quart casserole. Bake at 350 degrees for 25 minutes.
Serves: 6 to 8

CRAWFISH FETTUCCINE ORLEANS

5 green onions, chopped
2 cups sliced fresh mushrooms
2 cloves garlic, minced
½ cups butter, divided
2 Tablespoons vegetable oil
1 pound cooked and peeled
  crawfish tails
2 teaspoons salt

8 ounces fettuccine noodles,
  cooked al dente and drained
¾ cup freshly grated Romano
  cheese
¾ cup freshly grated Parmesan
  cheese
1 cup half-and-half cream
¼ cup chopped fresh parsley

In large skillet sauté onion, mushrooms and garlic in ¼ cup butter with oil. Add
crawfish and heat until just warm. Pour off excess liquid. Season with salt, cover and
keep warm. In saucepan melt remaining butter. Add noodles, cheeses and cream.
Mix well and combine with crawfish mixture. Sprinkle with parsley, toss and serve
immediately.
Serves: 4 to 6

One half cup cooked pasta has only about 100 calories, but go easy on the sauce!

ARTICHOKE AND TOMATO PASTA

2 Tablespoons oil
1 small onion, finely chopped
1 clove garlic, minced
8½ ounce can artichoke hearts, drained and chopped
3 medium tomatoes, peeled, seeded and chopped
1 Tablespoon chopped parsley

1½ teaspoons basil
Salt to taste
Freshly ground pepper to taste
16 ounces spaghetti, cooked al dente and drained
½ cup freshly grated Parmesan cheese

Heat oil in heavy skillet. Cook onion and garlic until transparent. Add artichokes, tomatoes, parsley, basil, salt and pepper. Cook slowly, stirring occasionally, for 1 hour or until thickened. Serve over spaghetti and sprinkle with Parmesan cheese.
Serves: 6

Excellent as a sauce over veal.

VERMICELLI WITH SHRIMP AND AVOCADO SAUCE

3½ Tablespoons butter, divided
½ teaspoon minced garlic
1 cup shrimp, peeled and deveined
2 Tablespoons chopped parsley
2 Tablespoons dry vermouth or white wine
¼ cup freshly grated Parmesan cheese

½ cup whipping cream
Dash of freshly ground black pepper
4 ounces vermicelli, cooked al dente and drained
1 cup diced ripe avocado

In a large skillet or medium saucepan heat 1 Tablespoon butter over moderately high heat. Do not brown. Add garlic and cook 1 minute, stirring constantly. Add shrimp, parsley and vermouth. Cook 2 minutes longer, stirring constantly, until shrimp turns pink or is just tender. Do not overcook. Transfer shrimp mixture to bowl. Add remaining butter to skillet and heat until melted. Reduce heat to low. Add cheese, cream and pepper. Cook 2 to 3 minutes longer, stirring constantly, until cheese melts and sauce is smooth. Remove from heat. Add hot vermicelli, avocado and shrimp mixture and toss gently. Serve immediately on heated plates.
Serves: 2

FETTUCCINE WITH BUTTER SAUCE

6 quarts water
1 Tablespoon salt
16 ounces fettuccine
½ cup butter
Salt to taste

¼ teaspoon pepper
⅛ teaspoon oregano
2 cloves garlic, minced
¼-½ cup grated Parmesan or
   Romano cheese

Bring water and 1 Tablespoon salt to a rolling boil in a large pot. Cook fettuccine until just al dente. While fettuccine is cooking, melt butter in saucepan; add salt, pepper, oregano and garlic. Simmer together on very low heat. Sprinkle cooked and drained fettuccine with cheese. Pour butter sauce over fettuccine. Toss and serve.
Serves: 6

SPAGHETTI WITH EGGPLANT SAUCE

½ cup olive oil
1 eggplant, peeled and cubed
½ cup chopped onion
⅛ teaspoon garlic powder
2 Tablespoons chopped fresh
   parsley
16 ounce can Italian tomatoes,
   undrained
6 ounce can tomato paste

¼ cup dry red wine
4 ounce can mushrooms
Pinch of oregano
1 teaspoon salt
1 teaspoon sugar
8 ounces thin spaghetti, cooked al
   dente and drained
Grated Parmesan cheese

In a large skillet or Dutch oven heat oil over medium heat. Add eggplant cubes, onion, garlic and parsley. Cook until transparent and tender, about 5 minutes. Stir in tomatoes, tomato paste, wine, mushrooms, oregano, salt and sugar. Break up tomatoes with a fork. Reduce heat to low and simmer 45 minutes, stirring occasionally. Serve over spaghetti and sprinkle with Parmesan cheese.
Serves: 6

If preparing dried pasta that is to be eaten as a main dish, one pound pasta will serve 4. When served as an accompaniment or side dish, one pound is sufficient for 6 to 8.

If preparing fresh pasta, allow ½ pound per person as a main dish and ¼ pound or less if a first course or side dish.

BREADS

BASIC YEAST BREAD

1 Tablespoon sugar	**3 Tablespoons vegetable oil**
1 package dry yeast	**4 cups all-purpose flour**
1½ cups hot water	**Butter, melted**
1½ teaspoons salt	

In a large mixing bowl dissolve sugar and yeast in water. Let mixture stand 10 minutes. Add the salt and oil. Gradually add flour using a wooden spoon to beat. After the dough is well mixed, leave the spoon in the dough and cover with a damp cloth or paper towel. Stir well or agitate to remove air bubbles at 15 minute intervals, 4 or 5 times. Divide dough into 2 balls and place on a floured board. Let rest for 10-15 minutes. Roll each ball into a 9X12-inch rectangle. Then roll up along the long side like a jelly roll. Place rolls on greased cookie sheet, seal the ends and score the tops diagonally with a knife. Cover again with towel and let rise until double in size, approximately 1 hour. Bake at 400 degrees for 25 minutes. Remove from oven and brush with melted butter. Variation: Whole wheat or other grain flours can be substituted up to a 1 to 1 ratio with the all-purpose flour. The sugar can be replaced by honey or molasses for multi-grained breads.
Yield: 2 loaves

NO KNEAD ROLLS

1 cup vegetable shortening	**1 cup warm water**
⅔ cup sugar	**6 cups all-purpose flour**
1½ teaspoons salt	**2 packages dry yeast**
1 cup boiling water	**Butter, melted**
2 eggs, beaten	

Mix shortening, sugar, salt and boiling water together. Set aside and cool. Add beaten eggs and warm water to shortening mixture. Mix yeast with 3 cups flour and sift into shortening mixture. Add the 3 remaining cups of flour, blending well. Cover and refrigerate for at least 4 hours or overnight. Three hours before serving, roll dough on a lightly floured surface to ½-inch thickness and cut out rolls with a small biscuit cutter. Dip rolls in melted butter, fold over and place rolls, sides touching, on any desired cookie sheet or pan sprayed with no-stick cooking spray. Allow rolls to rise until almost double in size. Bake at 425 degrees for 12-15 minutes.
Yield: 6 dozen small rolls

These rolls can be baked, then frozen.

REFRIGERATOR ROLLS

2 cups milk
½ cup vegetable shortening
½ cup sugar
½ cup lukewarm water
1 package dry yeast
4¼ cups all-purpose flour

2 teaspoons salt
1 heaping teaspoon baking
  powder
½ teaspoon baking soda
Butter, melted

Bring milk, shortening and sugar to a boil, let cool to lukewarm, approximately 112 degrees, stirring occasionally. Dissolve yeast in lukewarm water and add to cooled milk mixture. Add 3 cups flour to milk mixture, 1 cup at a time, and mix well with mixer at medium speed. Set in warm place until dough rises and then begins to fall, approximately 1½ hours. Add salt, baking powder and baking soda to remaining flour and stir into batter with a spoon. Refrigerate at least 8 hours or overnight. Dough will be very sticky. Divide dough in half, leaving one half in refrigerator. On lightly floured board, roll each half into ¼-inch thickness. Cut rolls using a small biscuit cutter. Dip in melted butter and fold over. Place in a lightly greased 8X8-inch pan, leaving room between rolls for rolls to rise. Let rise 1-1½ hours. Bake at 425 degrees for 7 minutes or until golden.
Yield: 5 dozen

Rolls can be cut bigger if desired. The secret to light rolls is to use very little flour when rolling out and handle as gently and as little as possible.

DATE NUT BREAD

1½ cups boiling water
1½ cups dates, chopped
2 Tablespoons butter or
  margarine
1½ cups sugar
1 teaspoon salt

1 egg
2¾ cups all-purpose flour
1 teaspoon baking soda
1 teaspoon cream of tartar
1 teaspoon vanilla extract
1 cup chopped walnuts

Mix boiling water, dates, butter, sugar and salt together and let cool. Add remaining ingredients, mixing well. Pour into 3 lightly greased miniature loaf pans. Bake at 350 degrees for 30 minutes.
Yield: 3 small loaves

Nice to give at Christmas.

GRAHAM WHEAT ROLLS

½ cup sugar
½ cup vegetable shortening, melted
1 teaspoon salt
1 cup boiling water
1 package dry yeast
1 teaspoon sugar

1 cup cool water
3 cups sifted all-purpose flour
2 cups whole wheat flour, unsifted
1 egg, well beaten
1 cup graham cracker crumbs
Butter, melted

In large bowl combine sugar, shortening and salt. Add boiling water. Stir and cool. Dissolve yeast and 1 teaspoon sugar in cool water. Add to first mixture. Combine flours. Add ½ of the flour, stirring until smooth. Gradually add remaining flour, egg, and cracker crumbs, stirring after each addition. Let rise until double. Cover and refrigerate dough until chilled thoroughly. May be refrigerated for up to 24 hours. Roll out dough on lightly floured board to ¼-inch thickness. Cut with biscuit cutter. Brush with butter and fold over; place on lightly greased baking sheet. Cover and let rise for 2 hours. Bake at 350 degrees for 25-30 minutes. Additional butter may be brushed on rolls and graham cracker crumbs sprinkled on top before baking. These rolls may be frozen. Allow an extra hour for rising if frozen.
Yield: 4 dozen

YEAST BISCUITS

¼ cup lukewarm water
2 packages dry yeast
5½ cups self-rising flour
⅓ cup sugar

1 teaspoon baking soda
1 cup vegetable shortening
2 cups buttermilk

Mix water and yeast, set aside. Sift and measure flour. Add sugar and baking soda to flour. Cut shortening into flour mixture with pastry blender. Add buttermilk, then yeast mixture, stirring after each addition. Place in refrigerator in covered bowl and allow mixture to rise at least 4 hours. The dough can be rolled and cut into biscuits or dropped by teaspoon onto greased cookie sheet. Bake at 400 degrees for 10-15 minutes.
Yield: 3 dozen

Dough may be stored for 1 week refrigerated, pinching off desired amount as needed.

MONTE JACK BREAD

**1 large loaf French bread,
   thinly sliced**
½ cup margarine
1 Tablespoon poppy seeds

1 teaspoon garlic powder
**6 ounces Monterey Jack cheese,
   sliced thinly**

Place bread on large piece of aluminum foil. Melt margarine in microwave. Add poppy seeds and garlic powder. Place a thin slice of cheese between each slice of bread. Spoon margarine mixture between each slice of bread. Pour any remaining margarine over top of loaf. Seal foil and bake at 350 degrees for 10-15 minutes. Open foil the last 5 minutes to brown bread.
Yield: 1 loaf

BOSTON BROWN BREAD

2 cups buttermilk
¾ cup dark molasses
¾ cup seedless raisins
1 cup rye flour
**1 cup whole wheat or graham
   flour**

1 cup yellow cornmeal
¾ teaspoon baking soda
1 teaspoon salt
1 Tablespoon butter, softened
**2 (1 pound) cans, washed and
   dried**

In deep bowl beat buttermilk and molasses together vigorously with a spoon. Stir in raisins. Combine flours, cornmeal, baking soda and salt. Sift into buttermilk mixture 1 cup at a time, stirring well after each addition. Grease bottom and sides of each can with butter. Pour batter into cans to within 1 inch of top. Cover each can loosely with a circle of buttered waxed paper and then a larger circle of heavy-duty aluminum foil. The foil should be puffed, allowing an inch of space above the top edge of cans so batter can rise as it steams. Tie paper and foil in place with kitchen string. Stand cans in a large pot. Add enough boiling water to come up to ¾ of the can height. Return water to a boil over high heat. Cover pan tightly and reduce heat to low. Steam 2 hours and 15 minutes. Remove foil and paper at once and turn bread out on a heated platter. May leave in cans with foil and paper still attached to store and steam 10-15 minutes to reheat before serving.
Yield: 2 loaves

POPPY ONION LOAF

6 Tablespoons butter
1 Tablespoon instant minced
  onions

1 Tablespoon poppy seeds
24 canned refrigerated
  butterflake rolls or biscuits

Melt butter, add onions and poppy seeds. Separate each roll into 2 or 3 rolls. Dip each roll in butter mixture, turning to coat. Place rolls on edge in a 8x4-inch loaf pan, arranging rolls in two rows. Bake at 350 degrees for 30-35 minutes. Serve warm.
Serves: 8 to 10

HOLLAND CARROT BREAD

2 cups sifted all-purpose flour
2 teaspoons baking soda
2 teaspoons cinnamon
½ teaspoon salt
1½ cups sugar

1½ cups vegetable oil
3 eggs, beaten
2 teaspoons vanilla extract
2 cups grated carrots
1 cup nuts or raisins

Sift together in large bowl the sifted flour, soda, cinnamon and salt. Add sugar, oil, eggs and vanilla. With mixer, beat until well blended. Fold in carrots, nuts or raisins. Pour into 2 greased and floured 9X5-inch loaf pans. Bake at 300 degrees for 1 hour or until wooden pick inserted in center comes out clean.
Yield: 2 loaves

This bread stays moist and is delicious served with cream cheese.

CARROT APRICOT BREAD

17 ounce can apricots, undrained
1½ cups grated carrots
½ cup nuts, chopped
3 cups all-purpose flour, sifted
2 teaspoons baking soda

2 cups sugar
4 eggs
1 cup vegetable oil
2 teaspoons vanilla extract

Mash apricots. Add carrots and nuts to apricots. Sift together flour, baking soda and sugar. Add eggs, oil and vanilla to dry ingredients. Beat until well blended. Fold in apricot mixture. Pour into 2 greased 8X5-inch loaf pans. Bake at 325 degrees for 1 hour and 15 minutes.
Yield: 2 loaves

CORN LIGHT BREAD

2 cups cornmeal
1 cup all-purpose flour
1 cup sugar
1 teaspoon salt

1 teaspoon baking soda
2 cups buttermilk
1 Tablespoon vegetable
  shortening, melted

Mix cornmeal, flour, sugar and salt together. Add soda to buttermilk. Gradually add buttermilk to dry ingredients. Stir in vegetable shortening. Pour into a greased 9X5-inch loaf pan. Cover with foil. Bake at 350 degrees for 20 minutes. Remove foil and continue baking for 40 minutes. Remove from oven and let sit for 10 minutes before serving.
Yield: 1 loaf

This is a sweet, heavy cornbread. This recipe was brought to Tupelo years ago from Tennessee. Especially good served with ham and black-eyed peas.

CORNBREAD DRESSING

10-inch skillet of cornbread
7 slices white bread
2 cups chopped celery
1 large onion, chopped
3-4 cups turkey broth or 3 (10¾
  ounce) cans chicken broth

4 eggs, beaten
1 Tablespoon sage
1 teaspoon black pepper
Salt to taste

Prepare cornbread a day ahead. Let cornbread and white bread sit uncovered to become dry before making dressing. In large bowl crumble cornbread and bread slices and mix together. In a medium saucepan cover celery and onion with water. Boil until tender. Drain vegetables. Add vegetables to bread mixture. Stir. Add enough chicken broth to bread mixture to make the consistency of uncooked cornbread. Add eggs and seasonings. Mix well. Pour into a greased 9X13-inch pan. Bake uncovered at 350 degrees for 45 minutes. Stir from the sides at least twice while baking.
Serves: 10 to 12

Just like your grandmother used to make.

MRS. BROWN'S SOUR CREAM CORNBREAD

½ cup margarine
1 cup cream-style corn
1 cup sour cream

1 cup self-rising cornmeal
2 eggs, beaten
1 small onion, grated

Preheat oven to 350 degrees. Melt margarine in an 8X8-inch pan in preheating oven. In a bowl mix remaining ingredients until well blended. Add melted margarine to batter. Pour batter into pan and bake for 35 minutes.
Serves: 8

CORNBREAD EASY

¾ cup self-rising cornmeal
¼ cup biscuit mix
1 egg

¾ cup milk or buttermilk
1 Tablespoon vegetable oil

Combine cornmeal and biscuit mix in a bowl. Break egg into a 1 cup measuring cup. Beat well and add enough milk to measure 1 cup. Add oil to milk, stir and add to dry ingredients. Mix well. Immediately pour into a hot, oiled 8-inch skillet and bake at 425 degrees for 20-25 minutes. Bread should be very lightly browned on top. This recipe can easily be doubled and cooked in a 10-inch skillet.
Serves: 4 to 6

Corn bread batter should sizzle when poured into hot skillet or pan. This prevents sticking and assures a nice crust.

For better corn bread, muffins or cornsticks, always blend the egg, shortening and meal before adding milk. Beat batter until creamy and free of all lumps.

To raise yeast bread in the microwave, place prepared dough in a well-greased microwave-proof bowl, large enough to hold it when doubled. Turn dough to coat with fat, and cover loosely with waxed paper that has been dusted inside with flour. Set one cup of boiling water beside bowl and use 50% power or defrost cycle for 1 minute. Let stand in oven one hour or until dough has doubled.

MARSHMALLOW POPOVERS

8 ounce can refrigerated crescent dinner rolls
½ cup sugar

1 teaspoon cinnamon
½ cup margarine, melted
8 marshmallows

Separate rolls into 8 triangles. In a small bowl combine sugar and cinnamon. Dip each marshmallow into margarine and then into sugar mixture. Wrap one sugared marshmallow in each triangle, pinching dough edges together securely. Dip each into margarine and place in muffin tins. Bake at 375 degrees for 13 minutes.
Yield: 8 rolls

To put a smile on a child's face, make these!

APPLESAUCE PUFFS

2 cups biscuit mix
¾ cup sugar
1½ teaspoons cinnamon
¾ cup applesauce

¼ cup milk
2 eggs, slightly beaten
3 Tablespoons vegetable oil

In mixing bowl combine biscuit mix, sugar and cinnamon. Add applesauce, milk, eggs and oil. Mix well. Spoon into greased muffin tins, filling cups ⅔ full. Bake at 400 degrees for 12 minutes or until browned. Cool slightly. Remove from pan and dip into topping.

Topping
¼ cup sugar
½ teaspoon cinnamon

2 Tablespoons margarine, melted

Combine sugar and cinnamon. Dip tops of muffins into butter and then into sugar-cinnamon mixture.
Yield: 12 muffins

OATMEAL MINI MUFFINS

¾ cup margarine
¾ cup packed light brown sugar
1 egg
1 cup all-purpose flour

¼ teaspoon baking powder
¼ teaspoon baking soda
1 cup oatmeal
1 cup chopped pecans

Cream margarine and sugar. Add egg and stir well. Combine flour, baking powder and baking soda. Add to creamed mixture. Fold in oatmeal and pecans. Pour batter into greased miniature muffin tins. Bake at 350 degrees for 10-12 minutes or until lightly browned. Remove from pan and frost.

Frosting
2 Tablespoons margarine, softened
1¾ cups powdered sugar

2 Tablespoons milk
1 teaspoon vanilla extract

Mix all ingredients until smooth. Spread on muffins when they have cooled slightly.
Yield: 4 dozen

ORANGE MUFFINS

1 cup sour cream
⅔ cup margarine, softened
2 eggs
6 Tablespoons orange juice
2 Tablespoons grated orange rind

2⅔ cups all-purpose flour
2 cups sugar
1 teaspoon salt
1 teaspoon baking soda
1 Tablespoon poppy seeds

Grease 24 muffin tins or line with paper baking cups. Combine sour cream, margarine, eggs, orange juice and orange rind in mixing bowl. Beat until smooth. Combine remaining ingredients and blend into creamed mixture just until all ingredients are moistened. Spoon into prepared muffin cups, filling cups ⅔ full. Bake at 400 degrees for 15-20 minutes or until a wooden pick inserted in center comes out clean. Let stand on wire rack 5 minutes before removing muffins from pan. Best served warm.
Yield: 2 dozen

CRISPY WAFFLES

2 cups biscuit mix
½ cup vegetable oil

1 egg
1⅓ cups club soda

Mix all ingredients until smooth. Cook in pre-heated waffle iron.
Serves: 3

Very light, crispy waffles.

ORANGE BREAKFAST RING

1 cup sugar
3 Tablespoons grated orange rind
20 canned refrigerated biscuits
⅓ cup butter, melted

3 ounces cream cheese, softened
½ cup powdered sugar
2 Tablespoons orange juice
Orange slices for garnish

Combine sugar and orange rind. Dip each biscuit in melted butter and coat with sugar-orange mixture. Stand biscuits on sides, overlapping edges in an ungreased 9-inch tube pan. Bake at 350 degrees for 30 minutes. Invert pan on serving plate. Combine cream cheese, powdered sugar and orange juice, mix until smooth. Spread over top while ring is hot. Serve warm. Garnish with fresh orange slices.
Serves: 8 to 10

BERNIE'S CREAM CHEESE COFFEE CAKE

2 cups all-purpose flour
⅛ teaspoon salt
¾ cup margarine, softened
1 package dry yeast
¼ cup warm water

1 egg, beaten
16 ounces cream cheese, softened
1½ cups sugar
2 Tablespoons grated lemon rind

Mix flour, salt and margarine until crumbly. In a cup dissolve yeast in warm water. Add beaten egg to yeast mixture and mix well. Slowly add yeast mixture to flour mixture. Blend. Divide dough in half and roll out on a floured board into 2 (12X14-inch) rectangles. Combine cream cheese, sugar and lemon rind, beat until smooth. Spread cream cheese mixture evenly over dough. Roll each in jelly roll fashion. Place rolls on an ungreased cookie sheet. Split tops crosswise to allow steam to escape. Place 2-inch wide strip of aluminum foil between rolls of dough to prevent sticking together. Bake at 370 degrees for 25-30 minutes. Dust with powdered sugar, cool and serve.
Yield: 2 loaves

RASPBERRY CREAM CHEESE COFFEE CAKE

3 ounces cream cheese
4 Tablespoons butter
2 cups biscuit mix
⅓ cup milk

½ cup raspberry preserves
1 cup sifted powdered sugar
½ teaspoon vanilla extract
Milk

Combine cream cheese, butter and biscuit mix. Blend well with pastry cutter until crumbly. Blend in milk. Turn dough onto lightly floured waxed paper and knead 8-10 strokes. Roll dough into a 8X12-inch rectangle. Turn over onto greased baking sheet. Spread preserves down center of dough. Make 2½-inch cuts at intervals on sides of dough. Braid strips over filling. Bake at 425 degrees for 15 minutes. Combine powdered sugar and vanilla and enough milk to make a stiff frosting. Spread on coffee cake while still warm. Variation: Substitute apricot preserves and sliced almonds using ½ teaspoon almond extract in glaze for a different flavor.
Serves: 6

CINNAMON ROLL UPS

2 loaves very thin sliced white
  bread
8 ounces cream cheese, softened
1 egg yolk
1 cup sugar

¼ teaspoon lemon juice
¼ cup sugar
1 teaspoon cinnamon
3 Tablespoons butter, melted

Remove crust from bread. With rolling pin roll each bread slice ⅛-inch thin. Mix cream cheese, egg yolk, sugar and lemon juice. Spread on bread and roll up. Cut each roll in half. Combine sugar and cinnamon. Dip each roll into melted butter and then into sugar-cinnamon mixture. Place on ungreased cookie sheet. Bake at 375 degrees for 8-10 minutes.
Yield: 80 pieces

A nice Saturday morning treat with fresh fruit and sausage.

ACCOMPANIMENTS

RASPBERRY JAM

Green tomatoes
4 cups sugar

6 ounces raspberry gelatin

Peel and cut up tomatoes. Place in blender and purée. Measure 5 cups of tomato purée. Mix with sugar. Bring to a boil and cook 15 minutes. Remove from heat and skim off foam. Stir in gelatin. Pour into sterile jars and seal. Cool. Let stand for a week before serving.
Yield: 2½ pints

A real surprise!

BANANA FRUIT JAM

1 cup mashed ripe bananas
3¼ cups peaches, peeled and
**   mashed or 2 (20 ounce) cans**
**   sliced peaches, drained**
8 ounce can crushed pineapple,
**   undrained**

2 Tablespoons fresh lemon juice
1¾ ounce package powdered
**   fruit pectin**
6 cups sugar

Place fruits and lemon juice in a large saucepan. Add powdered pectin to fruit. Mix well. Bring to a full boil. Add sugar and boil for 1 minute, stirring constantly. Remove from heat and skim off foam. Cool slightly. Pour into hot, sterilized jars, filling to within ½ inch of top. Seal.
Yield: 4 half pints

APRICOT PRESERVES

½ pound dried apricots
Water
8 ounce can crushed pineapple

1 Tablespoon fresh lemon juice
2½ cups sugar
¼ teaspoon salt
½ cup sliced almonds, optional

Cover apricots with water and simmer for 35 minutes. Cool. Drain and chop apricots. Add pineapple, lemon juice, sugar and salt. Boil slowly until thickened, stirring frequently so it does not scorch. Cook for 20 minutes. Add almonds. Store in refrigerator or pour into hot, sterilized jars and seal.
Yield: 3 half-pints

LEMON PEAR HONEY

1 quart ripe pears, peeled, cored and chopped

3 lemons, seeded, unpeeled and quartered

4 cups sugar

Place pears and lemons in food processor and grind. Pour mixture into a heavy pan and add sugar. Bring to a boil. Cook over low heat until mixture is very thick. Pour immediately into hot, sterilized jars and seal.
Yield: 3 pints

This recipe is easily doubled.

CRANBERRY CHUTNEY

1 cup water
1 cup sugar
¼ cup seedless raisins
1 Tablespoon light brown sugar
¼ teaspoon ginger

¼ teaspoon garlic salt
¼ teaspoon red pepper
2 cups fresh cranberries
2 Tablespoons vinegar

Combine water and sugar in saucepan. Bring to a boil. Add remaining ingredients and simmer gently, stirring occasionally, until thickened. Cool. Store in refrigerator until ready to use. Do not freeze.
Serves: 12

This is good with turkey or ham.

JALAPEÑO RELISH

3 cups vinegar
1 cup sugar
3 Tablespoons salt
2 teaspoons mustard seed
1 teaspoon celery seed

2 cups finely chopped green bell peppers
1 cup finely chopped jalapeño peppers
2 cups chopped onions

Mix vinegar, sugar, salt, mustard seed and celery seed together. Bring to a boil. Pour over chopped vegetables. Let stand overnight. Next day, bring to a boil and simmer 10 minutes. Pour into hot, sterilized jars and seal.
Yield: 2 pints

PEAR RELISH

2 quarts pears, peeled, cored and quartered
9 green bell peppers, chopped
1 red bell pepper, chopped
6 small green or red pepper pods, chopped
6 medium onions, chopped

½ cup salt
4 cups sugar
8 Tablespoons all-purpose flour
4 Tablespoons dry mustard
1 Tablespoon turmeric
1½ quarts cider vinegar
2 ounce jar diced pimientos

Grind pears, peppers and onions. Pour salt over mixture and let stand for 1 hour. Drain. Sift dry ingredients together and stir in cider vinegar. Bring to a boil. Add ground pear mixture and pimiento. Boil 5 minutes. Spoon into hot, sterilized jars. Seal.
Yield: 6 pints

FRENCH PICKLES

4 quarts green tomatoes, sliced
3 large white onions, sliced
¼ cup salt
2 cups cider vinegar

2 cups sugar
2 Tablespoons whole mustard seeds
1 Tablespoon allspice
1 Tablespoon cinnamon

In a large pan place layers of tomatoes, onions and salt alternately. Cover and let stand overnight. Next morning, drain thoroughly. Mix together the vinegar, sugar, mustard seed and spices. Heat this mixture thoroughly, then add tomatoes and onions. Boil exactly 15 minutes. Pour into sterilized jars and seal.
Yield: 4 pints

EASY PICKLES

1 gallon jar sour pickles
4 sticks cinnamon
2 Tablespoons whole cloves
2 Tablespoons mustard seeds

2 Tablespoons celery seeds
1 Tablespoon alum
6 cloves garlic
5 pounds sugar

Pour pickles into colander and drain. Rinse under running water. Slice pickles and rinse again. Drain well. Place a layer of pickles, spices and sugar in a gallon jar. Repeat layers until all ingredients have been used. Let stand 6 days before serving. Flavor improves with time.
Yield: 1 gallon

Pack into small jars for gifts.

PEAR CHUTNEY

3 cups packed light brown sugar
3 red hot peppers, crushed
2 cups cider vinegar
4 cups water
1 Tablespoon cloves
1 Tablespoon allspice

1 Tablespoon cinnamon
4 Tablespoons ginger
12 to 14 large pears, peeled and chopped
2 cups seedless golden raisins

In a large pan combine all ingredients, except pears and raisins. Bring to a boil and cook for 30 minutes. Add pears and raisins. Cook slowly for 3 hours. Pour into hot, sterilized jars and seal. You may substitute 6 green mangoes for a delicious mango chutney.
Yield: 6 pints

Excellent served with game, turkey or beef.

YELLOW CUCUMBER PICKLES

7 pounds overripe pickling cucumbers
2 gallons water
2½ cups lime
2½ ounce jar powdered alum
2 gallons water
2 gallons ice water

2 quarts vinegar
5 pounds sugar
1 Tablespoon salt
1 Tablespoon pickling spice
3 to 4 jalapeño peppers, sliced, optional
Green food coloring

Peel and seed cucumbers. Cut into strips; should yield approximately 2 gallons. Mix water with lime and soak cucumbers in lime water for 24 hours. Rinse 3 times. Mix powdered alum in 2 gallons water and soak cucumbers in alum water for 12 hours. Remove cucumbers from alum water and rinse well. Soak cucumbers in 2 gallons ice water for 6 hours. Drain. Make syrup with vinegar, sugar, salt, pickling spice and jalapeño peppers. Pour over pickles. Let stand overnight. Next morning, boil for 35 minutes. Add a few drops of green food coloring. Pour into hot jars and seal.
Yield: 5 to 6 quarts

ACCOMPANIMENTS

RIPE TOMATO RELISH

5 pounds tomatoes, peeled and
   chopped
3½ cups yellow onions, chopped
2 cups sugar
3 cups chopped celery

2 teaspoons salt
¾ teaspoon allspice
1¼ teaspoons cinnamon
2 cups cider vinegar

In a heavy pot combine all ingredients. Bring to a boil. Cook on low heat for 1 hour or until thickened, stirring every 15 minutes. Ladle into hot, sterilized jars and seal. Yield: 3 to 4 pints.

Good served over green beans and black-eyed peas.

CANDIED SWEET PICKLES

2-gallon crock container
2 gallons pickling cucumbers,
   5-7 inches in length
2½ quarts water
1 cup salt
3 quarts water

2½ ounce jar powdered alum
Cider vinegar with 4 to 6 percent
   acid
Green food coloring
3 teaspoons pickling spice
8 to 10 cups sugar

Place whole cucumbers in crock. Mix 2½ quarts water with salt. Stir until dissolved. Pour over packed cucumbers. Be sure to cover completely with salted water. Place lid on crock and place weight on top of lid, if necessary, to hold cucumbers under liquid. Let stand for 10 days. Remove cucumbers from crock, rinse and slice. Dissolve alum in 3 quarts water. Pour over cucumbers and soak overnight. Make sure cucumber slices are completely covered with liquid. Next day, drain and rinse well. Add vinegar and 1 to 2 drops food coloring. Cover and let stand overnight. Drain and place a layer of sliced cucumbers and a heavy layer of sugar in a gallon jar. Continue layering. When jar is ⅓ full, place spice in cheesecloth bag; tie securely. Add spice bag to pickles. Continue with cucumbers and sugar. Add another spice bag when ⅔ full. Continue until completed, making sure sugar is on top. Jar does not have to be sealed. Let stand for 2 weeks. Cloth bags may be removed before serving. Yield: 1 gallon

English dry mustard has a fiery bite. French dry mustard is a milder version. Choose accordingly!

MUSTARD SAUCE

3 egg yolks
½ Tablespoon all-purpose flour
½ cup sugar
1 Tablespoon dry mustard

2 beef bouillon cubes
½ cup hot water
¼ cup vinegar
¼ cup butter

In the top of a double boiler combine all ingredients. Cook, stirring until thickened.
Yield: 1½ cups

Delicious served on ham.

RAVIGOTE SAUCE

1 cup mayonnaise
2 Tablespoons chopped fresh
  parsley
2 Tablespoons chopped capers
1 Tablespoon dry mustard

1 Tablespoon horseradish
2 Tablespoons chopped pimiento
1 hard-boiled egg; mash yolk,
  chop white
½ teaspoon fresh lemon juice

Combine all ingredients. Chill before serving.
Yield: 1½ cups

Stuff half an avocado with fresh shrimp or crabmeat. Serve with sauce.

SAUCE MEUNIERE

½ cup butter
1 Tablespoon minced fresh parsley
1 Tablespoon chopped green bell
  pepper
2 Tablespoons Worcestershire
  sauce

2 Tablespoons fresh lemon juice
½ teaspoon salt
½ teaspoon pepper
Dash of hot sauce

In a small saucepan combine all ingredients. Simmer over low heat for 5 minutes.
Yield: ¾ cup

This sauce is great for basting broiled catfish fillets or shrimp.

FRESH TOMATO SAUCE

4 pounds ripe tomatoes
1 cup best quality olive oil
3 medium onions, chopped
3 carrots, chopped
6 cloves garlic, chopped

6 fresh basil leaves or 1½
   teaspoons dried basil
4 anchovy fillets, mashed,
   optional
Pepper to taste

Coarsely chop tomatoes and simmer covered in Dutch oven for 10-15 minutes. Heat oil in a skillet and sauté onion and carrots until soft. Add garlic to onions and carrots and sauté for 5 minutes. Pour vegetable mixture into the tomatoes. Add basil and simmer uncovered for 20 minutes more. Cool. Pour mixture through a food mill or sieve to remove skins, seeds and pulp. Do not use a food processor. To serve, reheat and toss with pasta.
Yield: 6 cups

MUSHROOM SAUCE SUPREME

2 Tablespoons minced shallots
1 clove garlic, minced
2 Tablespoons chopped green
   bell pepper
1 pound fresh mushrooms; if
   large, cut in half
2 Tablespoons butter
1 Tablespoon olive oil

1 Tablespoon all-purpose flour
½ cup dry red wine
¼ teaspoon salt
⅛ teaspoon pepper
½ teaspoon Worcestershire sauce
1 Tablespoon chopped fresh
   parsley

Sauté shallots, garlic, bell pepper and mushrooms in butter and olive oil. Cook for 5 minutes. Add flour and mix well. Stir in wine and seasonings. Continue cooking until sauce thickens.
Yield: 1 cup

Serve over chicken, beef, fresh vegetables, pasta or fish.

Four ounces, or about 1½ cups fresh mushrooms will yield about ½ cup cooked, sliced mushrooms.

SPICY SHRIMP SAUCE

1½ cups mayonnaise
4 Tablespoons mustard with
   horseradish
1 cup olive oil
Juice of 1-2 lemons

3 cloves garlic, minced
1 medium onion, grated
3 Tablespoons vinegar
5 Tablespoons A-I Steak sauce

Mix all ingredients in a quart jar. Shake to mix well. Refrigerate.
Yield: 1 quart

This is good and will keep a long time refrigerated. Great sauce for fresh peeled shrimp.

TED'S MARINADE

¼ cup sherry
2 Tablespoons Worcestershire
   sauce
2 Tablespoons teriyaki sauce
2 Tablespoons soy sauce
Juice of 3 lemons
½ cup margarine
¾ teaspoon Kitchen Bouquet
¾ teaspoon Liquid Smoke

1 teaspoon bacon bits
½ teaspoon oregano
½ teaspoon Accent
½ teaspoon salt
½ teaspoon seasoned salt
½ teaspoon lemon pepper
¼ teaspoon garlic salt
⅛ teaspoon pepper

Combine all ingredients and simmer over low heat for 10 minutes. Use sauce for marinating and basting.
Yield: 2 cups

Good for meat, poultry or fish.

REBECCA SAUCE

1½ cups sour cream
¼ cup packed light brown sugar
1 Tablespoon light rum

1 Tablespoon bourbon
¼ cup golden seedless raisins

Combine sour cream, brown sugar, rum, bourbon and raisins. Blend well. Cover and chill. Best made 2 hours before serving.
Yield: 2 cups

Serve over fresh honeydew melon, blueberries or strawberries.

AMARETTO SAUCE

3 egg yolks
½ cup powdered sugar

¼ cup Amaretto
½ cup whipping cream, whipped

Place egg yolks, sugar and Amaretto in blender. Blend until smooth. Fold whipped cream into egg mixture. Chill.
Yield: 3 cups

Serve over fresh strawberries, peaches or blueberries.

FUDGE SAUCE

1 cup sugar
4 Tablespoons cocoa
2 Tablespoons all-purpose flour
½ teaspoon salt

1 cup hot water
1 Tablespoon butter
1 teaspoon vanilla extract

Blend sugar, cocoa, flour and salt in small saucepan. Add hot water, stirring constantly. Cook until thickened. Remove from heat and add butter and vanilla.
Yield: 1½ cups

Delicious served over poached pears.

OLD FASHIONED ORANGE SAUCE

1 cup sugar
½ cup fresh orange juice
Grated rind of 1 orange
1 Tablespoon lemon juice

¼ cup butter
3 eggs, beaten
Salt to taste

Combine all ingredients in the top of a double boiler. Simmer until thickened. Keep warm until serving time or make ahead and refrigerate.
Yield: 1½ cups

A very good and rich sauce. Serve warm over ice cream, pound cake or gingerbread.

Reheat sauces gently over hot, not boiling water to avoid separation.

DESSERTS

ELEGANT PARTY DESSERT

2 ounces unsweetened chocolate
1 cup sugar, divided
¼ cup water
4 egg yolks, beaten until light
¾ cup butter, softened

1 cup powdered sugar, sifted
1 teaspoon vanilla extract
⅔ cup chopped pecans
4 egg whites, room temperature
2 dozen ladyfingers, split

Melt chocolate in top of double boiler. Add ½ cup sugar, water and egg yolks. Stir until thickened. Remove from heat and beat until smooth. Cool. Cream butter and powdered sugar. Add cooled chocolate mixture, vanilla and pecans. Beat egg whites, gradually adding ½ cup sugar. Beat until stiff peaks form. Fold egg whites into chocolate mixture. Set chocolate filling aside. In a 9-inch springform pan arrange split ladyfingers over bottom and sides. Alternate layers of chocolate filling with ladyfingers ending with ladyfingers on top. Cover and refrigerate for 24 hours. To serve remove sides of pan and place on serving dish. Frost top and sides of cake with icing. Garnish with cherries or strawberries.

Icing
1 cup whipping cream
¼ cup sugar
½ teaspoon vanilla extract
6 marshmallows, cut up

1 banana, chopped
Cherries for garnish
Strawberries for garnish

Whip cream, adding sugar and vanilla. Add marshmallows and banana. Mix well.
Serves: 10 to 12

A very rich and elegant dessert.

HEAVENLY STRAWBERRIES

2 quarts fresh strawberries, hulled
   and halved
1 cup powdered sugar

1 cup whipping cream
1 teaspoon almond extract
1 Tablespoon orange liqueur

Toss strawberries in sugar and let sit for at least 1 hour. When ready to serve, whip cream and flavor with almond and orange liqueur. Fold strawberries into cream and spoon into sherbet bowls. Serve immediately.
Serves: 6

A celestial treat.

RASPBERRY FLUFF

6 ounces raspberry gelatin
2 cups boiling water
20 ounces frozen raspberries
4 cups whipping cream

4 Tablespoons sugar
1 large angel food cake, torn into
small pieces

Dissolve gelatin in hot water. Cool by adding frozen raspberries. Whip cream and add sugar. Fold whipped cream into cooled gelatin mixture. Pour a layer of gelatin mixture into a 10-inch tube pan with removeable bottom. Add a layer of cake pieces. Repeat layers until pan is full. Refrigerate overnight. To serve, lift stem from pan and slice. Variation: Use frozen strawberries and strawberry gelatin. Prepare and serve from a trifle bowl.
Serves: 24

Easy to make and "party pretty".

APRICOT REFRIGERATOR CAKE

6 ounces dried apricots
2 cups water
1 cup butter, softened
2 cups powdered sugar, sifted
4 eggs, separated

Juice of 1 lemon and rind, grated
¾ cup sugar
2 dozen ladyfingers, split
Whipped cream for garnish
Toasted almonds for garnish

Combine apricots and water. Cook uncovered 20 minutes or until tender. Pour into food processor and process until smooth. (There should be 1½ cups.) Cool. Cream butter and powdered sugar until light and fluffy. Add egg yolks and beat well. Blend in cooled apricot purée, lemon juice and rind; mix well. Beat egg whites until stiff, gradually adding ¾ cup sugar. Fold into apricot mixture. Line bottom and sides of 9-inch springform pan with ladyfingers. Spoon in half of apricot mixture, a layer of ladyfingers, continuing layers until full. Refrigerate overnight. To serve, remove sides of pan and garnish with whipped cream and toasted almonds.
Serves: 10

A delicious taste of apricots.

For successful whipped cream, whip very slowly to incorporate smaller air bubbles into the cream, making the foam more stable. Whip one pint of cream for 12 to 14 minutes at the slowest mixer speed.

GRAND MARNIER CHOCOLATE MOUSSE

8 ounces semi-sweet chocolate
2 Tablespoons black coffee
2 Tablespoons butter
6 eggs, separated
1 teaspoon vanilla extract

3 Tablespoons Grand Marnier
Whipped cream for garnish
Toasted slivered almonds for
  garnish

Melt chocolate in a heavy saucepan over low heat. Add coffee and mix well. Remove from heat and add butter. Beat egg yolks until light. Stir into chocolate mixture. Add vanilla and Grand Marnier. Beat egg whites until stiff and fold into chocolate mixture. Pour into individual compotes. Chill until firm. Garnish with a dollop of whipped cream and toasted almonds.
Serves: 6 to 8

A spectacular chocolate dessert.

MALAKOFF

6 ounces semi-sweet chocolate
⅓ cup hot water
⅓ cup hot coffee
4 egg yolks
2 Tablespoons brandy or
  Amaretto
¾ cup powdered sugar
½ cup butter, cut into pieces

2 egg whites
1 cup whipping cream
2 Tablespoons powdered sugar
1 teaspoon vanilla extract
2 dozen ladyfingers, sprinkled
  with rum or Amaretto
Whipped cream for garnish
Chocolate shavings for garnish

Mix chocolate and hot water in food processor for thirty seconds. Add coffee and mix for additional thirty seconds. Transfer mixture to a mixing bowl. Blend egg yolks, brandy, sugar and butter for 1 minute in processor. Add to chocolate mixture. Beat egg whites until stiff peaks form. Set aside. Whip cream with 2 Tablespoons powdered sugar until stiff. Fold egg whites, whipped cream and vanilla into chocolate mixture. Split half of ladyfingers. Line trifle bowl on bottom and sides with ladyfingers. Pour half of chocolate mixture into trifle bowl. Crumble remaining ladyfingers and place on top of chocolate layer. Pour remaining chocolate mixture over crumbled ladyfinger layer. Cover with additional whipped cream and decorate with chocolate shavings.
Serves: 8

Easy and chocolatey!

LEMON MOUSSE WITH RASPBERRY SAUCE

6 large eggs
6 large egg yolks
1½ cups sugar
1 cup fresh lemon juice, strained
2 Tablespoons minced lemon peel

14 Tablespoons well-chilled
    unsalted butter, cut into
    small pieces
¾ cup whipping cream, chilled
Fresh mint for garnish

Whisk eggs and yolks in heavy non-aluminum saucepan until foamy. Whisk in sugar, lemon juice, and lemon peel. Cook over low heat until mixture thickens to consistency of heavy custard, about 10 minutes. Do not boil. Remove from heat and stir in butter. Transfer mixture to a bowl and cool until very thick, about 50 minutes, stirring occasionally. Whip cream to soft peaks. Fold into lemon mixture just until combined. Spoon mousse into individual serving glasses. Cover and refrigerate until set, about 2 hours. Garnish with fresh mint. Serve with raspberry sauce.

Raspberry Sauce
1½ cups fresh raspberries, or 10
    ounces frozen, unsweetened
    raspberries

2 Tablespoons sugar

Place raspberries in food processor or blender and process until smooth. Strain to remove seeds. Add sugar. Taste, adding more sugar if desired. Cover and refrigerate 1 hour. Spoon sauce over center of lemon mousse. Sauce and mousse may be prepared one day ahead.
Serves: 8 to 10

Elegant dessert with a gentle lemon flavor.

Egg whites may be successfully beaten until stiff in the food processor by the following method. Put 6 large egg whites in a work bowl and turn on the machine. After 8 seconds, pour 1 Tablespoon white wine vinegar mixed with 1 Tablespoon water through the feed tube and process for 1½ minutes, or until the egg whites are whipped and hold their shape. You can't make a meringue shell by this method, but spongecakes, mousses, soufflés, waffles and fluffy omelettes can be prepared with whites beaten by this method.

CHOCOLATE POTS DE CRÈME

6 ounces semi-sweet chocolate
  chips
1 egg
1 teaspoon sugar
1 teaspoon vanilla extract

¾ cup half-and-half cream,
  scalded
Whipped cream for garnish
Chocolate shavings for garnish

In blender place chocolate chips, egg, sugar and vanilla. Blend well. Slowly add scalded cream and blend until smooth. Pour into 4 pots de crème cups. Refrigerate. Can be prepared a day in advance. May be doubled. Garnish with whipped cream and chocolate shavings. Variation: Before adding scalded cream, add any of the following: 1 teaspoon instant coffee, cognac, or Crème de Cacao.
Serves: 4

A delicious classic favorite.

CHOCOLATE MOUSSE WITH APRICOT SAUCE

6 ounces semi-sweet chocolate
2 ounces bitter chocolate
½ cup honey
3 teaspoons instant coffee

2 Tablespoons Cognac
6 cups whipping cream, divided
Shaved chocolate for garnish

In top of double boiler over hot water, melt semi-sweet and bitter chocolate. Add honey, stirring until mixture is smooth. Add coffee and Cognac. Cool. Whip 4 cups of cream and fold into chocolate mixture. Pour into serving bowl or individual dessert bowls, if desired. Whip remaining 2 cups cream. Spread over top of mousse and sprinkle with shaved chocolate.

Apricot Sauce
1½ cups apricot jam
½ cup water
2 Tablespoons sugar

1½ Tablespoons brandy or
  favorite liqueur

Combine apricot jam, water and sugar. Bring to a boil and cook 5-6 minutes, stirring constantly to keep from scorching. Add brandy. Cool. Serve over chocolate mousse.
Serves: 10 to 12

This chocolate mousse is delicious with or without the sauce.

PINEAPPLE MERINGUE TORTE

⅓ cup vegetable shortening
½ cup sugar
4 egg yolks
⅔ cup all-purpose flour

1 teaspoon baking powder
1 teaspoon salt
¼ cup pineapple juice, reserved
   from crushed pineapple

Cream shortening and sugar. Add egg yolks and beat well. Sift flour, baking powder and salt together and add gradually, alternating with pineapple juice to cream mixture. Divide the batter in half and pour into 2 (9-inch) cake pans that have been lined with waxed paper, greased and floured. Set aside.

Meringue Layer
4 egg whites, room temperature
½ cup sugar
½ teaspoon salt

1 teaspoon vanilla extract
1½ cups flaked coconut
½ cup finely chopped pecans

Beat egg whites until soft peaks form. Gradually beat in sugar until stiff peaks form. Fold in salt, vanilla, coconut and pecans. Spread on top of batter in each pan. Bake at 325 degrees for 25 minutes. Cool. Place bottom layer with meringue side down on serving plate. Spread with half of pineapple filling, reserving enough filling to ice sides of torte. Place remaining layer on top with meringue side up . Ice sides of torte with remaining filling. Refrigerate. Prepare at least 6-8 hours before serving or 1 day ahead to let pineapple flavor permeate the whipped cream.

Filling
1 cup whipping cream
2 Tablespoons powdered sugar
1 teaspoon vanilla extract

8 ounce can crushed pineapple,
   drain and reserve juice

Whip cream, slowly adding sugar. Fold in vanilla and pineapple.
Serves: 10 to 12

Light and refreshing.

Egg whites should always be at room temperature when beaten. They will whip to higher volumes.

BASIC TORTE

6 egg whites, room temperature
1¼ teaspoons cream of tartar
2 teaspoons vanilla extract
2 cups sugar
2 cups crushed saltine crackers

1½ cups finely chopped pecans
Vanilla ice cream, softened
21 ounce can cherry or blueberry
  pie filling

Beat egg whites, cream of tartar and vanilla until foamy. Slowly add sugar and beat until stiff. Fold in crackers and pecans. Pour into a 9X13-inch buttered pan. Bake at 350 degrees for 25-30 minutes. Cool completely. Refrigerate. Cover with softened ice cream. Freeze. When ready to serve cover top with pie filling or whipped cream topping.

Whipped Cream Topping
1 cup whipping cream
¼ cup powdered sugar
1 teaspoon vanilla extract

½ pound white chocolate, grated
Chopped pecans for garnish

Whip cream. Add powdered sugar and vanilla. Beat until stiff. Spread over torte. Sprinkle chocolate over whipped cream. Garnish with chopped pecans.
Serves: 12 to 15

Different and good!

FRUIT SURPRISE

1 quart fresh seasonal fruit
Cinnamon
Nutmeg
6 slices white bread
½ cup butter, melted

1½ cups sugar, depending on
  sweetness of fruit
1 Tablespoon all-purpose flour
1 egg
1 teaspoon vanilla extract

Place fruit in bottom of 9X13-inch baking dish. Sprinkle with cinnamon and nutmeg. Cut crusts from bread and place on top of fruit. Mix remaining ingredients and pour over bread. Bake at 325 degrees for 25-30 minutes.
Serves: 8

Try this. It is unbelievable! The bread makes a delicious crust.

POACHED PEARS IN RASPBERRY SYRUP

3 cups water
1½ cups sugar

3-4 Tablespoons raspberry vinegar
4 firm, ripe pears

Combine water and sugar in saucepan; cook over low heat, stirring constantly, until sugar melts. Add vinegar and mix well. Peel, halve, and core pears. Add immediately to syrup and simmer for 15-20 minutes. Turn several times while cooking. Let cool in syrup. To serve, remove pears from syrup and place in compotes and pour sauce over. If thicker syrup is preferred, remove pears and boil syrup until thick.
Serves: 4

Simplicity in its most elegant form.

HOLIDAY TORTE

6 egg whites
½ teaspoon cream of tartar
¼ teaspoon salt
1½ cups sugar

⅛ teaspoon almond extract
1 teaspoon vanilla extract
8 ounces frozen strawberries or
raspberries, thawed

Two hours before baking, place egg whites in large mixing bowl. Let stand to reach room temperature. Preheat oven to 450 degrees. Grease bottom only of a 10-inch tube pan, do not use Bundt pan. Add cream of tartar and salt to egg whites. Beat until whites are foamy. Gradually add sugar, ½ teaspoon at a time. Add almond and vanilla. Continue beating until meringue forms stiff glossy peaks and no granules of sugar remain, approximately 15-20 minutes. Spread mixture into pan. Place in oven. Turn off immediately. Let stand in oven overnight. Don't peek! Next morning loosen edge of torte with sharp, thin knife. Remove from pan. Frost torte with frosting. Refrigerate. When ready to serve, ladle strawberries over individual servings.

Frosting
1 cup whipping cream
2 Tablespoons powdered sugar

½ teaspoon vanilla extract

Whip cream, adding powdered sugar and vanilla.
Serves: 10 to 12

A pretty holiday dessert.

APRICOT CREAM CRÊPES

1½ cups all-purpose flour
¾ cup milk
¾ cup cold water
2 eggs
¼ cup butter, melted

2 Tablespoons sugar
Pinch of salt
3 Tablespoons brandy, rum or favorite liqueur

Combine all ingredients in blender and blend until smooth. Refrigerate at least 2 hours. Use crêpe pan, according to manufacturer's instructions to make crêpes. Crêpes may be made in advance, stacked between layers of waxed paper, and refrigerated or frozen until ready to use. Divide filling evenly among crêpes. Roll up and place seam side down in rectangular dish. Cover and refrigerate. Pour hot apricot sauce over crêpes to serve. Best to bring crêpes to room temperature before adding sauce.

Filling
17 ounce can apricots, well-drained
¼ cup powdered sugar

3 ounces cream cheese, softened
1 cup whipping cream
1 Tablespoon apricot brandy

Dice apricots and drain again. Set aside. In large mixing bowl, cream sugar and cream cheese. Slowly add whipping cream and beat until smooth and thick. Fold in brandy and diced apricots.

Apricot Sauce
12 ounce can apricot nectar
4 teaspoons cornstarch

4 teaspoons cold water

Over medium heat bring apricot nectar to boiling point. Mix cornstarch and water. Stir into hot nectar. Cook until thickened.
Serves: 12

A truly delicious way to enjoy apricots.

To avoid having whipped cream "weep" or become watery, do not use ultra-pasteurized cream, and be sure that cream, bowl and beaters are all well chilled.

FRESH FRUIT CRUNCH

1 cup sugar
1 egg, beaten
1 cup chopped pecans or walnuts
5¼ ounce package instant vanilla
    pudding mix

1 cup milk
1 cup sour cream
3 bananas or 2 cups fresh
    peaches, sprinkled with lemon
    juice

Combine sugar, egg and nuts. Mix well. Place on a cookie sheet and bake at 350 degrees for approximately 18-20 minutes. Reserve enough crumbs for topping. Set aside. Mix pudding, milk and sour cream together. In a 2-quart casserole or Trifle bowl, layer bananas, pudding and crumb mixture. Top with reserved crumbs.
Serves: 6 to 8

This is a new twist for banana pudding and so easy. Can layer in parfaits or sherbet glasses.

APPLE STRUDEL

½ cup butter
2 cups + 1 Tablespoon
    all-purpose flour
3 eggs, separated
2 Tablespoons white vinegar
¼ cup water
4 large cooking apples, peeled
    and finely diced

1 Tablespoon all-purpose flour
4 Tablespoons sugar
¼ teaspoon cinnamon
Butter
Sugar

Cut butter into 2 cups flour and add egg yolks, vinegar, and water. Mix well. Cover and refrigerate overnight or at least 3 hours. Divide dough in half. Roll out one half at a time to a 9X13-inch rectangle. Combine apples, 1 Tablespoon flour, sugar and cinnamon. Divide and arrange mixture on dough. Dot with butter. Roll up dough jelly roll fashion. Arrange rolls on an ungreased cookie sheet. Beat whites of eggs lightly and brush on top of each roll. Sprinkle with sugar. Bake at 375 degrees for 40 minutes.
Serves: 10

Good hot or cold.

DESSERTS

APPLE NUT PUDDING WITH RUM SAUCE

2 cups sugar
½ cup margarine, softened
2 eggs
2 teaspoons vanilla extract
½ teaspoon butter flavoring
2 cups all-purpose flour
2 teaspoons baking soda

2 teaspoons cinnamon
¼ teaspoon salt
2 Tablespoons water
4 apples, peeled, cored and
  chopped (Jonathan or Winesap)
1 cup chopped pecans

Cream sugar, margarine, eggs, vanilla and butter flavoring. Sift together flour, soda, cinnamon and salt. Add to creamed mixture. Add water and beat 2 minutes. Stir in apples and pecans. Pour into a greased 9X13-inch pan and bake at 350 degrees for 1 hour.

Rum Sauce
1 cup water
½ cup margarine
1 cup sugar
2 Tablespoons all-purpose flour

⅛ teaspoon salt
2 teaspoons vanilla extract
¼ teaspoon butter flavoring
2 teaspoons rum flavoring

Bring water and margarine to a boil. Sift dry ingredients together and add to liquid mixture. Add flavorings. Cook, stirring constantly, until sauce bubbles and thickens. Serve hot over pudding.
Serves: 12

Perfect for a cold winter evening.

GRAHAM MARSHMALLOW ROLL

12 whole graham crackers
¾ cup sliced dates
1 cup chopped pecans

14 marshmallows, cut-up
Whipped cream for garnish
Cherries for garnish

Roll crackers with a rolling pin. Chop fruit, nuts and marshmallows. Mix with ⅔ of the crumb mixture. Shape into a roll. Roll in remaining ⅓ cup crumbs. Refrigerate or freeze. To serve, top with whipped cream and cherries.
Serves: 6 to 8

A good holiday dessert.

BREAD PUDDING WITH CARAMEL RUM SAUCE

¼ cup butter
3 eggs
3 cups milk
½ cup sugar
1 Tablespoon vanilla extract

¼ teaspoon salt
½ cup chopped dates or raisins
4 cups cubed day-old French
   bread

Melt butter. Pour half of butter into a 1½-quart casserole dish to coat. Set aside. In a medium bowl, beat eggs . Add milk, sugar, vanilla, salt, dates and remaining butter. Mix well. Stir in bread. Let stand 5 minutes. Pour into casserole and bake in a water bath at 325 degrees for 1½ hours, or until knife inserted in center comes out clean. Best served warm with caramel rum sauce.

Caramel Rum Sauce
1½ cups sugar, divided
⅔ cup evaporated milk
4 Tablespoons butter

1 egg, beaten
1 Tablespoon rum extract

In a heavy skillet cook ½ cup sugar over moderately high heat, stirring constantly, until sugar has melted completely and turned a deep golden color. Pour milk into the side of skillet carefully, as caramel will harden when the milk is added. Cook mixture, stirring, until the caramel is dissolved. Add remaining sugar and butter, stirring very fast. Cook over low heat, stirring until mixture thickens. Cool slightly. Add rum. Serve warm over bread pudding.
Serves: 6 to 8

A real Southern delight!

Two egg whites may be substituted for one whole egg in most recipes, including egg dishes and baked goods, to lower the cholesterol level.

CARAMEL FLAN

2 cups milk
1 cinnamon stick
1 vanilla bean
1 cup sugar
2 ounces cream cheese, softened

14 ounces sweetened condensed
  milk
3 eggs
4 egg yolks

Scald milk with cinnamon stick and vanilla bean. Let cool. Strain and set aside. Caramelize sugar in iron skillet until a rich brown and immediately pour into a 10-inch glass pie plate. Place remaining ingredients in blender, along with cinnamon-vanilla milk. Blend until smooth. Pour over caramelized sugar and bake in a water bath at 350 degrees for 1 hour and 15 minutes or until knife inserted in middle comes out clean. Cool in pan. Run knife around edge and turn out onto a flat rimmed dish. Serves: 8

A tasty Mexican dessert.

DATE ORANGE PUDDING

½ cup butter, softened
1 cup sugar
2 eggs
1 teaspoon baking soda
⅔ cup buttermilk

2 cups all-purpose flour
1 teaspoon salt
1 Tablespoon orange rind
1½ cups chopped dates
1 cup chopped pecans

Cream butter and sugar; then add eggs, one at a time, beating until smooth. Combine soda and buttermilk. Set aside. Mix flour, salt, orange rind, dates and pecans. Add to sugar mixture alternately with the buttermilk. Pour into a greased 9X9-inch pan. Bake at 350 degrees for 40 minutes. Serve with topping.

Topping
¾ cup orange juice
1 Tablespoon grated orange rind

1 cup sugar
Whipped cream for garnish

In small saucepan combine orange juice, rind and sugar. Bring to a boil. Remove from heat and pour over warm cake. Serve with whipped cream.
Serves 10 to 12

Makes a nice autumn dessert.

GRAHAM CRACKER PUDDING WITH
LEMON CARAMEL SAUCE

½ cup butter, softened
1 cup sugar
2 eggs, beaten
2 cups graham cracker crumbs

2 teaspoons baking powder
Pinch of salt
1 cup milk
1 cup chopped pecans

Cream butter and sugar. Add beaten eggs. Mix crumbs, baking powder and salt. Add to creamed mixture alternately with milk. Fold in nuts. Grease and flour a 9X9-inch pan. Pour in batter and bake at 350 degrees for 30 minutes.

Lemon Caramel Sauce
2 cups packed light brown sugar
2 Tablespoons all-purpose flour
1 cup boiling water

2 Tablespoons butter
Juice and grated rind of 1 lemon

In small saucepan combine sugar and flour. Pour boiling water over mixture and stir until creamy. Add butter, lemon juice and rind. Cook 5 minutes. Serve warm.
Serves: 12

Favorite autumn dessert.

SHERRY NUT PUDDING

½ cup butter, softened
1 cup sugar
4 eggs
1 cup chopped pecans

⅓-½ cup sherry
2 cups vanilla wafer crumbs
Whipped cream for garnish
Maraschino cherries for garnish

Cream butter and sugar. Add eggs one at a time, mixing well after each addition. Add pecans and sherry. Place a layer of crumbs in a greased 1½-quart dish. Add layer of sherry-nut mixture. Continue layers, ending with crumbs on top. Refrigerate 48 hours. Serve with whipped cream and cherries.
Serves: 8 to 10

Improves with age.

DESSERTS

HONEY AMARETTO DESSERT

½ gallon vanilla ice cream
½ gallon chocolate ice cream
½ gallon coffee ice cream
8 Tablespoons cinnamon, or less
  to taste

½ cup Amaretto
1 cup honey
Toasted, sliced almonds for
  garnish

Allow vanilla ice cream to soften enough to thoroughly mix in cinnamon. Layer this into a 10-inch tube pan with removable bottom or springform pan. Place in freezer. Soften chocolate ice cream and layer over vanilla. Return to freezer. Repeat with coffee ice cream. Cover and refreeze. When ready to serve, remove from freezer. If using tube pan, place in warm water for a few minutes. Remove stem and unmold. Garnish with almonds. Cut with a knife dipped into warm water. Combine Amaretto and honey. Ladle over slices of ice cream dessert and sprinkle almonds on top
Serves: 12 to 15

Just the right summer dessert to complement any meal.

CHOCOLATE COFFEE FREEZE

1½ cups vanilla wafers, finely
  crushed
¾ cup butter, divided
1 quart coffee ice cream, softened
2 ounces unsweetened chocolate
3 eggs, separated

1¼ cups powdered sugar, sifted
1 cup chopped pecans or walnuts
1 teaspoon vanilla extract
Whipped cream for garnish
Chopped pecans for garnish

Combine cookie crumbs and ¼ cup melted butter. Press into bottom of greased 9-inch springform pan. Spread with ice cream and freeze. Melt remaining ½ cup butter and chocolate together. Gradually stir into well-beaten egg yolks. Add sugar, pecans and vanilla. Cool thoroughly. Beat egg whites until stiff. Beat cooled chocolate mixture until smooth and fold into egg whites. Spread chocolate mixture over ice cream and freeze until firm. Before serving, top with additional whipped cream and pecans.
Serves 8 to 10

Perfect finale to a grand dinner.

Egg whites will not whip if they contain any egg yolk.

FROZEN GRAND MARNIER SOUFFLÉ

6 egg yolks
¾ cup sugar
2¾ cups whipping cream,
  whipped and divided

⅓ cup Grand Marnier
Shaved chocolate
Fresh mint for garnish
Twisted orange slices for garnish

Beat egg yolks and sugar until stiff. Fold in 2 cups whipped cream. Gently fold in Grand Marnier. Pour into small dessert cups and freeze. When ready to serve, top with remaining ¾ cup whipped cream and shaved chocolate. Garnish each plate with a sprig of mint and twisted orange slices.
Serves: 10 to 12

Make a fancy dessert, serve in orange cups.

FROZEN MOCHA TOFFEE DESSERT

1 dozen ladyfingers, split
2 Tablespoons instant coffee
  crystals
1 Tablespoon boiling water
1 quart vanilla ice cream,
  softened

1½ cups (4-6 bars) toffee candy,
  frozen and crushed
½ cup whipping cream
2 Tablespoons white Crème de
  Cacao

Line bottom and sides of 9-inch springform pan with ladyfingers. Dissolve coffee crystals in boiling water. Cool. Combine coffee, ice cream and candy bars, reserving 1½ Tablespoons crushed candy for garnish. Spoon into pan, cover and freeze until firm. Before serving, whip cream with Creme de Cacao until soft peaks form. Spread over frozen ice cream. Remove springform pan rim and garnish with reserved crushed candy.
Serves: 8 to 10

Toffee lover's delight!

In baked goods, substitute unsweetened cocoa powder for unsweetened chocolate squares. Replace a 1 ounce square of chocolate with 1 Tablespoon cocoa and 1 Tablespoon vegetable oil, which is less saturated than cocoa butter, the fat which is in chocolate.

COFFEE PARFAITS

12 coconut macaroons
⅓ cup orange juice or light rum

½ gallon coffee ice cream
Sliced almonds

Crumble macaroons in bowl. Stir in orange juice or rum. Spoon into individual parfait glasses, reserving some crumbs to sprinkle on top. Add ice cream and top with almonds. Cover and freeze several hours or overnight. Take out of freezer 30 minutes before serving. Sprinkle with reserved macaroon crumbs.
Serves: 8 to 10

Light enough to accompany any meal.

FRENCH MINT MOUSSE

Crumb crust
1¼ cups graham cracker crumbs
½ cup cocoa
½ cup sugar

¼ cup butter, melted
Chocolate curls for garnish
Sprigs of mint for garnish

Mix crumbs, cocoa, and sugar. Stir in butter. Place paper liners in muffin tins. Cover bottom of liners with crumb mixture. Spoon mint filling on top of chocolate crumbs and freeze. Take out of freezer 15 minutes before serving. Remove paper liners, garnish with chocolate curls and a sprig of mint.

Mint filling
1 cup butter or margarine,
   softened
3½ cups powdered sugar

4 eggs
1 teaspoon mint flavoring
5 drops green food coloring

Cream butter and sugar. Add eggs, one at a time, beating thoroughly after each addition. Add mint flavoring and food coloring. Mix well.
Serves: 12

A tingling delight.

BRANDY FREEZE

3 cups quality vanilla ice cream
3 Tablespoons brandy
1 Tablespoon Cointreau

1½ Tablespoons Crème de Cacao
  or Crème de Mênthe
Nutmeg for garnish

Mix all ingredients in blender, keeping ice cream as frozen as possible. Put into sherbet or wine glasses. Cover tightly and freeze. Can be made one week prior to serving. Sprinkle with nutmeg before serving.
Serves: 4

So easy and delicious.

CRUNCHY FROZEN DELIGHT WITH FUDGE SAUCE

½ cup butter
2½ cups Rice Krispies
1½ cups flaked coconut

1 cup chopped pecans
¾ cup packed light brown sugar
½ gallon vanilla ice cream

Preheat oven to 300 degrees. In a 9X13-inch pan, melt butter. Add cereal, coconut and pecans. Stir to coat. Toast for 30 minutes, stirring occasionally. Add brown sugar and mix well, reserving half of mixture. Cut ice cream into 1 inch thick slices and place on top of remaining toasted mixture in pan. Sprinkle reserved crumb mixture over top and pat down. Freeze. Cut ice cream into squares and ladle warm sauce over top of each serving.

Fudge Sauce
3 ounces unsweetened chocolate
½ cup butter
14 ounces sweetened condensed
  milk

Pinch of salt
1 teaspoon vanilla extract

In top of double boiler melt chocolate and butter. Blend in milk, salt and vanilla. Stir until smooth and thickened.
Serves: 16 to 18

Palate pleaser for all ages.

KING LEO PEPPERMINT ICE CREAM

**1½ pounds King Leo Peppermint
  sticks**

**1 quart milk
4 cups whipping cream**

Dissolve peppermint sticks in milk in a 2-quart saucepan over low heat; stirring constantly. Cool and add whipping cream. Pour into a 4-quart electric ice cream freezer. Freeze according to manufacturer's instructions.
Serves: 10

Delicious topped with chocolate sauce or served on top of fudge pie.

RASPBERRY SHERBET

**½ cup water
2 cups sugar
Pinch of salt
2 (16 ounce) cans raspberries,
  drain and reserve juice**

**2 cups whipping cream
4 drops red food coloring
3 cups milk**

Bring water to a boil. Add sugar and salt until sugar dissolves completely. Set aside. Using a large strainer, mash raspberries with spoon against side of strainer, mashing out as much pulp as possible. May have to do this several times, but be careful not to get any seeds in juice and pulp. Discard seeds. Add raspberry juice and pulp to sugar water. Add whipping cream, stirring to blend. Add food coloring. Pour mixture into ice cream freezer cannister. Add milk and stir. Freeze according to manufacturer's instructions. Remove sherbet from freezer cannister and pour into a large plastic bowl. Cover and freeze.
Serves: 8 to 10

Take half a watermelon and remove all meat and seeds. Drain well upside down. Freeze until hull is frozen. Pack sherbet into watermelon hull. Cover with aluminum foil. Refreeze. When ready to serve, decorate with chocolate chips to resemble watermelon seeds. Serve immediately.

Freeze whipped cream in dollops on a cookie sheet lined with waxed paper. When frozen, put in plastic bags to be taken out and used as needed for garnishing.

CRANBERRY ICE

1 quart whole cranberries
Juice of 2 lemons
Sugar

6 ounces frozen lemonade,
thawed

Cover cranberries with water and cook until they burst open. Remove from heat and strain well, reserving juice. Press berries gently but do not mash. Add juice of lemons to cranberry juice and measure. Add 1 cup sugar for each cup of cranberry juice. Mix lemonade according to directions. Add 1 cup sugar. Combine with cranberry juice. Freeze in electric freezer. Can be doubled.
Yield: 3 quarts

A delicious sorbet.

FROZEN LADYFINGER DESSERT

2 dozen ladyfingers, split
½ gallon vanilla ice cream,
divided
6 ounces frozen orange juice,
partially thawed
10 ounces frozen strawberries,
partially thawed and drained

8 ounce can crushed pineapple,
well drained
½ cup pecans, lightly toasted
and chopped
½ teaspoon almond extract
Fresh strawberries for garnish

Line bottom of angel food cake pan or a 9-inch springform pan with split ladyfingers. Stand ladyfingers upright around edge with split toward center. Set aside. Cut ice cream in half. Return one half to freezer. Slightly soften ice cream and fold in orange juice. Blend with mixer on low, working quickly. Pour into pan and freeze until firm. Thoroughly mix strawberries with pineapple and spoon on top of orange ice cream layer. Refreeze. Slightly soften remaining ice cream and fold in pecans and almond extract. Pour over fruit layer. Cover and freeze. Remove from freezer 15-20 minutes before serving. Lift stem from pan to remove dessert. Slice into wedges and garnish with strawberries.
Serves: 12 to 16

Simply divine.

APRICOT PARFAITS

½ gallon vanilla ice cream,
  softened
6 ounces frozen lemonade,
  thawed

12 ounces frozen whipped
  topping
½ cup apricot preserves
Fresh mint for garnish

Use mixer to blend ice cream, lemonade, whipped topping and apricot preserves.
Spoon into parfait glasses. Cover and freeze. Before serving garnish with mint. Variation: Combine ice cream, lemonade and whipped topping. Layer in parfait glasses
with preserves and top with chocolate cookie crumbs.
Serves: 8 to 10

Cool and refreshing.

ICE CREAM CAKE WITH CHOCOLATE SAUCE

1 large angel food cake
½ gallon vanilla ice cream,
  softened

2 cups whipping cream
1 Tablespoon Amaretto, optional

Tear angel food cake into ½-inch pieces and mix with ice cream. Whip cream and
add Amaretto. Fold into ice cream mixture. Pour into a 10-inch springform pan and
freeze. When ready to serve, remove rim from pan. Slice and spoon warm chocolate
sauce over each piece.

Chocolate Sauce
1 ounce semi-sweet chocolate
½ cup butter
¾ cup evaporated milk

¾ cup sugar
½ teaspoon vanilla extract

Melt chocolate and butter over low heat. Add milk, sugar and vanilla and bring to a
boil. Stir constantly until just thick enough to coat the back of a spoon.
Serves: 8

Never fails to elicit praise.

GRAPE JUICE SHERBET

1 pint grape juice
15½ ounce can crushed
   pineapple, drained

1 cup sugar
4 egg whites
1 cup whipping cream, whipped

Combine grape juice, pineapple and sugar and mix well. Place in refrigerator freezer while preparing remaining ingredients. Beat egg whites until stiff. Fold in whipped cream. Fold cream mixture into chilled fruit. Blend well. Freeze. Stir several times while freezing. Serve in sherbet dishes with butter cookies.
Serves: 8

BURGUNDY ICE

2¾ cups water
1 cinnamon stick
1½ cups sugar
Pinch of salt
¼ cup applejack liqueur or
   apple brandy

2 cups Burgundy wine
4 Tablespoons fresh strained
   lemon juice
1 Tablespoon grated orange rind

In a saucepan, combine water, cinnamon stick, sugar, salt and applejack liqueur. Bring to a boil. Boil approximately 5 minutes without stirring. Strain into a large bowl and allow to cool. Stir in wine, lemon juice and orange rind. Cool thoroughly. Chill for at least 2 hours, stirring every half hour. Pour into container and place in refrigerator freezer. Serve in stemmed glasses.
Serves: 8

Simple and dazzling.

To make chocolate leaves for decorating fancy desserts, melt 1 ounce semi-sweet baking chocolate in top of double boiler. Pour onto a waxed paper-lined pan, spreading thinly. Chill until almost firm, then cut out leaves with a cookie cutter. Let chocolate stand until firm before removing leaves.

ANISE BUTTER CAKE

2 cups all-purpose flour
1½ teaspoons baking powder
½ teaspoon baking soda
¼ teaspoon salt
1 Tablespoon ground aniseed
1 cup unsalted butter, softened

2 cups sugar
½ teaspoon vanilla extract
2 eggs, room temperature
1 cup sour cream, room
 temperature
¾ cup apricot preserves

Preheat oven to 350 degrees. In a large bowl mix flour, baking powder, soda, salt and aniseed. In a separate bowl beat butter until light and fluffy. Add the sugar and mix well. Add vanilla; add eggs one at a time. After adding last egg, beat for 3 minutes. Stir in sour cream. Fold in dry ingredients just until blended. Spoon batter into a greased and floured 10-inch tube pan. Bake 50-60 minutes. Cool 5 minutes before removing from pan. In saucepan, melt apricot preserves over low heat. Brush over cooled cake.

APPLE CAKE

½ cup vegetable oil
3 eggs
2 cups sugar
2 teaspoons vanilla extract
3 cups all-purpose flour, divided
1 teaspoon baking soda

½ teaspoon salt
1 teaspoon cinnamon
1 cup chopped pecans
3 cups peeled and chopped
 apples

Preheat oven to 350 degrees. Mix oil, eggs, sugar and vanilla. Add 2¾ cups flour, soda, salt and cinnamon. Roll pecans in remaining ¼ cup flour. Fold nuts and apples into batter. Pour into a greased and floured 10-inch tube pan. Bake 1 hour. While cake is still in pan, prick holes all over and slowly pour hot glaze over cake, allowing glaze to soak through. Leave cake in pan 2 hours to cool.

Glaze
1 cup packed dark brown sugar
½ cup margarine

¼ cup milk

Combine ingredients in saucepan. Bring to a boil. Boil for 2-3 minutes.

BLACK RUSSIAN CAKE

1 box chocolate cake mix
½ cup vegetable oil
4 ounce package instant chocolate pudding mix

4 eggs, at room temperature
¾ cup strong coffee
⅜ cup Kahlua
⅜ cup Crème de Cacao

Preheat oven to 350 degrees. Combine cake mix, oil, pudding mix, eggs, coffee, Kahlua and Crème de Cacao in a large mixing bowl. Beat about 4 minutes at medium speed of electric mixer, or until smooth. Pour into a greased and floured 10-inch tube pan. Bake for 45-50 minutes, or until cake tests done. Remove from pan to cool. Punch holes in cake with cake tester or meat fork. Spoon topping slowly over cake, allowing to soak through.

Topping
1 cup sugar
½ cup butter

¼ cup water
1-1½ ounces Kahlua

In a heavy saucepan combine sugar, butter and water. Bring to a boil. Boil for 1 minute. Remove from heat. Stir in Kahlua.

FESTIVE BANANA-SPICE CAKE

½ cup vegetable oil
½ cup butter, softened
1½ cups sugar
4 eggs, well-beaten
3 cups all-purpose flour
2 teaspoons baking soda
2 teaspoons cinnamon
1½ teaspoons cloves

½ teaspoon salt
6 bananas, mashed fine
⅓ cup seedless raisins
½ cup strawberry jam
1½ cups chopped nuts
Whipped cream for garnish
Cherries for garnish

Preheat oven to 250 degrees. Blend oil and butter. Gradually add sugar to butter mixture. Add eggs and mix well. Combine flour, soda, cinnamon, cloves and salt; add to creamed mixture. Stir in mashed bananas, raisins, jam and nuts. Pour into a greased and floured 10-inch tube pan. Bake for 2 hours. Cool in pan 10 minutes before turning onto a wire rack to cool. Garnish each slice with a dollop of whipped cream and a cherry before serving.

A good moist cake.

BLACK WALNUT CAKE

½ cup butter, softened
½ cup vegetable shortening
2 cups sugar
5 eggs, separated
1 cup buttermilk
1 teaspoon baking soda

2 cups all-purpose flour
1 teaspoon vanilla extract
1½ cups chopped black walnuts, divided
1½ cups flaked coconut
½ teaspoon cream of tartar

Preheat oven to 350 degrees. Cream butter and shortening. Gradually add sugar, beat until light and fluffy, and sugar is dissolved. Add egg yolks, beating well. Combine buttermilk and soda; stir until soda is dissolved. Add flour to creamed mixture alternately with buttermilk mixture, beginning and ending with flour. Stir in vanilla, 1 cup nuts, and coconut, mixing well. Beat egg whites with cream of tartar until stiff peaks form. Fold into batter. Pour into 3 greased and floured 9-inch round cake pans. Bake 30 minutes. Cool 10 minutes before removing from pan. Cool completely before icing. Frost cake and sprinkle remaining ½ cup nuts on top.

Cream Cheese Icing
½ cup butter
8 ounces cream cheese, softened

3½ cups powdered sugar
1 teaspoon vanilla extract

Cream butter and cream cheese. Gradually add sugar, beating well. Add vanilla. Stir until well mixed.

POPPY SEED CAKE

1 box yellow cake mix
½ cup sugar
¾ cup margarine, melted
½ cup sour cream

½ cup unsweetened applesauce
¼ cup poppy seeds
1 teaspoon vanilla extract
4 eggs

Preheat oven to 350 degrees. Mix ingredients, adding one egg at a time. Grease a 10-inch tube pan and dust with additional sugar. Pour batter into prepared pan and bake 50 minutes.

A cup of water placed in the oven while baking a cake will help keep the cake moist.

DEVILISH CHOCOLATE CAKE WITH ANGEL FROSTING

6 ounces semi-sweet chocolate
2 egg yolks, well beaten
1 cup buttermilk
½ cup butter
2 cups sifted light brown sugar

3 cups cake flour
1½ teaspoons salt
1½ teaspoons baking soda
1 cup very strong coffee
2 teaspoons vanilla extract

Preheat oven to 325 degrees. Melt chocolate in top of large double boiler. Add small amount of melted chocolate to egg yolks to warm yolks. Quickly stir egg yolks back into chocolate. Stir in buttermilk and cook until thickened; cool. Cream butter and brown sugar. Add to chocolate mixture. Mix flour, salt and soda. Add dry ingredients and coffee alternately to batter. Stir in vanilla. Pour batter into 2 (9-inch) cake pans that have been lined with waxed paper, greased and floured. Bake for 30 minutes until layers test done. Pour glaze over cake layers in pans. Cool completely. Remove one cake layer from pan and spread on half of cream filling. Turn second layer out on top of first layer. Spread with remaining filling. Frost sides and top of cake with frosting. Refrigerate.

Rum Glaze
¼ cup butter
⅔ cup sugar

½ cup rum

Combine in saucepan. Cook over low heat until sugar is dissolved.

Cream Filling
6 ounces semi-sweet chocolate
   chips

¼ cup evaporated milk
1 egg, well-beaten

Mix ingredients in saucepan. Cook over low heat, stirring until smooth. Chill.

Angel Frosting
2 cups whipping cream

1 teaspoon almond extract

Whip cream with almond extract until stiff.

A chocolate lover's delight.

STRAWBERRY CAKE

1 box white cake mix
3 ounces strawberry gelatin
1 cup vegetable oil
4 eggs
½ cup milk

1 cup sliced strawberries or 10 ounces frozen strawberries, thawed
1 cup flaked coconut
1 cup chopped pecans

Preheat oven to 350 degrees. Mix cake mix and gelatin. Add oil, eggs and milk. When thoroughly mixed add strawberries, coconut and pecans. Stir well. Pour into 3 greased and floured 9-inch cake pans. Bake 30-35 minutes. Let cool completely before icing.

Icing

½ cup margarine, softened
3½ cups powdered sugar
1 cup sliced strawberries, or 10 ounces frozen strawberries

1 cup chopped pecans
1 cup flaked coconut

Cream margarine and powdered sugar until smooth. Add strawberries and mix until spreading consistency. Stir in pecans and coconut.

WHITE CITRONLESS FRUIT CAKE

½ pound candied pineapple, chopped
½ pound candied cherries, chopped
1 cup white seedless raisins
1 cup chopped dates
3 cups chopped pecans
1 cup butter, room temperature
5 eggs
¼ cup orange juice

¼ cup milk
¼ cup light corn syrup
1½ cups sugar
2¼ cups cake flour
½ teaspoon salt
1 teaspoon baking powder
¼ teaspoon cinnamon
¼ teaspoon allspice
1 teaspoon vanilla extract

Preheat oven to 250 degrees. Combine fruits and nuts. Cream together butter, eggs, juice, milk, syrup and sugar. Combine dry ingredients and spices. Slowly blend in combined dry ingredients. Fold in fruit and nut mixture. Add vanilla. Line the bottom of a 10-inch tube pan with waxed paper. Pour in batter and bake for 3 hours. Check for doneness with wooden pick.

PUMPKIN SPICE CAKE WITH MAPLE FROSTING

2 cups sifted all-purpose flour
1 Tablespoon baking powder
1 teaspoon salt
1 teaspoon cinnamon
½ teaspoon cloves
½ teaspoon nutmeg
1½ cups sugar

7 eggs, separated
¾ cup canned pumpkin
½ cup vegetable oil
½ cup water
½ teaspoon cream of tartar
1½ cups chopped pecans or
walnuts

Preheat oven to 325 degrees. Sift dry ingredients into mixing bowl; set aside. Separate eggs. Combine yolks with pumpkin, oil and water. Make a well in center of dry ingredients. Add liquid all at one time. Blend until smooth. Beat egg whites until foamy. Add cream of tartar, beat until stiff. Fold into batter. Bake in ungreased 10-inch tube pan for 55 minutes at 325 degrees, and then at 350 degrees for 15 minutes longer. Remove from oven and invert pan on cake rack. Let stand until cool, about 1 hour. Loosen sides and center of cake with a spatula. Frost with Maple Frosting. Cover with nuts.

Maple Frosting
¼ cup butter, softened
3½ cups sugar, divided

⅓ cup sweetened condensed milk
½ teaspoon maple flavoring

Cream butter. Add ½ of the sugar and mix until fluffy. Blend in milk, flavoring and remaining sugar until spreading consistency.

The secret of storing both in-shell nuts and nut meats is to keep them cool. The lower the temperature, the longer nuts keep. In the refrigerator nuts store satisfactorily for up to 9 months; in the freezer at 0 degrees, they remain in good condition for 2 years.

SUGAR PLUM CAKE

2 cups sugar
1 cup vegetable oil
3 eggs
2 cups all-purpose flour
2 teaspoons cinnamon
2 teaspoons nutmeg

2 teaspoons cloves
1 teaspoon baking soda
½ teaspoon salt
1 cup buttermilk
1 cup chopped nuts
1 cup chopped prunes

Preheat oven to 325 degrees. Mix sugar, oil and eggs. Sift flour, spices, soda and salt together. Add this mixture to the sugar, oil and eggs alternately with the buttermilk. Add nuts and prunes; mix well. Pour batter into a well-greased and floured 10-inch tube pan. Bake for 1 hour to 1 hour and 10 minutes. Cool cake slightly. Pierce top of cake with wooden pick. Slowly pour glaze over cake in pan, allowing glaze to be absorbed. Reserve some glaze to brush on top. Let cake cool 15 minutes before removing from pan. Apply remaining glaze to top of cake with pastry brush.

Glaze
½ cup margarine
½ cup buttermilk

1 cup sugar
½ teaspoon baking soda

Combine all ingredients in a saucepan. Bring to a boil and boil for 3 minutes, stirring constantly.

SOUTHERN GINGERBREAD

½ cup sugar
½ cup butter or margarine,
  softened
1 cup sorghum molasses
1½ teaspoons baking soda
1 cup boiling water

2½ cups all-purpose flour
1 teaspoon ginger
1 teaspoon cinnamon
2 eggs
1 teaspoon salt

Preheat oven to 350 degrees. Mix sugar, butter and molasses until well-blended. Combine soda and boiling water. While foaming, add to mixture. Sift together flour, ginger and cinnamon. Add dry ingredients to mixture. Beat eggs well, add salt and combine with other ingredients. Stir until well-mixed. Pour into greased and floured 9X13-inch pan and bake for 25-30 minutes. Good served with a dollop of whipped cream, applesauce, fresh peaches or a warm lemon-orange sauce.

Will stay fresh and moist for several days.

CHOCOLATE CAKE WITH WHITE FROSTING

2 cups sugar
¾ cup vegetable shortening
4 eggs, separated
½ cup cocoa

½ cup boiling water
1 cup buttermilk
2½ cups cake flour
1 teaspoon baking soda

Preheat oven to 350 degrees. Cream sugar and shortening, adding sugar a little at at time. Beat egg yolks until thick and lemon colored. Add to shortening and sugar. Dissolve cocoa in boiling water and add to mixture. Add buttermilk. Sift flour with soda and add a few spoonfuls at a time until well-mixed. Beat egg whites until stiff but not dry. Fold into batter. Pour into 2 greased and floured 9-inch cake pans. Bake for 25-30 minutes. Cool and frost.

White Frosting
2¼ cups sugar
½ cup water
3 Tablespoons light corn syrup

3 egg whites
3 Tablespoons powdered sugar
1 teaspoon vanilla extract

In a heavy saucepan, mix sugar, water and corn syrup and cook to soft ball stage, 238 degrees on a candy thermometer. Beat egg whites until stiff. Add sugar syrup mixture slowly to beaten egg whites and beat thoroughly with mixer until mixture is consistency of whipped cream. Add powdered sugar and vanilla. Continue beating until spreading consistency.

This cake freezes well and will keep several months in the freezer.

To make chocolate curls for dessert garnish, heat one 1-ounce chocolate square uncovered in microwave on medium 15 to 20 seconds until just warm. Using a swivel-bladed vegetable peeler, shave off curls. If chocolate hardens, simply rewarm.

BUTTERSCOTCH CAKE

⅔ cup butterscotch morsels
¼ cup boiling water
½ cup vegetable shortening
1 cup sugar
3 eggs

2¼ cups sifted all-purpose flour
1 teaspoon salt
1 teaspoon baking soda
½ teaspoon baking powder
1 cup buttermilk

Preheat oven to 375 degrees. Combine butterscotch morsels and water. Stir until morsels are melted; cool. Cream shortening and sugar until fluffy. Add eggs one at a time, beating well after each addition. Stir in butterscotch mixture. Sift flour, salt, soda and baking powder together. Add to creamed mixture alternately with butter-milk, blending at low speed of mixer. Pour batter into 2 greased and floured 9-inch cake pans. Bake for 25-30 minutes. Cool. Spread frosting between layers; then frost top and sides of cake.

Frosting
¾ cup sugar
1½ Tablespoons cornstarch
1 cup evaporated milk
½ cup butterscotch morsels

3 Tablespoons butter
1½ cups flaked coconut, optional
¾ cup chopped nuts, optional

In saucepan combine sugar and cornstarch; add milk. Cook, stirring constantly, until thick and boiling. Remove from heat. Add butterscotch morsels and butter; stir until melted. Add coconut and nuts, if desired.

EASY CARAMEL ICING

¾ cup butter
1½ cups packed brown sugar
¼ cup + 2 Tablespoons milk

¾ teaspoon salt
1½ teaspoons vanilla extract
3 cups powdered sugar

Melt butter and brown sugar in saucepan over low heat, stirring constantly. Add milk and stir until mixture comes to a boil. Remove from heat and cool. Add salt, vanilla, and powdered sugar. Beat with electric mixer until smooth and of spreadable consistency.

PUMPKIN CAKE

2 cups sugar
1¼ cups vegetable oil
4 eggs, beaten
2 cups sifted self-rising flour
2 teaspoons cinnamon

1 teaspoon baking soda
2 cups fresh cooked pumpkin or
  16 ounces canned pumpkin
Chopped nuts

Preheat oven to 350 degrees. Mix sugar, oil, eggs, flour, cinnamon, soda and pumpkin. Beat until thoroughly blended. Pour into a greased and floured 10-inch tube pan. Bake 1 hour and 15 minutes. Cool. Frost and sprinkle with nuts.

Frosting
8 ounces cream cheese, softened
½ cup margarine, softened
2 Tablespoons milk

1 teaspoon vanilla extract
3½ cups powdered sugar

Mix all ingredients and cream well.

This cake is better baked a day or two ahead of serving time.

PARKER BANANA NUT COFFEE CAKE

2½ cups sugar
1¾ cups butter
3 eggs
3 cups sifted all-purpose flour
Pinch of salt
6 Tablespoons buttermilk

¾ teaspoon baking soda
1 cup mashed ripe bananas
2 cups chopped pecans
2 teaspoons vanilla extract
2 teaspoons banana flavoring

Preheat oven to 350 degrees. Cream butter and sugar well. Add eggs one at a time. Add salt to flour. Add soda to buttermilk. Add flour and buttermilk alternately to creamed mixture, starting and finishing with flour. Fold in bananas, nuts and flavorings. Pour into greased and floured 10-inch tube pan and bake for 50-60 minutes, or until cake tests done. A 9X13-inch pan may be used. Optional: Frost with caramel icing.

One cup of shelled pecans equals about 3 ½ ounces.

OVERNIGHT COFFEE CAKE

¾ cup butter, softened
1 cup sugar
2 eggs
1 cup sour cream
2 cups all-purpose flour
1 teaspoon baking powder

1 teaspoon baking soda
½ teaspoon salt
¾ cup packed light brown sugar
¾ cup chopped walnuts
1 teaspoon cinnamon

Combine butter and sugar. Cream until light and fluffy. Add eggs and sour cream, mixing well. Combine flour, baking powder, soda and salt. Add to batter and mix well. Pour batter into a greased and floured 9X13-inch pan. Combine brown sugar, nuts and cinnamon. Sprinkle evenly over batter. Cover and refrigerate overnight. Bake uncovered at 350 degrees for 35-40 minutes or until cake tests done.

Impress your house guests with this delicious cake.

SOUR CREAM COFFEE CAKE

1 cup margarine, softened
2 cups sugar
2 eggs
1 cup sour cream
½ teaspoon vanilla extract
2 cups cake flour

1 teaspoon baking powder
¼ teaspoon salt
½ cup chopped nuts
¼ teaspoon cinnamon
3 Tablespoons dark brown sugar
Powdered sugar

Preheat oven to 350 degrees. Cream margarine, sugar and eggs. Fold in sour cream and vanilla. Sift dry ingredients; add to sour cream mixture . Mix together nuts, cinnamon and brown sugar for topping. Spoon half the batter into a greased and floured 10-inch tube pan. Sprinkle half the topping mix on the batter. Repeat layers. Bake for 55-60 minutes. Cool almost completely before removing from pan. Sift powdered sugar over cake. Variation: For a blueberry coffee cake, fold 1½-2 cups fresh blueberries into batter.

Best made the day before serving.

Plain low-fat yogurt (140 calories) may be substituted for sour cream (493 calories per cup) cup for cup in baked products without noticing much difference in taste.

CHOCOLATE POUND CAKE WITH CHOCOLATE ICING

3 cups sugar
½ cup vegetable shortening
1 cup margarine, softened
6 eggs, room temperature
3 cups all-purpose flour

½ teaspoon baking powder
½ teaspoon salt
½ cup cocoa
1¼ cups milk, room temperature
2 teaspoons vanilla extract

Preheat oven to 325 degrees. Cream sugar, shortening and margarine. Add eggs, one at a time, beating well after each addition. Sift together flour, baking powder, salt and cocoa. Add dry ingredients alternately with milk and vanilla to the creamed mixture. Pour into a greased 10-inch tube pan. Bake for 1½ hours. Cool 10 minutes and remove from pan. Frost with chocolate icing.

Chocolate Icing
2 cups sugar
¼ cup cocoa
¼ teaspoon salt

⅔ cup milk
½ cup vegetable oil
1 Tablespoon vanilla extract

In a saucepan combine cocoa and sugar. Add salt, milk and oil and bring to a full boil. Boil rapidly for 2 minutes, stirring constantly. Remove from heat and add vanilla. Beat until creamy.

A very rich chocolate cake.

DIVINITY ICING

2 cups sugar
¾ cup water
Pinch of salt

4 egg whites
5 large marshmallows

In a large saucepan dissolve sugar and salt in water. Heat to boiling. Boil until mixture spins a thread. Beat egg whites until stiff. Pour cooked syrup over egg whites, beating until thick. Add marshmallows. Excellent icing for coconut, banana or chocolate cakes.

BUTTERMILK POUND CAKE

5 eggs, separated
1 cup butter
3 cups sugar
½ teaspoon baking soda

1 cup buttermilk, divided
3 cups sifted all-purpose flour
1 teaspoon vanilla extract

Preheat oven to 325 degrees. Beat egg whites until stiff but not dry; set aside. Cream butter and sugar thoroughly. Add egg yolks one at a time, beating well after each addition. Add soda to ½ cup buttermilk; mix well and add to butter mixture. Add flour and remaining buttermilk alternately. Add vanilla. Fold in beaten egg whites. Pour into greased and floured 10-inch tube pan. Bake in center of oven for 1 hour and 15 minutes. Immediately turn cake out of pan and quickly invert right side up on another plate to cool. This cake has a nice crust on top.

COCONUT SOUR CREAM POUND CAKE

1½ cups margarine
3 cups sugar
6 eggs
3 cups all-purpose flour
1 cup sour cream
¼ teaspoon baking soda

¼ teaspoon salt
2 teaspoons vanilla extract
6 ounces frozen coconut, thawed
1 teaspoon coconut flavoring,
  optional

Preheat oven to 500 degrees. Cream margarine and sugar. Beat thoroughly 6 eggs; add eggs and flour alternately to creamed mixture. Add sour cream, soda, salt, vanilla and flavoring, mixing well. Fold in coconut. Pour into greased and floured 10-inch tube pan. Place cake in oven and immediately turn temperature down to 325 degrees. Do not open door before 1 hour and 10 minutes. When cake tests done, let cool in pan 20-30 minutes. Remove from pan. Slowly spoon glaze over cake.

Glaze
½ cup sugar
½ cup water

1 teaspoon coconut flavoring

In a small saucepan bring all ingredients to a boil.

Absolutely wonderful!

MILKY WAY POUND CAKE

6 (2.15 ounce) Milky Way
  candy bars
1 cup margarine, divided
2 cups sugar
4 eggs

2½ cups sifted all-purpose flour
½ teaspoon baking soda
1¼ cups buttermilk
1 cup chopped pecans

Preheat oven to 325 degrees. Melt candy bars with ½ cup margarine in microwave or in top of double boiler. Set aside. In a large bowl cream sugar and ½ cup margarine. Add eggs one at a time to creamed mixture, beating well after each addition. Sift flour and soda together; add alternately with buttermilk to batter. Add melted candy bars and pecans. Pour into greased and floured 10-inch tube pan. Bake for 1 hour and 10 minutes. Cool 10 minutes and remove from pan. When completely cool, frost with Milky Way Icing.

Milky Way Icing

3 (2.15 ounce) Milky Way
  candy bars
½ cup margarine

2 cups powdered sugar
1-2 Tablespoons milk

Melt candy bars and margarine in microwave or in top of double boiler over low heat. Remove from heat and beat in sugar. Thin with milk until spreading consistency.

SOUR CREAM POUND CAKE

1 cup butter, room temperature
3 cups sugar
6 eggs
½ teaspoon almond extract

1 teaspoon vanilla extract
3 cups sifted cake flour
¼ teaspoon baking soda
1 cup sour cream

Preheat oven to 350 degrees. Cream butter and sugar. Add eggs one at a time, beating after each addition. Add vanilla and almond extracts. Sift flour and soda together. Add alternately with sour cream. Pour into greased and floured 10-inch tube pan. Bake 1 hour and 15 minutes. Cool 10 minutes in pan and remove.

SOUR CREAM PEACH CAKE

3 cups sifted cake flour
2½ teaspoons baking powder
1 teaspoon salt
¾ cup margarine, softened
1½ cups sugar

4 eggs
1 teaspoon vanilla extract
1 cup milk
1 cup sour cream

Preheat oven to 350 degrees. Grease and flour 2 (9-inch) cake pans. Sift flour, baking powder and salt together and set aside. At high speed beat together margarine, sugar, eggs and vanilla for 5 minutes. At low speed alternately add flour mixture and milk. Pour into prepared pans and bake 30-35 minutes. Surface should spring back when pressed with finger. Cool in pans 10 minutes before turning out onto wire racks to cool. When cake layers are completely cooled, split each layer horizontally to make four thin layers. Spoon ⅓ cup sour cream over 1 split cake layer. Spread ⅓ of peach filling over sour cream. Add another split cake layer and repeat procedure until 3 split cake layers have been assembled. Place remaining split cake layer on top. Frost cake with whipped cream frosting and garnish with fresh peach slices. Store in refrigerator.

Peach Filling
1½ cups sugar
4 Tablespoons cornstarch
4 cups peeled and chopped fresh
  peaches

½ cup water

Combine sugar and cornstarch in saucepan. Add peaches and water. Cook over medium heat stirring constantly until thickened. Cool completely.

Whipped Cream Frosting
2 cups whipping cream

2-3 Tablespoons powdered sugar

Beat whipping cream with powdered sugar until stiff peaks form.

Best made several hours before serving.

CARAMEL POUND CAKE

2⅓ cups packed light brown
  sugar
1 cup sugar
1 cup margarine
½ cup vegetable shortening
5 eggs

1 teaspoon vanilla extract
1 teaspoon vanilla, butter and nut
  flavoring
3 cups sifted all-purpose flour
½ teaspoon baking powder
1 cup milk

Preheat oven to 325 degrees. Cream both sugars, margarine, and shortening. Add eggs one at a time, mixing well after each addition. Add flavorings. Add flour and baking powder alternately with milk. Blend well. Pour into greased and floured 10-inch tube pan. Bake for 1 hour and 10 minutes or until cake tests done. Cool and frost with caramel frosting or serve with praline sauce.

Caramel Frosting

1 cup packed light brown sugar
1 cup sugar
½ cup margarine
½ cup evaporated milk

1 teaspoon vanilla extract
1 teaspoon vanilla, butter and nut
  flavoring
1 cup chopped pecans

Mix sugars, margarine and milk together. Cook over medium heat, stirring constantly, until mixture comes to a boil. Boil for 1 minute. Remove from heat. Add flavorings. Beat until spreading consistency. Add nuts.

Praline Sauce

1 cup light corn syrup
½ cup sugar
⅓ cup butter

1 egg, beaten
1 Tablespoon vanilla extract
1 cup chopped pecans

Combine syrup, sugar, butter and egg in a heavy saucepan. Bring to a boil over medium heat, stirring constantly. Boil 2 minutes without stirring. Remove from heat and add vanilla and pecans.
Yield: 2 cups

PEACH POUND CAKE

1 cup butter, softened
3 cups sugar
6 eggs, room temperature
1 teaspoon vanilla extract
½ teaspoon almond extract

3 cups all-purpose flour
¼ teaspoon baking soda
½ teaspoon salt
½ cup sour cream
2 cups peeled, chopped peaches

Preheat oven to 350 degrees. In large mixing bowl cream butter and sugar until light and fluffy. Add eggs one at a time, beating well after each addition. Stir in vanilla and almond extracts. In a small bowl combine flour, soda and salt; add to creamed mixture. Fold in sour cream and peaches. Pour into a greased and floured 10-inch tube pan. Bake for 1 hour and 15 minutes or until wooden pick inserted in center comes out clean. Cool for 10 minutes and remove from pan.

Sinful with homemade ice cream.

CARAMEL ICING

3 cups sugar, divided
⅔ cup evaporated milk

½ cup margarine
1 teaspoon vanilla extract

In a deep saucepan mix 2½ cups sugar with milk and bring to a boil over medium heat. While this is heating, measure ½ cup sugar and put into a small iron skillet. Over medium heat allow sugar to melt, no need to stir. When sugar has dissolved completely, continue cooking until golden brown in color. When caramelized sugar is the desired color, pour into the boiling sugar and milk mixture in saucepan. Stirring constantly bring to a full rolling boil, reduce heat slightly and cook 1 minute. Remove from heat. Add margarine and vanilla. Beat with an electric mixer until cool enough to spread. Frosting for a 2 layer 8-inch cake or a 10-inch tube cake.

A caramel icing easy enough for a beginning cook!

All-purpose flour may be substituted for cake flour. If the recipe calls for one cup of cake flour, use one cup less two Tablespoons of all-purpose flour. The cake flour is made from softer wheats, producing a finer textured cake.

PINEAPPLE REFRIGERATOR CAKE

2 Tablespoons unflavored gelatin
½ cup cold water
3 eggs, separated
1 cup sugar
2 cups milk
9 ounce can crushed pineapple, drained

2 cups whipping cream, whipped
½ cup chopped walnuts
10-inch angel food cake
Pineapple slices for garnish
Maraschino cherries for garnish
Whipped cream for garnish

Soften gelatin in cold water. Combine well-beaten egg yolks, sugar and milk in top of double boiler; mix well. Cook over hot, not boiling, water, stirring constantly until mixture coats spoon. Add softened gelatin and stir until dissolved. Cool. Add drained pineapple. Fold in whipped cream, stiffly-beaten egg whites and walnuts. Remove crust from angel food cake, break cake into large pieces. Line bottom of greased 10-inch tube pan with half the pieces. Pour half the gelatin mixture over cake. Repeat layers. Chill. When set, unmold and garnish with pineapple and cherries. Additional whipped cream may be used to fill center of cake or to frost cake.

Served icy cold, this rich dessert is nice for an Easter brunch or a hot summer day!

DELUXE CHEESECAKE

1¼ cups graham cracker crumbs
2 Tablespoons sugar
4 Tablespoons butter, melted
24 ounces cream cheese, softened
1½ cups sugar
2 cups sour cream

14 ounces sweetened condensed milk
2 Tablespoons lemon juice
2 teaspoons vanilla extract
8 eggs

Preheat oven to 325 degrees. Mix graham cracker crumbs with sugar and butter. Press on bottom and partially up sides of a 10-inch springform pan. Beat cream cheese until smooth. Add sugar, sour cream, milk, lemon juice and vanilla. Add eggs one at a time until thoroughly mixed. Bake for 1 hour and 10 minutes. Turn oven off and leave cheesecake in oven for 1 hour. Remove cheesecake from oven and cool to room temperature. When cooled remove cheesecake from pan and refrigerate. Top with fresh fruits, such as strawberries, kiwi or pineapple.

FANTASTIC CHEESECAKE

2 cups vanilla wafer crumbs   ¼ cup sugar
1 teaspoon cinnamon   ½ cup butter, melted
1 teaspoon ginger

Combine wafer crumbs, cinnamon, ginger and sugar. Stir in melted butter. Press in bottom and about 1½ inches up the sides of a 9-inch springform pan.

Filling
4 eggs   1 teaspoon lemon juice
1 cup sugar   32 ounces cream cheese, softened
⅛ teaspoon salt

Preheat oven to 375 degrees. Beat eggs. Add sugar and beat until thick. Add salt, lemon juice and cream cheese. Continue to beat until smooth. Pour over prepared crust and bake 35-45 minutes.

Topping
2 cups sour cream   4 Tablespoons sugar
1 teaspoon vanilla extract

Combine all ingredients. Pour over cheesecake and return to oven to bake at 475 degrees for 10-15 minutes. Cool. Refrigerate overnight. Serve cold topped with sliced kiwi, strawberries and blueberries.

Very colorful and attractive.

To test for doneness when baking a cheesecake, go by the cake's appearance. The sides will be raised and show a hint of turning brown. The center may be a little soft at this stage, but will become firm as the cake cools. Allow the cake to cool in the turned-off oven, door open, for about an hour; then refrigerate.

TRIPLE CHOCOLATE CHEESECAKE

2 cups chocolate wafer cookie
  crumbs
½ cup butter
1 cup sugar + 2 tablespoons,
  divided
40 ounces cream cheese, divided
3 eggs
1 teaspoon vanilla extract,
  divided

2 ounces semi-sweet chocolate,
  melted
1⅓ cups sour cream, divided
⅓ cup + 2 Tablespoons packed
  dark brown sugar
1 Tablespoon all-purpose flour
¼ cup chopped pecans
¼ teaspoon almond extract

Blend cookie crumbs, butter and ½ cup sugar. Press into bottom and up the sides of a 9-inch springform pan. Set aside. For layer 1: Combine 16 ounces cream cheese and ⅓ cup sugar. Beat until fluffy. Add 1 egg and ¼ teaspoon vanilla. Blend well. Stir in melted chocolate and ⅓ cup sour cream. Spoon over chocolate crust. For layer 2: Combine 16 ounces cream cheese, brown sugar and flour. Beat until fluffy. Add 1 egg and ½ teaspoon vanilla. Blend well. Stir in pecans. Spoon gently over chocolate layer. For layer 3: Combine 8 ounces cream cheese with ¼ cup sugar and beat until fluffy. Add 1 egg and blend well. Stir in 1 cup sour cream, ¼ teaspoon vanilla and almond extract. Spoon gently over pecan layer. Bake at 325 degrees for 1 hour. Turn off oven and leave cheesecake in oven for 15 minutes with the door closed. Open oven and leave cheesecake in oven an additional 30 minutes. Cool. Chill 8 hours. Remove from pan. Spread warm chocolate glaze over cheesecake. Let glaze run down the sides about every 1½ inches. Garnish with chocolate leaves.

Glaze

6 ounces semi-sweet chocolate
¼ cup butter
¾ cup sifted powdered sugar

2 Tablespoons water
1 teaspoon vanilla extract

Combine chocolate and butter in top of a double boiler. Cook until melted. Remove from heat and stir in remaining ingredients. Stir until smooth.

Very good and different.

PRALINE CHEESECAKE

1¼ cups graham cracker crumbs
¼ cup sugar

¼ cup chopped pecans, toasted
¼ cup butter, melted

Combine all ingredients, mixing well. Press mixture on bottom and 1½ inches up sides of 9-inch springform pan. Bake at 350 degrees for 5 minutes.

Filling
24 ounces cream cheese, softened
1 cup packed light brown sugar
⅔ cup evaporated milk
2 Tablespoons all-purpose flour

3 eggs
1½ teaspoons vanilla extract
1 cup pecan halves, toasted

Beat cream cheese at medium speed of mixer until light and fluffy. Gradually add sugar, milk and flour; mix well. Add eggs, one at a time, beating well after each addition. Stir in vanilla. Pour into prepared crust. Bake at 350 degrees for 55-60 minutes. Let cool in pan 30 minutes. Loosen and remove sides of pan. Cool completely. Cover loosely and refrigerate overnight. Serve with warm glaze and pecan halves arranged on top.

Glaze
1 cup dark corn syrup
2 Tablespoons packed light brown sugar

1 Tablespoon cornstarch
1 teaspoon vanilla extract

Combine first 3 ingredients in a small saucepan; bring to a boil. Reduce heat and simmer 1-2 minutes, stirring constantly. Remove from heat; cool slightly and stir in vanilla. Serve warm over cheesecake. Glaze can be made ahead and reheated.

Everyone will rave over this cheesecake.

One pound unshelled pecans equals about 4½ cups shelled.

APPLE PIE

2 unbaked 10-inch pie crusts	1 teaspoon cinnamon
5 medium apples, peeled, cored and sliced	1 teaspoon allspice
	1 teaspoon cloves
3 Tablespoons all-purpose flour	2 eggs, beaten
1½ cups sugar	⅔ cup butter

Fill pastry-lined 10-inch pie plate with apples. Mix flour, sugar and spices together. Add beaten eggs and mix well. Spread over apples. Melt butter and drizzle over filling. Cut second pie crust into strips and make a lattice top for pie. Bake at 300 degrees for 50 minutes. Increase temperature to 400 degrees and continue to bake for 10 minutes or until crust is golden brown.
Serves: 8

Delicious served warm with vanilla ice cream.

APPLE PECAN CRUMB TOP PIE

1 unbaked 10-inch pie crust	2 teaspoons all-purpose flour
4-5 medium apples	½ teaspoon cinnamon
¼ cup chopped pecans	¼ teaspoon nutmeg
1 cup sugar	2 Tablespoons butter

Peel, core and slice apples. Set aside. Sprinkle pecans on bottom of unbaked pie crust. Mix sugar, flour and spices together. Toss with apple slices. Pour apple mixture into pie crust. Dot with butter and top with crumb topping. Bake at 425 degrees for 10 minutes. Reduce oven temperature to 350 degrees and bake for 20-25 minutes.

Crumb Topping

½ cup packed light brown sugar	¼ teaspoon cinnamon
¼ cup butter, softened	¼ cup chopped pecans
⅓ cup sifted all-purpose flour	

Mix brown sugar, butter, flour and cinnamon with fork until lumps are size of peas. Stir in pecans.
Serves: 8

One pound of apples will yield 3 cups diced or 2¾ cups sliced apples.

CRÈME LIQUEUR PIE

1¼ cups finely crushed chocolate
   wafers
¼ cup butter, melted
¾ cup milk
20 large marshmallows
1 cup whipping cream, whipped

2 Tablespoons Crème de Menthe
3 Tablespoons white Crème de
   Cacao
Whipped cream for garnish
Shaved chocolate for garnish

Mix chocolate wafer crumbs and melted butter. Press into a 9-inch pie pan. Chill. In a saucepan heat milk. Add marshmallows, stirring until melted. Place in refrigerator and let cool completely. Combine whipped cream with liqueurs and fold into cooled marshmallow mixture. Pour into pie crust and chill. Serve with whipped cream and chocolate shavings.
Serves: 8

LEXIE'S INKBERRY TARTS

2½ cups sifted all-purpose flour
¼ cup vegetable shortening

½ teaspoon salt
Ice water

Mix flour, shortening and salt using spoon to work together. Add ice water as needed, until mixture cleans bowl. Place dough on floured surface; do not knead. Roll out and cut into 5-inch circles. Place pastry circles on back of muffin tins to shape. Cut off excess dough. Prick pastry with fork and bake on back of muffin tins at 325 degrees until golden brown.

Filling
3 (16 ounce) cans blueberries in
   heavy syrup
3 Tablespoons all-purpose flour

¼ cup sugar
1 teaspoon margarine
1 teaspoon vanilla extract

Drain blueberries, reserving juice and setting aside ¼ cup. In a large saucepan heat remaining juice until hot, but do not boil. Mix flour and sugar in small bowl. Add reserved ¼ cup of juice and mix well. Add sugar mixture slowly to hot juice in saucepan. Add margarine and vanilla to hot mixture. Let mixture cool. Fold in blueberries. Fill tart shells with filling and top with vanilla ice cream.
Serves: 12 to 14

LEMON CHESS PIE

1 unbaked 9-inch deep-dish
  pie crust
2 cups sugar
1 Tablespoon all-purpose flour
1 Tablespoon cornmeal

2 Tablespoons grated lemon rind
4 eggs
¼ cup butter, melted
¼ cup evaporated milk
¼ cup fresh lemon juice

Combine sugar, flour, cornmeal and grated lemon rind. Toss lightly with a fork. Beat eggs and add butter, milk and lemon juice. Add to sugar mixture and mix well. Pour into pie crust and bake at 350 degrees for 35-40 minutes.
Serves: 8

This pie is best served at room temperature.

LEMON SOUR CREAM PIE

1 baked 9-inch pie crust
1 cup sugar
5 Tablespoons cornstarch
Dash of salt
1 cup milk

3 egg yolks, slightly beaten
4 Tablespoons butter
1 teaspoon grated lemon rind
¼ cup lemon juice
½ cup sour cream

Combine sugar, cornstarch and salt in top of double boiler. Gradually stir in milk. Cook over medium heat, stirring constantly, until mixture thickens (approximately 10 minutes). Add small amount of hot mixture to egg yolks, blending well. Stir egg yolks into custard. Cook, stirring 2 minutes longer or until very thick. Add butter, lemon juice and grated lemon rind. Remove from heat, cover and cool. Fold in sour cream. Pour into pie crust. Spread meringue over filling. Bake at 350 degrees for 12 minutes or until golden brown. Chill before serving.

Meringue
3 egg whites
¼ teaspoon cream of tartar

4 Tablespoons sugar

Beat egg whites until stiff peaks form. Gradually add cream of tartar and sugar.
Serves: 8

RAISIN PIE

1 baked 9-inch pie crust
1 cup sugar
½ cup water
1 cup seedless raisins

3 Tablespoons cornstarch
½ cup whipping cream
3 egg yolks, beaten
⅛ teaspoon salt

Cook sugar, water and raisins until raisins are tender. Mix cornstarch with whipping cream. Add beaten egg yolks and salt. Add cream mixture to raisin mixture and cook until thickened. Pour into pie crust. Spread meringue on top of pie, sealing around crust. Bake at 400 degrees until golden brown.

Meringue
3 egg whites
¼ teaspoon cream of tartar

⅓ cup sugar

Beat egg whites and cream of tartar until foamy. Gradually add sugar and beat to form stiff peaks.
Serves: 6 to 8

PEACH COBBLER

2 unbaked 9-inch pie crusts
8 medium-large peaches, peeled and sliced (reserve peelings and pits)
Juice of 1 lemon

1 cup powdered sugar
1 cup water
1 cup sugar
Butter
Sugar

Place peaches in 9X13-inch baking dish and cover with lemon juice to prevent turning brown. Sprinkle with powdered sugar. In a saucepan combine peelings, pits, water and sugar. Boil approximately 15 minutes to make a syrup. Strain and pour syrup over peaches. Use desired amount of crust to form lattice design on top. Take remaining crust and cut into small pieces. Push pastry pieces into cobbler. Dot with butter and sprinkle with sugar. Bake at 375 degrees for 20-30 minutes or until crust is brown. Serve with vanilla ice cream if desired.
Serves: 6 to 8

Peach cobbler at its best!

PINEAPPLE AND CREAM PIE

1 unbaked 9-inch pie crust
1 cup sugar, divided
1 Tablespoon cornstarch
8 ounce can crushed pineapple, undrained
8 ounces cream cheese, softened
½ teaspoon salt
2 eggs
½ cup milk
½ teaspoon vanilla extract
¼ cup chopped pecans

Blend ½ cup sugar with cornstarch and add crushed pineapple. Cook over medium heat, stirring constantly, until mixture is thick and clear. Set aside to cool. Blend cream cheese with remaining sugar and salt. Add eggs, one at a time, stirring well after each addition. Blend in milk and vanilla. Spread cooled pineapple mixture into pie crust. Pour in cream cheese mixture and sprinkle top with pecans. Bake at 425 degrees for 10 minutes. Reduce oven temperature to 325 degrees and continue baking for 50 minutes. Cool before serving.
Serves: 8

PUMPKIN TARTS

24 baked tart shells
3½ cups sugar, divided
1 teaspoon salt
4 cups milk
4 eggs
8 Tablespoons all-purpose flour
16 ounce can pumpkin
1 cup packed dark brown sugar
1 teaspoon cinnamon
½ teaspoon ginger
¾ teaspoon cloves
1 teaspoon allspice
Whipped cream for garnish

Scald 1½ cups sugar, salt and milk. In a separate bowl beat eggs. Sift 2 cups sugar with flour and add to eggs. Combine this mixture with scalded milk mixture. In a separate pan cook pumpkin, brown sugar and spices until most of moisture is gone. Mix all ingredients together and cook, stirring until thickened, approximately 40-50 minutes. Refrigerate until ready to serve. Fill tart shells and serve with dollop of whipped cream.
Serves: 24

FRENCH CREAM PIE

1 unbaked 9-inch pie crust
⅓ cup butter or margarine
2¼ cups sugar
3 eggs
⅛ teaspoon salt
⅔ cup evaporated milk
⅓ cup whipping cream

¼ teaspoon almond extract
½ teaspoon vanilla extract
Sweetened whipped cream for garnish
Toasted slivered almonds for garnish

Melt butter and add next 7 ingredients, beating well after each addition. Continue beating for 3 minutes. Pour into pie crust and bake at 350 degrees for 40-50 minutes. Let stand for 1 hour before serving. Garnish with whipped cream and toasted almonds.
Serves: 8

CHOCOLATE ANGEL STRATA PIE

1 baked 9-inch pie crust
2 eggs, separated
½ teaspoon vinegar
¼ teaspoon salt
¾ cup sugar, divided

¼ cup water
1 cup semi-sweet chocolate chips, melted
1 cup whipping cream

Beat egg whites with vinegar and salt. Gradually add ½ cup sugar until meringue stands in glossy peaks. Spread on bottom and sides of pie crust. Bake at 325 degrees for 15-18 minutes, or until lightly browned. Add slightly beaten egg yolks and ¼ cup water to melted chocolate chips. Spread 3 Tablespoons chocolate mixture over cooled meringue. Whip ¼ cup sugar and whipping cream until stiff. Spread ½ cream mixture over chocolate layer. Combine remaining whipped cream with chocolate mixture and spread on top. Chill at least 4 hours before serving.
Serves: 8

PEAR PIE

1 unbaked 9-inch pie crust
2 (16 ounce) cans pears, drained
  and sliced
1 cup sugar
½ cup butter or margarine,
  melted

⅓ cup all-purpose flour
1 egg
½ Tablespoon grated lemon rind
1 Tablespoon lemon juice
½ teaspoon ginger
Whipped cream for garnish

Arrange pears in a circle in pie crust. Mix remaining ingredients and pour over pears. Bake at 325 degrees for 50-60 minutes or until set. Cool and serve with a dollop of whipped cream.
Serves: 8

CREAMY COCONUT PIE

1 baked 9-inch pie crust
¾ cup sugar
⅓ cup all-purpose flour
¼ teaspoon salt
2 cups milk

3 egg yolks, slightly beaten
2 Tablespoons margarine
1¼ cups flaked coconut, divided
1 teaspoon vanilla extract

In saucepan combine sugar, flour and salt. Gradually stir in milk. Cook over medium heat until mixture begins to boil, stirring constantly. Continue cooking 2 more minutes. Add small amount of hot mixture to beaten egg yolks and blend well. Pour egg yolk mixture back into hot mixture in saucepan. Continue to cook 2 more minutes. Remove from heat and add margarine, 1 cup coconut and vanilla. Cool. Pour into baked pie crust. Spread meringue over pie and sprinkle with ¼ cup coconut. Bake at 350 degrees for 10 minutes or until meringue is golden brown.

Meringue
3 egg whites
¼ cup sugar

½ teaspoon vanilla extract

Beat egg whites until foamy. Gradually add sugar until mixture begins to form stiff peaks. Beat in vanilla.
Serves: 8

SOUTHERN CARAMEL PIE

1 baked 9-inch pie crust
3 egg yolks, beaten
1½ cups sugar, divided
3 rounded Tablespoons all-
    purpose flour

1½ cups milk
2 Tablespoons butter
1 teaspoon vanilla extract

In top of a double boiler over hot water combine beaten egg yolks, ¾ cup sugar, flour and milk. Cook until thickened, approximately 5-7 minutes. In a cast iron skillet caramelize remaining ¾ cup sugar. In a thin stream slowly pour caramelized sugar into custard, stirring with a wire whisk. Whisk until well blended. Remove from heat, add butter and vanilla. Pour into pie crust. Spread meringue over filling, sealing to edge of crust. Bake at 350 degrees for 10 minutes, or until golden brown.

Meringue
3 egg whites, room temperature
½ teaspoon cream of tartar

6 Tablespoons sugar

Beat egg whites until foamy. Gradually add cream of tartar and sugar, beating until stiff peaks form.
Serves: 8

PEANUT BUTTER PIE

1 cup graham cracker crumbs
1 Tablespoon sugar
6 Tablespoons margarine, melted
3 ounces cream cheese, softened
⅓ cup milk
½ cup peanut butter

1 teaspoon vanilla extract
⅔ cup powdered sugar
12 ounces frozen whipped
    topping, thawed
8 ounces frozen whipped
    topping, thawed

Mix crumbs, sugar and margarine. Press mixture on sides and bottom of a 9-inch pie plate. Combine cream cheese, milk, peanut butter, vanilla and powdered sugar. Fold in 12 ounces whipped topping. Pour into pie crust. Top with 8 ounces whipped topping. Freeze. Thaw before serving.
Serves: 8 to 10

FUDGE PIE

1 unbaked 9-inch pie crust	**1 teaspoon vanilla extract**
2 eggs	**⅛ teaspoon salt**
1 cup sugar	**Toasted pecan halves**
½ cup all-purpose flour	**Whipped cream for garnish**
¼ cup butter	**Peppermint ice cream for garnish**
2 ounces semi-sweet chocolate	

Beat eggs with sugar and flour. In top of double boiler melt butter and chocolate. Add vanilla and salt. Combine the two mixtures and pour into pie crust. Top with pecan halves and bake at 350 degrees for 30 minutes. Serve with dollop of whipped cream or peppermint ice cream.

Serves: 8

EASY CARAMEL PIE

1 baked 9-inch pie crust	**1 Tablespoon cornstarch**
14 ounce package caramel candy	**¼ teaspoon salt**
2 cups milk, divided	**1½ teaspoons vanilla extract**
5 eggs, separated	

Place unwrapped candies and 1 cup milk in glass bowl. Microwave for 2 to 3 minutes or until melted, stirring after each minute. In top of double boiler thoroughly beat egg yolks. Add remaining milk and cornstarch; blend well. Add caramel mixture and salt. Cook until thick, stirring constantly. When thickened add vanilla and mix well. Pour into pie crust. Spread meringue over pie filling. Bake at 350 degrees for 8-10 minutes.

Meringue

1 Tablespoon cornstarch	**5 egg whites**
2 Tablespoons milk	**6 Tablespoons sugar**
½ cup boiling water	**1½ teaspoons vanilla extract**

Blend cornstarch and milk in saucepan. Add boiling water and cook until thick and clear. Cool. Beat egg whites until foamy. Gradually add sugar and beat until stiff. Add cooled milk mixture and vanilla. Beat until blended.

Serves: 8

No browning sugar for this caramel pie!

CHOCOLATE PIE

1 baked 9-inch pie crust	3 egg yolks
1 cup sugar	1 cup water
4 Tablespoons cornstarch	3 Tablespoons margarine
3 Tablespoons cocoa	1 teaspoon vanilla extract
1 cup evaporated milk, divided	

Combine sugar, cornstarch and cocoa in heavy saucepan. Add ¼ cup evaporated milk, egg yolks and mix well. Add remaining milk and water. Add margarine and vanilla. Stir constantly over medium heat until mixture is thick and creamy. Pour into pie crust. Spread meringue over filling, sealing to edge of crust. Bake at 350 degrees for 15-20 minutes or until golden brown. Cool before serving.

Meringue

3 egg whites	7 ounce jar marshmallow creme
Dash of salt	

Beat egg whites with salt, until soft peaks form. Gradually add marshmallow creme and beat until stiff peaks form.
Serves: 6 to 8

WHITE CHOCOLATE PIE

3 egg whites	½ cup chopped pecans
1 cup Ritz Cracker crumbs	2 cups whipping cream
Pinch of salt	¼ cup powdered sugar
1 cup sugar	8 ounces white chocolate, grated
2 teaspoons vanilla extract, divided	Chopped pecans for garnish

Beat egg whites to stiff peaks. Combine cracker crumbs, salt, sugar, 1 teaspoon vanilla and chopped pecans. Fold into beaten egg whites. Spread in buttered and floured 9-inch deep-dish pie plate. Bake at 325 degrees for 30 minutes. Cool. Whip cream with powdered sugar and 1 teaspoon vanilla. Spread over crust. Sprinkle grated white chocolate over whipped cream. Garnish with chopped pecans.
Serves: 6 to 8

OATMEAL PIE

1 unbaked 9-inch deep-dish pie
 crust
½ cup butter
⅔ cup sugar
2 eggs

⅔ cup dark corn syrup
⅔ cup quick-cooking oats
1 teaspoon vanilla extract
½ cup chopped pecans

Melt butter and add sugar. Beat eggs and add to butter and sugar mixture. Add syrup, oats, vanilla and pecans. Blend all ingredients until smooth. Pour into pie crust and bake at 325 degrees for 40 minutes.
Serves: 8

MYSTERY PECAN PIE

1 unbaked 9-inch pie crust
8 ounce cream cheese, softened
⅔ cup sugar, divided
4 eggs

2 teaspoons vanilla extract,
 divided
1-1½ cups chopped pecans
1 cup light corn syrup

Beat cream cheese with ⅓ cup sugar, 1 egg and 1 teaspoon vanilla until creamy. Pour into pie crust and sprinkle with pecans. Beat together remaining eggs, sugar and vanilla with corn syrup. Gently pour mixture over pecan layer. Bake at 375 degrees for 45 minutes or until firm.
Serves: 8

COFFEE FUDGE ICE CREAM PIE

1 9-inch graham cracker crust
1 pint coffee ice cream
1⅔ cups fudge topping

1 cup chopped pecans
1 cup whipping cream
2 Tablespoons powdered sugar

Soften ice cream and beat with mixer. Pour into pie crust and freeze. Heat fudge topping; pour on top of ice cream. Top with pecans and refreeze. Whip cream with powdered sugar until just stiff. Spread on top of pie. Freeze. Just before serving, remove from freezer and slice.
Serves: 6 to 8

Easy and good.

CRUMBLY CRUNCH ICE CREAM PIE

1 cup all-purpose flour
½ cup packed light brown sugar
½ cup margarine, softened
½ cup chopped pecans

6 ounces semi-sweet chocolate chips
1½ cups evaporated milk
1 cup miniature marshmallows
½ gallon vanilla ice cream

In oven-proof pan mix flour, sugar, margarine and pecans until crumbly. Bake at 350 degrees for 25 minutes. Stir often until mixture looks like toasted nuts. Cool. In top of double boiler combine chocolate chips, evaporated milk and marshmallows. Cook over boiling water, stirring constantly, until smooth. Remove from heat and cool. In a 9X13-inch pan spread ⅔ of the crumb mixture; then pour ½ of the chocolate sauce over crumbs. Remove top and sides from ice cream carton. Cut into 1 inch thick slices and cover chocolate sauce. Pour remaining sauce over ice cream and sprinkle remaining crumbs on top. Freeze.
Serves: 12

KAHLUA PARFAIT PIE

2½ cups flaked coconut
1 cup finely chopped pecans

⅓ cup margarine, melted

Spread coconut on cookie sheet and lightly brown in a 350 degree oven. Watch closely, stirring once or twice. Cool. Combine toasted coconut, chopped pecans and margarine. Press into bottom and sides of 9 or 10-inch pie pan. Bake at 350 degrees or until golden brown, about 10 minutes. Cool completely.

Ice Cream Filling
½ gallon vanilla ice cream
1 Tablespoon instant coffee
  crystals
½ teaspoon water

Whipped cream for garnish
Shaved semi-sweet chocolate
Kahlua

Slightly soften ice cream. Place coffee crystals into small bowl and add water to dissolve coffee and make a smooth paste. With electric mixer, blend dissolved coffee into softened ice cream, working quickly. Spoon into coconut crust to make pretty swirls. Freeze. Remove from freezer shortly before serving. Top each slice with dollop of whipped cream and sprinkle with chocolate curls. Pour 1-2 Tablespoon Kahlua over each serving, or serve each guest Kahlua in an individual liqueur glass.
Serves: 8

BURGESS BARS

¾ **cup butter**
1 cup sugar
2 eggs, slightly beaten
2½ cups graham cracker crumbs

2 cups miniature marshmallows
1½ cup chopped pecans
12 ounces butterscotch morsels
½ cup peanut butter

In saucepan cook butter, sugar and eggs until thick. Cool. Add cracker crumbs, marshmallows and pecans, mixing well. Pack loosely in very lightly oiled 9X13-inch baking dish. Over low heat slowly melt morsels and peanut butter. Blend well and spread over first mixture. Bake at 350 degrees for 6 minutes. Cool. Cut into 1-inch bars.
Yield: 5 dozen

BUTTERY BITTERS BARS

½ cup sugar
3 cups graham cracker crumbs
1 cup butter
2 cups packed dark brown sugar
1 Tablespoon all-purpose flour

1 teaspoon baking powder
1 cup flaked coconut
1 cup chopped pecans or walnuts
3 eggs, well beaten
1 Tablespoon angostura bitters

Combine sugar and cracker crumbs. Cut butter into mixture until well blended. Press firmly into 2 (9X9-inch) pans. Set aside. Combine brown sugar, flour and baking powder. Mix in coconut and pecans. Add bitters to beaten eggs and beat thoroughly into brown sugar mixture. Divide mixture and spread evenly over crumb layer in each pan. Bake at 350 degrees for 35-40 minutes or until top layer is set. Cool in pan on wire rack. While warm cut into small bars.
Yield: 20

People who can not eat chocolate will enjoy these bars. The bitters add an interesting flavor.

The freshness of unsalted butter may be maintained for six to eight weeks by storing it in the freezer.

COOKIES

CINNAMON COFFEE BARS

¼ cup vegetable shortening
1 cup packed dark brown sugar
1 egg
½ cup hot coffee
1½ cups sifted all-purpose flour
1 teaspoon baking powder

¼ teaspoon soda
¼ teaspoon salt
½ teaspoon cinnamon
½ cup seedless raisins
¼ cup chopped nuts

Cream shortening, brown sugar and egg thoroughly. Stir in coffee. Sift flour, baking powder, soda, salt and cinnamon together and add to creamed mixture. Blend in raisins and nuts. Spread in greased 9X13-inch baking pan. Bake at 350 degrees for 20 minutes. Spread while warm with thin coating of Easy Creamy Icing.

Easy Creamy Icing
1 cup sifted powdered sugar
¼ teaspoon salt

½ teaspoon vanilla extract
2 Tablespoons milk

Mix all ingredients; spread over warm cookies. Cut into bars to serve.
Yield: 2 dozen

OATMEAL CARAMELETTES

1 cup all-purpose flour
1 cup quick oats
¾ cup packed light brown sugar
¾ cup butter, melted

1 cup chocolate chips
½ cup chopped pecans
32 caramel candies
5 Tablespoons milk

Combine flour, oats and brown sugar. Add melted butter; mix well. Place ½ of mixture in greased 9X13-inch pan. Bake at 350 degrees for 10 minutes. Sprinkle chocolate chips and pecans on top of baked mixture. In top of double boiler melt caramels in milk. Cool and pour over chocolate chips and pecans. Sprinkle with remaining flour mixture. Bake at 350 degrees for 20-25 minutes. Chill 1-2 hours. Cut into bars.
Yield: 18-20

DATE BAR DELIGHTS

1 cup packed light brown sugar
¾ cup butter, melted
½ teaspoon vanilla extract

1¼ cups all-purpose flour
1 teaspoon baking soda
1¼ cups oatmeal

Mix together brown sugar, butter, vanilla, flour, baking soda and oatmeal until well blended. Grease a 9X13-inch pan. Press ½ of crust mixture into pan. Set aside.

Filling
½ cup water
1 cup sugar

8 ounces chopped dates
1 cup chopped pecans

In medium saucepan bring water and sugar to a boil. Stir in dates and pecans. Cool. Spread cooled filling over crust. Top with remaining crust mixture. Bake at 350 degrees for 25 minutes. Variation: Substitute 1½ cups peach or apricot preserves for filling.
Yield: 4 dozen

A good old-fashioned bar cookie.

TRULY DIFFERENT CUPCAKES

4 ounces semi-sweet chocolate
1 cup margarine
¼ teaspoon butter flavoring
1½ cups chopped pecans

1¾ cups sugar
4 eggs
1 cup all-purpose flour
1 Tablespoon vanilla extract

Melt chocolate and margarine in small saucepan. Remove from heat and add butter flavoring and pecans. Stir until pecans are coated. Set aside to cool slightly. By hand mix sugar, eggs, flour and vanilla until well blended, but do not beat. Stir in chocolate mixture and blend well. Place paper liners in muffin tins and fill ½ full. Bake exactly 25 minutes at 350 degrees.
Yield: 24

CHOCOLATE DREAM BARS

1 cup all-purpose flour   **½ cup butter**
½ cup packed light brown sugar

Mix flour and sugar; cut in butter with a pastry blender. Press into a shallow greased 10X15-inch pan. Bake at 350 degrees 10-12 minutes or until slightly brown.

Filling
1 cup packed light brown sugar   **2 eggs**
12 ounces semi-sweet chocolate   **½ teaspoon baking powder**
** chips**   **1 teaspoon vanilla extract**
2 Tablespoons all-purpose flour   **¼ teaspoon salt**

Mix brown sugar and chocolate chips with flour. Add eggs, baking powder, vanilla and salt. Mix well. Pour evenly over crust. Bake at 350 degrees for 25-30 minutes. Cool and cut into bars.
Yield: 5 dozen

BUTTERSCOTCH BROWNIES

2 cups all-purpose flour   **4 eggs**
2 teaspoons baking powder   **1 teaspoon vanilla extract**
1½ teaspoons salt   **1 cup chopped pecans**
12 ounces butterscotch morsels   **6 ounces semi-sweet chocolate**
½ cup margarine   ** chips**
2 cups packed light brown sugar

Preheat oven to 350 degrees. In small bowl combine flour, baking powder and salt; set aside. In top of double boiler melt butterscotch morsels and margarine; remove from heat. Stir in brown sugar and cool at room temperature for 5 minutes. Beat in eggs and vanilla. Stir in flour mixture and pecans. Spread evenly in greased 15X10-inch baking pan. Sprinkle chocolate chips on top. Bake for 30-35 minutes. Cool completely before cutting. Cut into 2-inch squares.
Yield: 3 dozen

CHOCOLATE LINZER BROWNIES

6 Tablespoons butter
3 ounces unsweetened chocolate
1 cup sifted all-purpose flour
3 Tablespoons cocoa
½ teaspoon salt
1½ cups sugar
3 Tablespoons powdered sugar

2 large eggs, room temperature
6 Tablespoons seedless raspberry jam, divided
1 teaspoon red wine vinegar, divided
½ cup slivered almonds, toasted

Stir butter and unsweetened chocolate in heavy small saucepan over low heat until melted and smooth. Cool. Sift flour, cocoa and salt into small bowl. Set aside. Sift sugars together in a large bowl. Add eggs to sugars and beat with mixer until pale yellow. Add 2 Tablespoons jam and ½ teaspoon vinegar and beat 1 minute. Fold into melted chocolate. Fold in dry ingredients. Add almonds and stir. Grease and flour a 9X9-inch pan. Spread batter evenly in pan. Bake at 325 degrees for 30 minutes or until a wooden pick inserted in center comes out almost clean. Mix 4 Tablespoons jam with ½ teaspoon vinegar. Spread over hot brownies. Cool brownies completely. Spread cool glaze over brownies. Let stand until chocolate sets, at least 2 hours. Cut into squares. Top each with a raspberry. May be prepared 1 day ahead. Store in airtight container.

Glaze

2 ounces semi-sweet chocolate, chopped
3 Tablespoons seedless raspberry jam

2 Tablespoons unsalted butter
⅛ teaspoon red wine vinegar

In heavy small saucepan melt chocolate, jam, butter and vinegar over low heat, stirring until smooth. Cool.
Yield: 2 dozen

To toast raw nuts for serving, place them in a shallow pan in 200 degree oven. When the nuts are warm, add 2 Tablespoons melted butter for 8 ounces nuts, or 4 Tablespoons melted butter for 16 ounces nuts. Stir to coat nuts, and salt to taste while stirring. Toast in oven for at least 4 hours.

WHITE CHOCOLATE CITRUS BROWNIES

½ cup finely chopped dried
  apricots
2 Tablespoons Grand Marnier
1 Tablespoon frozen orange juice,
  thawed
1 Tablespoon grated orange peel
1 teaspoon lemon juice
1 teaspoon grated lemon peel
½ teaspoon vanilla extract

8 ounces white chocolate, divided
2 Tablespoons unsalted butter
3 ounces cream cheese
1 cup sifted all-purpose flour
½ teaspoon salt
½ teaspoon ginger
2 large eggs, room temperature
⅔ cup sugar

Mix apricots, Grand Marnier, orange juice, orange peel, lemon juice, lemon peel and vanilla in medium bowl. In food processor finely chop 4 ounces of white chocolate and set aside. Melt butter and cream cheese in heavy small saucepan over low heat, stirring constantly. Remove from heat, and add the finely chopped white chocolate. Stir and mix well to melt white chocolate. Set aside to cool. Sift flour, salt and ginger into small bowl. Beat eggs and sugar in large bowl until thickened, about 1 minute. Add cream cheese mixture and mix well. Fold in apricot mixture. Coarsely chop remaining 4 ounces of white chocolate. Mix white chocolate into cream cheese and apricot mixture. Add dry ingredients. Grease and flour a 9X9-inch pan. Spread batter in pan. Bake at 350 degrees for 25 minutes, or until wooden pick inserted in center comes out clean. Cool. Spread with glaze. Let stand 20 minutes or until glaze is set. Cut into squares. May be prepared 1 day ahead and stored in airtight container.

Glaze
⅔ cup powdered sugar
1 Tablespoon Grand Marnier

3 teaspoons frozen orange juice,
  thawed

Mix all ingredients in small bowl.
Yield: 2 dozen

DECADENT CHOCOLATE BROWNIES

3½ ounces unsweetened
  chocolate
1 cup margarine
2 cups sugar
3 eggs, well beaten

1 cup sifted all-purpose flour
1 teaspoon vanilla extract
1 teaspoon salt
1 cup chopped pecans
Powdered sugar

In top of double boiler melt chocolate and margarine; add sugar and eggs. Cook until mixture begins to thicken. Slowly stir in flour, vanilla, salt and pecans. Mix well. Pour into a greased 7X11-inch metal pan. Bake at 350 degrees for 30-35 minutes. Cool before cutting into 1-inch squares. Dust with powdered sugar.
Yield: 2 dozen

A very moist delicious brownie.

VANILLA REFRIGERATOR COOKIES

1½ cups sifted all-purpose flour
½ teaspoon baking soda
½ teaspoon salt
½ cup vegetable shortening

1 cup sugar
1 egg
2-3 teaspoons vanilla extract or
  ½ teaspoon almond extract

Sift together flour, baking soda and salt. Set aside. Cream shortening and sugar until light and fluffy. Add unbeaten egg and vanilla. Gradually add flour mixture to shortening mixture. Turn dough out onto a large piece of waxed paper. Shape into a 2-inch roll. Wrap tightly and chill several hours or overnight. When ready to bake slice ¼-inch thick. Place on greased cookie sheet. Bake at 375 degrees for 10 minutes. Cool before storing in airtight container. Variations: Lemon Cookies—follow vanilla cookie recipe substituting 2 teaspoons lemon extract for vanilla. Cherry Cookies—make vanilla cookie recipe adding ½ cup chopped candied cherries. Chocolate Cookies—make vanilla recipe adding 1 ounce melted unsweetened chocolate.
Yield: 4 dozen

Good old-fashioned cookie.

EASY COOKIES

1 box yellow cake mix
½ cup margarine, softened
1 egg

1 teaspoon vanilla extract
½ cup chopped pecans

In large bowl thoroughly blend cake mix, margarine and egg. Combine with remaining ingredients to make a very stiff dough. Divide into 2 rolls. Roll back and forth on waxed paper to form long smooth rolls approximately 1½-inches in diameter. Wrap in waxed paper and place in refrigerator or freezer. To bake, slice very thin. Place on ungreased baking sheet. Bake at 350 degrees for 10-15 minutes or until lightly browned.
Yield: 4 dozen

Great slice and bake cookies—ready for the children coming home from school or when the homeroom mother calls for refreshments.

FRUITCAKE COOKIES

3 slices candied pineapple, cut
into small pieces
1 cup chopped candied cherries
⅓ cup golden seedless raisins
½ cup chopped dates
3½ cups coarsely chopped
pecans
½ cup margarine, softened

½ cup packed light brown sugar
2 small eggs, beaten
1 teaspoon vanilla extract
1½ cups sifted all-purpose flour
½ teaspoon cinnamon
½ teaspoon baking soda
¼ teaspoon salt
¼ cup milk

Combine pineapple, cherries, raisins, dates and pecans. Mix well and set aside. In a separate bowl cream margarine and sugar. Add eggs and vanilla, beating well. Sift together dry ingredients. Stir dry ingredients into creamed mixture alternately with milk. Add fruit mixture and mix well. Use teaspoon to drop dough onto greased cookie sheet. Bake at 300 degrees for 20-30 minutes.
Yield: 6 dozen

These cookies can be frozen. Great for a large crowd.

FRUIT NUT WREATH COOKIES

1 cup margarine, softened
½ cup packed light brown sugar
1 egg
2 cups all-purpose flour
½ teaspoon baking powder
1 cup rolled oats

¼ cup chopped pecans
¼ cup chopped candied cherries,
   red and green
Shredded coconut
Candied cherry halves

Cream margarine and sugar. Add egg and beat well. Sift together flour and baking powder. Add to creamed mixture, blending well. Fold in oats, pecans and cherries. Shape into wreaths by rolling 2 Tablespoons dough into a thin roll, connecting ends to form a circle. Place on a greased cookie sheet. Bake at 350 degrees for 10-15 minutes. When cool, remove and store in airtight container or freeze if not using immediately. Before serving, place cookies on serving tray and drizzle with icing. Sprinkle with coconut. Press 3 cherry halves on top of each cookie.

Icing

1 cup sifted powdered sugar
1 Tablespoon butter, softened

3 Tablespoons evaporated milk

Combine sugar, butter and milk. Stir until smooth.
Yield: 3 dozen

> *Colorful and pretty. Nice for Christmas.*

CHOCOLATE CHEWIES

12 ounces semi-sweet chocolate
   chips
14 ounces sweetened condensed
   milk

¼ cup butter
1 teaspoon vanilla extract
1 cup all-purpose flour
1 cup chopped pecans

In top of double boiler combine chocolate chips, condensed milk and butter. Stir until chips are melted and mixture is well blended. Add vanilla, flour and pecans. Mix until thoroughly blended. Drop by teaspoon onto ungreased cookie sheet. Bake at 350 degrees for 7-10 minutes. Remove cookies and place on wire rack to cool.
Yield: 5 dozen

COOKIES

GINGER COOKIES

⅔ cup vegetable oil
1¼ cups sugar, divided
1 egg
¼ cup dark molasses
2 cups sifted all-purpose flour

2 teaspoons baking soda
½ teaspoon salt
1 teaspoon cinnamon
1 teaspoon ginger

Mix oil, 1 cup sugar, egg and molasses. Sift together dry ingredients. Blend into sugar mixture. Mix thoroughly. Drop by teaspoon into ¼ cup sugar and roll into ball. Place 3 inches apart on ungreased cookie sheet. Bake at 350 degrees for 10-12 minutes or until the cookies are golden brown. Remove cookies from baking sheet while still warm. Cool on wire rack.
Yield: 5 dozen

CRINKLE COOKIES

1⅔ cups sugar
½ cup vegetable shortening
1 teaspoon vanilla extract
2 eggs
2 ounces unsweetened chocolate,
  melted

2 cups sifted all-purpose flour
2 teaspoons baking powder
½ teaspoon salt
½ cup chopped pecans
⅓ cup milk
Powdered sugar

Cream sugar, shortening and vanilla. Add eggs and beat well. Add melted chocolate. Sift together dry ingredients. Stir in pecans. Blend dry ingredients into creamed mixture alternately with milk, beating well. Chill 3 hours. Shape cookies into 1-inch balls and roll in powdered sugar. Space cookies 2 inches apart on greased cookie sheet. Bake at 350 degrees for 15 minutes. Cool slightly before removing.
Yield: 4 dozen

An attractive and delicious cookie.

CHERRY TWINKLES

½ cup butter, no substitute
¼ cup sugar
1 egg, separated
1 cup all-purpose flour

2 teaspoons fresh lemon juice
¾ cup finely chopped walnuts
Candied cherries or well drained
  maraschino cherries

Cream butter, sugar and egg yolk. Add flour and lemon juice. Chill for 1 hour. Shape into 1-inch balls. Dip each ball in beaten egg white and roll in walnuts. Place on ungreased cookie sheet. Press cherry half on top of each ball. Bake at 350 degrees for 15-20 minutes.
Yield: 2½ dozen

Great Christmas cookie. Many cookies look like this one, but this one has a wonderfully delicate taste.

FANTASTIC COOKIES

1 cup butter, softened
⅓ cup whipping cream

2 cups all-purpose flour
¾ cup sugar

In large mixing bowl combine butter, whipping cream and flour. Mix until well blended. Cover and chill for 1 hour. Divide dough into thirds. Work with one portion of dough at a time. Use just enough flour to work dough and roll to ⅛-inch thickness. Cut out each cookie using a 1½-inch round cookie cutter. Dip each cookie into sugar and place on ungreased cookie sheet. Pierce 5-6 times with a wooden pick. Bake at 350 degrees for 6-7 minutes. Do not brown. Remove from cookie sheet and cool. Place a small amount of filling between two cookies. Be gentle as these cookies are very fragile.

Filling
½ cup butter, softened
1½ cups powdered sugar
1½ teaspoons vanilla extract

1-2 drops food coloring, color of
  choice

Combine all ingredients. Mix until smooth.
Yield: 60 cookies

These cookies are very pretty at Christmas with red and green filling.
For a tea or coffee, make filling a pretty peach color.

CHOCOLATE MINT SNAPS

4 ounces semi-sweet chocolate
1¼ cups vegetable shortening
2 cups sugar
2 eggs
⅓ cup light corn syrup
2 teaspoons peppermint extract

1 teaspoon vanilla extract
4 cups all-purpose flour
2 teaspoons baking soda
½ teaspoon salt
Sugar

In top of double boiler melt chocolate. Cool. In large bowl cream shortening and sugar. Add eggs, syrup, peppermint and vanilla extracts and melted chocolate. Beat well. Sift flour, baking soda and salt. Add to creamed mixture. Mix until well blended. Shape into walnut-size balls and roll in sugar. Place on ungreased cookie sheet. Bake at 350 degrees for 10 minutes.
Yield: 6 dozen

PECAN CRISP

1 cup butter, softened
2½ cups packed light brown
  sugar
2 eggs, room temperature

2½ cups sifted all-purpose flour
¼ teaspoon salt
½ teaspoon baking soda
1 cup chopped pecans

Cream butter and sugar. Add eggs and beat well. Sift together dry ingredients. Add to creamed mixture. Stir in pecans. Drop by level teaspoon onto ungreased cookie sheet. Bake at 350 degrees for 8-10 minutes or until puffed cookie falls. After removing from oven let sit on cookie sheet for 1-2 minutes. Remove and cool on wire rack. Store in airtight container.
Yield: 6 dozen

TEACAKES

1¾ cups sugar
1 cup margarine
2 eggs, well beaten
¾ cup vegetable oil
4 cups all-purpose flour
1 teaspoon baking soda

1 teaspoon cream of tartar
1 teaspoon salt
2 teaspoons vanilla extract
Sugar
Nutmeg
Cinnamon

Cream sugar, margarine, eggs and oil. Add flour, soda, cream of tartar, salt and vanilla. Mix well. Drop by teaspoon or roll into balls the size of walnuts. Place on greased cookie sheet. Flatten with fork. Sprinkle with a mixture of sugar, nutmeg and cinnamon. Bake at 350 degrees for 10-12 minutes or until lightly browned.
Yield: 5-6 dozen

House smells wonderful while these are baking. Children love these cookies.

ZESTY APRICOT SHORTBREAD

1 cup packed light brown sugar
⅔ cup butter, softened
2 cups all-purpose flour
1½ cups dried apricots

2 teaspoons grated lemon rind
1⅓ cups sugar
4 teaspoons cornstarch
⅔ cup finely chopped pecans

Cream brown sugar and butter. Blend in flour. Press dough into a 9X13-inch pan. Bake at 350 degrees for 12 minutes. Cool. Cook apricots in water to cover for 15 minutes or until tender. Drain and reserve 3 Tablespoons of liquid. Chop cooked apricots. In a saucepan combine apricots, reserved liquid, lemon rind, sugar and cornstarch. Bring mixture to a boil and continue to boil 1 full minute, stirring constantly. Cool 10 minutes. Spread mixture on cooled shortbread crust. Sprinkle with pecans. Bake at 350 degrees for 20 minutes. Cool. Cut into small squares.
Yield: 48

AMBROSIA BARS

⅔ cup all-purpose flour
½ teaspoon baking powder
½ teaspoon salt
¼ cup butter
1 cup sugar
1 egg

1 Tablespoon milk
1 teaspoon grated orange rind
1 cup flaked coconut
4 ounces semi-sweet chocolate,
  melted

Mix flour, baking powder and salt. Set aside. Cream butter. Add sugar gradually, beating well after each addition. Add egg, milk and orange rind; blend well. Stir in flour mixture and coconut. Spread in a 8X8-inch pan or a 9x5-inch loaf pan which has been greased, bottom of pan lined with waxed paper and greased again. Bake at 350 degrees for 30 minutes or until lightly browned. Remove from pan; spread with melted chocolate and cool. Cut into bars.
Yield: 20

PEPPERMINT PARTY MERINGUES

2 egg whites
Pinch of salt
Pinch of cream of tartar
⅔ cup sugar
6 drops green food coloring

½ teaspoon peppermint extract
6 ounces miniature semi-sweet
  chocolate chips
½ cup finely chopped pecans,
  optional

Preheat oven to 375 degrees. Combine egg whites, salt and cream of tartar. Beat until fluffy. Gradually add sugar, beating until very stiff. Add food coloring and peppermint extract. Fold in chocolate chips and pecans. Line 2 large cookie sheets with aluminum foil. Drop by teaspoon onto cookie sheets. Place oven racks close together in center of oven. Turn oven off as soon as cookie sheets are placed in the oven. Leave cookies in oven with door closed for at least 3 hours or overnight. Store in airtight container.
Yield: 4 dozen

FRUIT ROLLS

2⅔ cups vanilla wafer crumbs
1 cup chopped candied pineapple
1 cup chopped candied cherries
2 cups chopped pecans or
    walnuts

14 ounces sweetened condensed
    milk
Powdered sugar

Combine all ingredients in bowl. Divide into three equal portions. Shape into three rolls approximately 11 inches long. Roll in powdered sugar. Wrap in waxed paper and refrigerate. To serve, slice into 1-inch rounds.
Yield: 5 dozen

PEANUT BUTTER BON BONS

16 ounces ready to spread vanilla
    frosting
1 cup peanut butter
¼ cup margarine, melted

2 cups graham cracker crumbs
16 ounces ready to spread
    chocolate frosting

Combine vanilla frosting, peanut butter and margarine with a fork until well blended. Stir in graham cracker crumbs until well mixed. Form into 1-inch balls. Chill 1 hour. In a saucepan melt chocolate frosting over low heat. Dip balls in melted frosting, allowing excess to drip off. Place on waxed paper to cool. Let stand at room temperature for 6 hours or until dry.
Yield: 50 balls

Any food processor may be used to make peanut butter. Shelled, skinned peanuts, either roasted or dry roasted, may be used. A regular processor will hold up to 3 cups. Process peanuts to the desired consistency 3 to 4 minutes, stopping 2 to 3 times to scrape down the sides of the work bowl. Refrigerate!

DATE NUT KRISPIES

½ cup butter
1 cup packed light brown sugar
8 ounces dates, chopped
2 cups Rice Krispies
1 teaspoon vanilla extract

½ teaspoon salt
1 cup chopped pecans
1 cup flaked coconut
Powdered sugar

In large skillet combine butter, brown sugar and dates. Cook over low heat until mixture bubbles. Simmer for 5 minutes. Remove from heat. Add remaining ingredients. Cool and shape into balls. Roll in powdered sugar. Store in airtight container.
Yield: 3-4 dozen

SPICE ROLLS

8 ounces whole nuts
8 ounces dates, diced
8 ounces candied cherries
3 cups graham cracker crumbs
8 ounces marshmallows
1 Tablespoon grated orange rind

⅓ cup orange juice
⅛ teaspoon cinnamon
⅛ teaspoon nutmeg
⅛ teaspoon cloves
⅛ teaspoon allspice
⅛ teaspoon ginger

Combine nuts, dates, cherries and cracker crumbs; set aside. In a saucepan melt marshmallows. Add remaining ingredients and mix well. Put crumb mixture into marshmallow mixture. Mix with hands and shape into 2 rolls. Refrigerate. Slice and serve. Variation: Rolls can be dusted in powdered sugar.
Yield: 2 large rolls

SUGAR AND SPICE NUTS

1 cup sugar
1 Tablespoon pumpkin pie spice
1 egg white

1 Tablespoon water
4 cups mixed nuts

Combine sugar and pumpkin pie spice. Set aside. Beat egg white and add water. Stir sugar and egg mixtures into nuts. Coat nuts gently. Spread nuts on buttered cookie sheets. Bake at 300 degrees for 15-20 minutes. Stir often to prevent burning.
Yield: 4 cups

BUTTER TOFFEE

1 cup sugar
½ cup butter
¼ cup water
½ teaspoon salt

1½ cups chopped pecans or
   walnuts, divided
12 ounces semi-sweet chocolate
   chips

In a large saucepan combine sugar, butter, water and salt. Cook to soft-crack stage or to 285 degrees on candy thermometer. Add ½ cup chopped nuts. Pour into 8X8-inch pan. Cool. Melt chocolate chips. Spread half of chocolate mixture on cooled candy. Sprinkle with ½ cup chopped nuts. Cool. Turn candy over and repeat with a layer of remaining chocolate and nuts. Cool. Break into pieces and store in airtight container.
Yield: 23-30 pieces

PRALINES

1 cup sugar
1 cup packed light brown sugar
⅛ teaspoon salt
½ cup evaporated milk

2 Tablespoons light corn syrup
2 Tablespoons butter
1 Tablespoon vanilla extract
½ cup pecan halves

Combine sugars, salt, milk and syrup in heavy 3 quart saucepan. Bring to boil. Reduce heat to medium and stir. Cook to soft-ball stage or to 240 degrees on candy thermometer. Remove from heat. Add butter and vanilla. Beat until cool. Add pecan halves and drop by Tablespoon onto waxed paper. When firm, store in airtight container.
Yield: 2 dozen

OPERA PATTIES

2 cups sugar
Pinch of salt
¾ cup whipping cream

2 Tablespoons dark corn syrup
⅓ teaspoon vanilla extract
2 cups chopped nuts

Combine sugar, salt and cream. Bring to boil and add corn syrup. Cook to soft-ball stage or to 240 degrees on candy thermometer. Cool slightly. Beat slightly. Add vanilla and nuts. Drop by heaping Tablespoon onto waxed paper. If candy gets too hard while dropping, add a small amount of warm water to mixture.
Yield: 30 pieces

DREAMY WHITE FUDGE

2¼ cups sugar
½ cup sour cream
¼ cup milk
2 Tablespoons butter
1 Tablespoon light corn syrup

¼ teaspoon salt
2 teaspoons vanilla extract
1 cup chopped pecans or walnuts
⅓ cup candied cherries,
  quartered

In a deep saucepan combine sugar, sour cream, milk, butter, corn syrup and salt. Boil to 240 degrees on candy thermometer or soft-ball stage. Remove from heat and let stand 1 hour or until lukewarm. Add vanilla and beat until mixture loses gloss. Add nuts and cherries. Line an 8X8-inch pan with aluminum foil. Pour in candy mixture. When set, cut into 1-inch squares.
Yield: 48 pieces

CARAMEL FUDGE

3 cups sugar
2 cups whipping cream
1 cup light corn syrup

¼ cup butter
½ cup all-purpose flour
2 cups coarsely chopped pecans

Cook sugar, cream and syrup to 240 degrees on a candy thermometer or soft-ball stage. Remove from heat. Add butter. Cool for 5 minutes. Blend in flour and beat for 10-15 minutes. Add nuts. Pour into a buttered 9X13-inch pan. Cool. Cut into squares.
Yield: 2¾ pounds

MICROWAVE FUDGE

½ cup butter
3½ cups powdered sugar
½ cup cocoa

¼ cup milk
1 Tablespoon vanilla extract
½ cup chopped nuts

In a small glass bowl melt butter for 40-60 seconds on high setting of microwave. Set aside. In a large glass bowl blend sugar and cocoa. Add milk and melted butter and blend thoroughly. Microwave for 2 minutes on high. Remove from oven and stir well. Add vanilla and nuts. Stir until well blended. Pour into lightly buttered 8X8-inch pan. Refrigerate until firm enough to slice smoothly.
Yield: 48 pieces

Super easy.

CARAMEL CANDY

6 cups sugar, divided
2 cups evaporated milk
1 Tablespoon light corn syrup
¼ teaspoon baking soda

½ cup butter or margarine
1 teaspoon vanilla extract
2 cups chopped pecans

Caramelize 2 cups sugar by melting in a cast iron skillet. Combine 4 cups sugar, milk and corn syrup in a large saucepan. Bring to boil while sugar is caramelizing. Slowly pour caramelized sugar into boiling mixture, stirring constantly. Cook to firm-ball stage or to 245 degrees on candy thermometer. Remove from heat and immediately add soda, stirring vigorously as it foams. Add butter and stir only until melted. Cool 20 minutes. Add vanilla and beat until thick and creamy. Add pecans. Pour into buttered 9X13-inch pan. Cool. Cut into 1 inch squares. Keeps indefinitely in airtight container. This recipe can be halved.
Yield: 120 pieces

ALMOND MINTS

1⅛ cups butter, melted, divided
½ cup cocoa
3½ cups powdered sugar, sifted,
   divided
1 egg, beaten

1 teaspoon almond extract
2 cups graham cracker crumbs
⅓ cup Amaretto
1½ cups semi-sweet chocolate
   chips

Combine ½ cup melted butter and cocoa. Add ½ cup sugar, egg and almond extract; blend well. Stir in crumbs. Press into an ungreased 9X13-inch pan. Combine 6 Tablespoons butter and Amaretto in small mixing bowl. Beat at medium speed and gradually add 3 cups powdered sugar. Beat until smooth. Spread over crumb layer. Cover and chill in refrigerator for 1 hour. Combine chocolate chips and ¼ cup butter in microwave-proof dish. Melt on high 1 minute. Stir until smooth and melted. Spread over Amaretto layer. Chill for 1 hour or until firm. Cut into 1 inch squares. Store in refrigerator.
Yield: 8 dozen

CRAZY COCOA KRISPS

24 ounces almond bark   **2 cups dry roasted peanuts**
2 cups Cocoa Krispies

Place almond bark in microwave dish and cook 1 minute on high. Stir and heat at 30 second intervals until melted, stirring at each interval. Stir in cereal and peanuts. Spread on jelly roll pan or cookie sheet and allow to cool. Break into pieces and store in airtight container. May be dropped by teaspoon.
Yield: 36 pieces

PEANUT BUTTER BARS

3½ cups powdered sugar   **1 cup peanut butter, plain or**
1 cup graham cracker crumbs   **crunchy**
1 cup margarine, melted   **1½ cups chocolate chips**

Combine all ingredients except chocolate chips. Press into a 9X13-inch pan. Melt chocolate chips and pour over other ingredients. Cool and cut into small squares.
Yield: 30 small pieces

ICED ALMONDS

2 cups whole blanched almonds   **½ teaspoon vanilla extract**
1 cup sugar   **½ teaspoon salt**
3 Tablespoons butter

In heavy skillet over medium heat, combine almonds, sugar and butter. Cook until almonds are toasted and sugar is a golden brown. Cook an additional 15 minutes, stirring constantly. Stir in vanilla. Spread on aluminum foil. Sprinkle with salt.
Yield: 2 dozen

Unsalted butter has a richer flavor than salted butter because of its higher ratio of cream to water. Butter is salted mainly to preserve it and extend its shelf life.

ACKNOWLEDGEMENTS
AND
INDEX

ACKNOWLEDGEMENTS

The Symphony League of Tupelo would like to thank all those who donated, tested, selected and proofed recipes for *Great Performances*. We are also indebted to a number of individuals and businesses for the help they provided.

ACKNOWLEDGEMENTS

Bank of Mississippi
Mr. Bruce Bigelow
Brookwood Furniture Co.
Mr. and Mrs. Norris V. Caldwell, Jr.
Community Federal Savings and
Loan Assn.
First National Bank
First United Methodist Church
Gizmo Gift Shop
Gum Tree Book Store
Dr. Julian B. Hill
Mr. B. J. Huddleston
Lee County Library
Mitchell, McNutt, Threadgill,
Smith and Sams, P.A.
Mr. and Mrs. Peter Maloney
Northeast Mississippi Daily Journal
Peoples Bank and Trust Co.
Mr. and Mrs. Jack R. Reed
Mr. and Mrs. Jack R. Reed, Jr.
Dr. A. Jack Stacey
Tupelo Art Gallery
Tupelo Community Theater
Uni-South Banking Corp.
Village Green Book Store
Weatherall's Inc.
Mr. and Mrs. Jimmy Westbrook, Jr.
Mrs. Jane Finger Whitfield
Dr. and Mrs. J. W. Williamson

CONTRIBUTORS

Gay Kelly Abney
Sherry Jones Abraham
Gay Wagoner Adams
Opal Huddleston Adams
Sharon Ford Albert
Martha Frances Allen
Ginger Bland Anger
Jacqueline Martin Ashford
Robert H. Aycock
Polly Gatlin Bailey
Eula Mae Baker
Ann Ballard
Renée Manning Ballard
Emily Rasberry Barber
Ann Irwin Barnes
Celia Grisham Barnett
Joyce McGuire Barnett
Roberto Tesh Barrett

Doris Jamison Bass
Julianne Sawyer Battaile
Ruth Traylor Baxter
Lynn Bernstein Beadles
Jeri Swift Beard
Linda Jobe Beasley
Joyce Hall Beasley
Jane Huggins Bell
Melinda Ray Bell
Paula Reed Bingham
Bob Black
Emily Vanessa Black
Jane Pope Black
Mary Margaret Black
Ruth Hussey Black
Julia Dodge Blakey
Louise Rodgers Bland
Sandra Pennington Bland
Dorothy Keeton Blankenship
Patty Wood Block
Kate St.Clair Boehringer
Carolyn Pierce Boggan
Hallie Loftin Boggan
Susan Shaw Booth
Ruth Swan Bornscheuer
Martha Watkins Bourland
Sunny Measells Bourland
Tommie Wright Bourland
Ellen Moore Boyd
Hilda Stewart Boyd
June Raff Bowes
Lucille Wigginton Bradley
Frances Guyton Brasfield
Beth Boozer Brevard
Shawn Stewart Brevard
Katherine Thomas Bridgman
Betty Clough Brooks
Bob R. Brooks
Cindy Jones Brooks
Susan Chustz Brooks
Betsy Lubis Brown
Kacky Salmon Brown
Rosemary Rich Bryan
Sadie Ringold Buchanan
Glenda Phillips Burk
Sara Adams Burnett
Roberta Fagin Burress
Marianne Calhoun Burrus
Katie Ruth Field Bush

Martie Hansen Bush
Betty Montgomery Cagle
Adrian Leist Caldwell
Cynthia Mayer Caldwell
Ellen White Caldwell
Kevin Caldwell
Lee Pryor Foster Caldwell
Mary Ann Lee Caldwell
Mary Elizabeth Cates Caldwell
Betsy Caldwell Campbell
Dorothy Shirley Campbell
Ann Massey Carden
Vicki Greenslade Carlisle
Elizabeth Lewellen Carnell
Patsy Payne Carr
Ruby Pettigrew Carr
Vickie Cole Carson
Peggy Moore Carter
Ruth Cummings Carter
Evelyn Newman Carroll
Peggy Chappell Causey
Jerry Cermack
Beverly Brisco Chappell
Wilma Williams Chisholm
Ann Clanton
Grace Strickland Clark
Mary Wigginton Clark
Martha Whiting Clay
Camille Reed Clayton
Mary Jo Puckett Cliatt
Jane Sear Cohn
Inez Cowsert Coggins
Cynthia Rieves Colburn
Macie Hamblin Coley
Nancy Adams Collins
Earline Gillespie Cooley
Carol Spiers Cottle
Terry Duncan Cox
Gloria Adams Crabtree
Ila Brown Craig
Barbara Ferrell Creekmore
Catherine Burke Crews
Barbara Hutcheson Crumpton
Ursula Ann Dannemiller
Bonnie Payne Davidson
Berylyn Stuckey Davis
Jean Smith Davis
Kay Murff Dawson
John W. Dear, Sr.

Carla Swofford Delgadillo
Margaret DeMoville
Helen Clark Dick
Lori Gallagher Dickerson
Jim Diffee
Mike Diffee
Nancy Bostic Diffee
Jean Zimmerly Disalvo
Annie Frances Hinds Dodge
Martha Tate Stokely Dodge
Sandra Aycock Dossett
Margaret Kelly Durham
Ivy Duvall
Sherry Saylors Eble
Pat Spangler Eckenrode
Leigh Eldridge
Harriet Hitt Ellett
Carol Richardson Elliott
Peggy Robinson Engel
Helen Thorne Eskridge
Susan Griffon Ethridge
Priscilla Watts Eubank
Martha Elizabeth Cook Evans
Rosemary Trevathen Evans
Thomas I. Evans
Cindy McCool Faucette
Phyllis Phipps Faucette
Jane Fielder
Cora Mullin Fields
Beth Harris Fisher
David Fisher
Lucy Allen Puckett Fisher
Martha Swayze Fisher
Carol Davis Flowers
Bill Ford
Sandy Heard Ford
Sandra Pannell Foster
Frances Workman Foy
Elise Trout Francis
Meredith McClanahan Fraser
Sue Houston Freeman
Mimi Scofield Frengs
Alice Virginia Daniel Furr
Sharon Cerutti Gaddo
Sue Overton Gardner
Tommy Gardner
Kay Lada Giles
Ann Bishop Godwin
Louise Nanney Godwin
Susan Beam Goff
Frances Power Goozen
Alice Gordon
Mary Lee Blaine Gordon
Teresa Walker Graham
Mimi Jones Gray
Cindy Latture Greer
Ethel E. Gove

Debra Smith Grubbs
Mary Faye Hall Gwin
Jackie Rainer Haguegood
Freida Smith Hall
Donna Neaves Hambrick
Catherine Fisher Hames
Kathy Schertz Hamilton
Elaine Graham Hancock
Jabus Lee Hardin
Frances Foose Harris
Louise Lambert Harris
Pam Moses Harris
Cherie Brown Harris
Merriam Wicks Hayes
Odelle Wood Heard
Mitzie Cockrell Henson
Sandy Tatum Henson
Shirley Phillips Herring
Mary Elizabeth Hester
Nancy Turner Hicks
Brenda Parker Hilbun
Lucy Ewing Hilbun
Emily Harrison Hill
Nan Roberts Hill
Sara Mieher Hinds
Mary Ann Guice Hitch
Judy Joyner Hodges
Linda Puckett Holden
Betty Puckett Holland
Julie Witter Holland
Leigh Holland
Babs Downing Holliman
Floy Simpson Holloman
Sandra Wilburn Hudson
Sara Key Hudson
Jo Hutchinson
Sue Oldham Imbler
Fred M. Ingellis
Virginia Christian Ingellis
Nancy Murray Ingram
Guy and Martha Jenkins
Sonja Anne Jenkins
Mary Hussey Jobe
Andrea Moss Johnson
Joyce Causey Johnston
Helen Reid Jones
Lee Ware Jones
Mary Burleson Jones
Frances Elkin Joyner
Janet Ellis Kahlstorf
Betty Jane Slocum Kellum
Jane Carr Kellum
Marce Darby Kellum
Margaret Ann Frazier Kennedy
Rebecca Rhoden Kent
Janice Rosser Kidd
Jill Swing Kieffer

Susan Threldkeld Kimbrough
Mildred Ware King
Linda Smith Kinsey
Viola King Kinsey
Jan Houck Kirk
Gayle Murphree Klauser
Eric W. Knight
Eugenia Jones Lagrone
Anne Gilpin Leake
Carol Spight Leake
Jayne Strain Leake
Pam Ledbetter
Mildred McWherter Lee
Juanita Haltiwanger Linton
Carolyn Swindle Livingston
Mary Jane Meadows Livingston
Ruth Beasley Livingston
Janice Hill Lomenick
Sharon Hawkins Long
William Lynn Long
Connie Cisco Lord
Pam Hodgson Lowery
Jeanne Moak Lummus
Susan Thompson Madden
Marian Fay Collums Maloney
Lynn Jordan Maners
Jo Willis Mark
Kay Barnes Martin
Jackie Avery Massey
Virginia Timbes Mathews
Cindy Little Mathis
Virginia Mathews Maxey
Chris Powell Maynard
Beth Rieves McAuley
Allison Kirby McCarty
Lou Ann Hartgraves McCarty
Richard Rhodes McCarty
Elise Dowling McClanahan
Erin McCarthy McCullough
Margaret Long McCullough
Susan Newton McDonald
Frances Nuckles McGaughy
Frances Walker McGill
Lina Farr McGwier
Jeannein Creasey McKenzie
Ann McLendon
Marjorie Milam
Linda R. Miller
Debbie Holloway Mills
Barbara Mitchell
Blewett Schlater Mitchell
Catherine Reed Mize
Susan Thomas Mobley
Melanie Basu Modak
Loretta Sharp Monts
Tot Savery Moore
Crystal Cameron Morgan

ACKNOWLEDGEMENTS

Neva McDowell Morris
Susan Neely Morris
Walter Morris
Beth Reid Moses
Belinda Long Mothershed
Irene Hendrick Mozingo
Margaret Ann Cooper Murphey
Mabel McClanahan Murphree
Cindy Pickle Murphy
Tootie Sims Murry
Martelle Leake Nash
Claudia Johnson Neelly
Shirley Swanstra Neuhaus
Sheila James Newell
Shirley Davis Newton
Ruth Kaefring Nichols
Ann Godwin Nunley
Melissa Markette Oakes
Peggy Crooks Oakes
Mary Lee Kemp O'Dell
Mary LaRue Omodt
Julia Griffin Otis
Mary Ellis Pace
Betty McKee Page
Merrimac Puckett Pannell
Karen King Parker
Sarah Hewitt Parker
Helen Cotting Partlow
Lottie Sample Payne
Ruth Hawkins Payne
Clara Mae Benn Pegues
Sylvia Owen Pegues
Jean Greene Pettis
Elizabeth Wilkins Phillips
Julie Singley Pinkston
Carol McKinney Pitts
Angela Grillo Poland
Marti Mann Posey
Lucy Lorick Powers
Mildred McCarthy Prather
Joy McClanahan Price
Ellie Baker Prude
Judy Cook Pryor
Judy Walters Puckett
Lucy McClanahan Puckett
Martha Ann Hawkins Puckett
Susan Hill Puckett
Nelle Brown Purnell
Jennifer Smith Quinlan
Gretchen Long Ramsey
Lucy Allen Fisher Ray
Margaret Stevenson Ray
Betty Dean Reece
Betty Fields Reed
Christine Thornton Reed
Frances Purvis Reed
Lisa White Reed

Lee Wilson Reeder
Betty Hemmen Reeves
Elizabeth Moss Rice
Linda Wells Rice
Margaret Mill Richardson
Jane Spight Riley
Lynda Stanford Riley
Margaret Joyner Milam Riley
Marion Topp Riley
Carole Hawkinson Ringoen
Fredda Stephens Robinson
Maxine Shepherd Robinson
Nancy Swanger Robinson
Rita Hill Robinson
Alice Bishop Rogers
Geraldine Wiley Rogers
Holly Ingram Rogers
Merrell Liveakos Rogers
Arvie Wood Roper
Dolores Bobo Rose
Odessa Eanes Rose
Helen McKenny Rousseau
Zellah Zent Ruff
Rosalie Cartagine Russo
Mary Alice Rutherford
Catherine Hunter Sadler
Mary Helen McClure Sams
Cindy Ross Sanders
Audrey Jerue Schreiner
Gail Piccolo Scoville
Ruth Meeks Shappley
Shelaine Evans Shappley
Carolyn Loper Sharp
Jan Ferguson Shirley
Flo Harrell Shultz
Mary Ann Ca Pece Skinner
Yvette Andries Slocum
Jeanette Welford Smith
Willa Searcy Smith
Pearline Tucker Smothers
Carolyn Stickerod Snyder
Martha McClanahan Southerland
Cathy Timbes Sparks
Theresa Sneed Spears
Virginia Toomer Spight
Ann Shannon Springfield
A. J. "Gus" Staub
Betty Bell Staub
Jerri Massey Stacey
Virginia Shaw Daniel Stanley
Dena Sheffield Steele
Deborah Stern
Mary Hall Stinson
Anneil Price Stringer
Bama Faust Strawn
Katheleen Amundson Stumme
Rita Mogish Suchanick

Julia White Swetland
Diane Evans Tannehill
Evelyn Davidson Tannehill
Margaret Jackson Tant
Betty Blair Taylor
Camae Purvis Tharp
Daintry Richmond Thomas
Edith Ruff Thomas
Helga Mays Thomas
Judy Bornscheuer Thomas
Barbara Blair Thompson
Molly Thomas Thompson
Annette Tiner Thornton
Carol Palmer Threadgill
Jane Sheffield Threldkeld
Gladys Shubert Timbes
Pamela Cox Tims
Barbara Poor Toft
Joann Batton Upchurch
Leslie Harris Van Buskirk
Jean Tedford Waldrop
Hazel Reeves Walker
Lucy Ann Puckett Walker
Peggy Robertson Walker
Lee Purnell Walsh
Sue Thomas Washburn
Lindell Tate Waters
Mary Ellis Purviance Waters
Brenda Pettis Warren
Lucy Purnell Weaver
Georgia Manning Webb
Mary Westmoreland Webb
Shirley Neaves Webb
Ann Herron Weir
Doris Jackson Welch
Sammye Massey Wells
Hope Chaney Wesson
Marcie Riekhoe West
Charlotte Tannehill Westbrook
Wes Westbrook
Shirley Threldkeld Wheeler
Mary Yates Whitehead
Norma Jean Martin Whiteside
Jane Finger Whitfield
Miriam Ellis Whitney
Libby Given Whittington
Linda Monroe Whitwell
Gayle Long Wicker
Buddy Wikle
Cathy Messer Wikle
Ned Wikle
Charlotte Meek Wilburn
Nancy Lee Wilkins
Frances Jernigan Williams
Mary Elizabeth Phillips Williams
Rosemary Taylor Williams
Margaret McCurley Williamson

Dorothy Pegram Wilson
Tillye Kinsley Wilson
Amanda Winders
Susan Shands Winkler
Ezelle Hurley Witt
Betty Childers Wood
June Ballog Woolard
Anne Roberts Worthen
Latitia Parham Wright
Janis Crow Wulfers
Jean Russell Yarborough
Sarah Bounds Young
Sharon McDaniel Young
Judy McClanahan Youngblood
Kay Williams Younk
Barbara Christensen Zander
Virginia Brock Zeigler

TESTERS

Polly Gatlin Bailey
Rosalie Reed Baker
Renée Manning Ballard
Emily Rasberry Barber
Joyce McGuire Barnett
Ruth Traylor Baxter
Melinda Ray Bell
Bernadette Sanchez Bernardy
Judy Townes Billups
Paula Reed Bingham
Julia Dodge Blakey
Louise Rodgers Bland
Patty Wood Block
Gerri Insogna Boehme
Susan Shaw Booth
Tommie Wright Bourland
Hilda Stewart Boyd
Nancy Williams Box
Frances Joyner Brasfield
Beth Boozer Brevard
Cindy Jones Brooks
Judy McGriff Brown
Rosemary Rich Bryan
Sadie Ringold Buchanan
Marianne Calhoun Burrus
Adrian Leist Caldwell
Lee Pryor Foster Caldwell
Mary Ann Lee Caldwell
Mary Elizabeth Caldwell
Betsy Caldwell Campbell
Camille Reed Clayton
Grace Strickland Clark
Helen Reed Collins
Kathy Webb Corban
Ila Brown Craig
Catherine Burke Crews
Ursula Dannemiller
Bonnie Payne Davidson

Carla Swofford Delgadillo
Betty Champion Dickey
Nancy Bostic Diffee
Martha Tate Stokely Dodge
Margaret Kelly Durham
Peggy Stokes Eckard
Pat Spangler Eckenrode
Harriet Hitt Ellett
Cindy McCool Faucette
Carol Davis Flowers
Sandy Heard Ford
Frances Workman Foy
Alice Virginia Daniel Furr
Sharon Cerutti Gaddo
Sally Shannon Gillentine
Cindy Latture Greer
Freida Smith Hall
Donna Neaves Hambrick
Kathy Schertz Hamilton
Cherie Brown Harris
Brenda Garner Hawkins
Merriam Wicks Hayes
Sandy Tatum Henson
Lori Trigg Hester
Susan Spicer Hester
Nancy Turner Hicks
Emily Harrison Hill
Jan Whiteside Hillen
Judy Joyner Hodges
Karen Kahler Holliday
Michelle Barnhill Hutto
Sue Oldham Imbler
Jenny Shultz Irwin
Sonja Anne Jenkins
Joyce Causey Johnston
Libby Burleson Jones
Janet Ellis Kahlstorf
Ginger Coffey Kellum
Betty Ruth Kemp
Margaret Ann Frazier Kennedy
JoAnne Radojcsics Kent
Rebecca Rhoden Kent
Linda Smith Kinsey
Gayle Murphree Klauser
Karen McKenzie Koons
Laura King Lackey
Eugenia Jones Lagrone
Carol Spight Leake
Gus Liveakos
Ruth Krudop Liveakos
Mary Jane Meadows Livingston
Jeanne Moak Lummus
Jackie Avery Massey
Cindy Little Mathis
Virginia Timbes Mathews
Amy Tanner McClellan
Margaret Moorhead McNutt

Catherine Reed Mize
Jeanette Barbour Mobley
Daphne Keith Montgomery
Loretta Sharp Monts
Neva McDowell Morris
Mabel McClanahan Murphree
Tootie Sims Murry
Claudia Johnson Neelly
Barby Robinson O'Hearn
Julia Griffin Otis
Karen King Parker
Jean Greene Pettis
Louise Feist Phillips
Dianne Gove Pittman
Belva O'Cain Poland
Gretchen Long Ramsey
Margaret Stevenson Ray
Betty Dean Reece
Betty Fields Reed
Frances Purvis Reed
Lisa White Reed
Merlene Everett Reedy
Elizabeth Moss Rice
Jane Spight Riley
Fredda Stephens Robinson
Nancy Swanger Robinson
Alice Bishop Rogers
Merrell Liveakos Rogers
Arvie Wood Roper
Rosalie Cartagine Russo
Catherine Hunter Sadler
Audrey Jerue Schreiner
Gail Piccolo Scoville
Carolyn Loper Sharp
Jan Ferguson Shirley
Mary Ann Ca Pece Skinner
Willa Searcy Smith
Cathy Timbes Sparks
Ann Shannon Springfield
Jerri Massey Stacey
Dale Scott Stanford
Debra Stern
Anneil Price Stringer
Diane Evans Tannehill
Evenlyn Davidson Tannehill
Camae Purvis Tharp
Daintry Richmond Thomas
Edith Ruff Thomas
Judy Bornscheuer Thomas
Molly Thomas Thompson
Carol Palmer Threadgill
Lynn Talley Tidwell
Pamela Cox Tims
Lee Purnell Walsh
Sue Thomas Washburn
Lindell Tate Waters
Ann Herron Weir

ACKNOWLEDGEMENTS

Charlotte Tannehill Westbrook
Emily Sims Westbrook
Shirley Threldkeld Wheeler
Libby Givens Whittington
Cathy Messer Wikle
Mary Elizabeth Phillips Williams
Margaret McCurley Williamson
Susan Shands Winkler
Betty Childers Wood
Latitia Parham Wright
Beth Gully Wynn
Sarah Bounds Young
Barbara Christensen Zander

COMMITTEES

Marketing
Shawn Stewart Brevard
Donna Neaves Hambrick
Karen Kahler Holliday
Sloan Stribling Hunter
Catherine Reed Mize
Mary Elizabeth Phillips Williams

Photography Arrangements
Julia Dodge Blakey
Sadie Ringold Buchanan
Mary Ann Lee Caldwell
Peggy Moore Carter
Camille Reed Clayton
Donna Neaves Hambrick
Marion Fay Collums Maloney
Catherine Reed Mize
Crystal Cameron Morgan
Garra Overly Owens
Margaret Stevenson Ray
Frances Purvis Reed
Lisa White Reed
Carolyn Loper Sharp
Camae Purvis Tharp
Sue Thomas Washburn
Margaret McCurley Williamson

Standardizing
Patty Wood Block
Hilda Stewart Boyd
Helen Reed Collins
Nancy Bostic Diffee
Martha Tate Stokely Dodge
Donna Neaves Hambrick
Judy Joyner Hodges
Ginger Coffey Kellum
Carol Spight Leake
Virginia Timbes Mathews
Betty Fields Reed
Frances Purvis Reed
Pamela Cox Tims
Charlotte Tannehill Westbrook

Margaret McCurley Williamson
Barbara Christensen Zander

Typing
Adrian Leist Caldwell
Helen Reed Collins
Pamela Cox Tims
Tammy Wright Wheeler

Proofing
Hallie Loftin Boggan
Marrianne Calhoun Burrus
Bonnie Payne Davidson
Margaret McDuffie Gratz
Lori Trigg Hester
Emily Harrison Hill
Marian Sigrest Hill
Sloan Stribling Hunter
Michelle Barnhill Hutto
Sonja Anne Jenkins
Susan Sudduth Mitchell
Julia Griffin Otis
Amelia Smith Perkins
Anniel Price Stringer
Diane Evans Tannehill
Ann Herron Weir
Hope Chaney Wesson
Emily Sims Westbrook
Cathy Messer Wikle
Margaret McCurley Williamson
Jean Russell Yarborough

INDEX

INDEX

GREAT
PERFORMANCES

presented by the Symphony League of Tupelo, Mississippi

GREAT
PERFORMANCES

p.o. box 474
TUPELO, MISSISSIPPI 38802-0474
phone orders (601) 842-8433

ordered by:

name _____

address _____

city _____ state _____ zip _____

phone (____) _____

shipped to (if different from purchaser)

name _____

address _____

city _____ state _____ zip _____

Please send _____ copies of

GREAT PERFORMANCES   at $18.95 each _____

postage and handling   at $2.00 each _____

please gift wrap   at   .50 each _____

                          Total $ _____

check enclosed ☐   Master Card ☐

charge to Visa ☐   Exp. Date _____

Acct No. _____

Signature _____

GREAT
PERFORMANCES

presented by the Symphony League of Tupelo, Mississippi

GREAT
PERFORMANCES

p.o. box 474
TUPELO, MISSISSIPPI 38802-0474
phone orders (601) 842-8433

ordered by:

name _____

address _____

city _____ state _____ zip _____

phone (____) _____

shipped to (if different from purchaser)

name _____

address _____

city _____ state _____ zip _____

Please send _____ copies of

GREAT PERFORMANCES   at $18.95 each _____

postage and handling   at $2.00 each _____

please gift wrap   at   .50 each _____

                          Total $ _____

check enclosed ☐   Master Card ☐

charge to Visa ☐   Exp. Date _____

Acct No. _____

Signature _____